A Carpenter's View
of the Bible

Charlie March

March Winds
Publishers

Unless otherwise indicated, Scripture quotations are taken from the *Holy Bible, New International Version® NIV®*, Copyright © 1973, 1978, 1984, 2011 by Biblica, Inc.™. Used by permission of Zondervan. All rights reserved. www.zondervan.com

Other Scripture quotations are from the New King James Version (NKJV). Copyright © 1982 by Thomas Nelson, Inc. Used by permission. All rights reserved.

Gen 1:1–2 reprinted from *Tenach: The Holy Scriptures: The New JPS Translation to the Tradional Hebrew Text*, 1985 by the Jewish Publication Society, with the permission of the publisher.

Permission to reproduce images of the house church at Dura Europos by Yale University Art Gallery, Dura Europos Archives.

Permission to reproduce Lachish relief drawings courtesy of the Institute of Archaeology, Tel Aviv University.

Jerusalem temple images with permission, Ritmeyer Archaeological Design.

My deep appreciation to Karen Lee Thorp and Susanne Lakin for their heartfelt efforts in editing this text.

Cover Portrait: James Jacques Tissot, "The Youth of Jesus," (1886–1894); permission to reproduce by the Brooklyn Museum.

Design: Dena Dahilig / Arts in Action LLC · Los Angeles

ISBN 13: 978-0-9824244-2-1
ISBN 10: 0-9824244-2-6
Library of Congress Control Number: 2011917458

CONTENTS

Preface to the Second Edition   vii

Acknowledgments   ix

Introduction   xiii

Chapter 1   Creation:
The Word of God and Our Natural Landscapes   1

Chapter 2   Creation II:
The Word of God as Architect and Builder   19

Chapter 3   The Arks of Noah and Moses:
The Passing Over of Chaos   39

Chapter 4   The Babel Job:
Miscommunication and Building the Wrong Vision   61

Chapter 5   A More Suitable Verticality:
Altars, Heaps, and Standing Stones   77

Chapter 6   Jericho and Rahab: *The Issue of Walls*   93

Chapter 7   God within a Tent: *The Fabric of Faith*   125

Chapter 8   Patterns in the Mind: *The Hand of God*   143

Chapter 9   Pride and Evil in Built Form:
Lessons from Sodom and Lachish   159

Chapter 10   Nehemiah: *Building Amidst Ridicule*   191

Chapter 11   A Carpenter's View of Jesus   223

Chapter 12   Herod's Temple:
A Description of Transcendent Architecture   239

Chapter 13   Herod's Temple II:
When a House of God is No Longer God's   267

Chapter 14   Stone Imagery: *Jesus, Peter, and Paul*   295

Chapter 15   The House Church at Dura Europos   311

Chapter 16   Under Construction: *The City of Heaven*   335

Chapter 17   Sawdust: *Last Words from the Job Site*   345

Appendix   351

Bibliography   357

Endnotes   363

PREFACE TO THE SECOND EDITION

THE PURPOSE for this second edition of *A Carpenter's View of the Bible* nearly a year after its first publication is to improve it overall (hopefully without damaging it), fix a few very annoying errors, and to add several vital chapters: "Nehemiah: Building Amidst Ridicule" (chapter 10), and "Herod's Temple I and II" (chapters 12 and 13). I have added devotional questions at the end of each chapter. The very positive response I received from my readers prompts me to extend the book to a more complete form under my publishing company, March Winds Publishers (www.marchwindspublishers.com).

I have to clarify what have become several points of confusion. First, though this book is factually a carpenter's view of the Bible (by a carpenter), some of the text is somewhat complex and much of it outside the discipline of carpentry. Though I have spent years in the trades, I am an ancient historian with a strong Bible background. *A Carpenter's View of the Bible* is a mix of these disciplines in the context of a personal memoir. The text is a blend of Bible narrative, theology, architectural theory, archaeology, and life application taken from my Christian life, and years in construction. As my old boss and friend Roy Lambert might say, "This book sure has a lot of moving parts!" *A Carpenter's View of the Bible* is not written in the genre of Christian feel-good literature that unfortunately seems to be sweeping the Christian marketplace. Rather, amidst varying perspectives, I build a case for a theology of biblical architecture. I write more along this line further in the Introduction.

Second, until the completion of this book, I did not comprehend the power of nostalgia. As we will see in future chapters, remembrance, particularly in regard to places and landscapes, saturates Scripture. It follows that the recollection of past things drove many chapters if not the entire book. My cunning plan behind relating my life-stories is simply so the reader may do the same with their stories. Above all I wish to make this an interactive study. Together we can probe the deep things of God, the God who builds. As fleshly and spiritual structures of his design, we know we are loved by him and in this we are truly free.

The process of writing *A Carpenter's View of the Bible* was equally therapeutic. The countless hours in contemplation and putting thoughts about the Lord into intelligible writing were a spiritual watershed for me. The process enabled me to abandon much destructive psychological baggage I carried for years.

Prepare for a metaphor.

I purged bitterness at the check-in counter and happily boarded the flight into the remaining years of my life with fewer emotional carry-ons.

My friend and software programmer Gene Dahilig told me that he sees his work very much like the construction process. He spoke in terms of laying a foundation with source codes and setting declarations, statements, and expressions over it to create an algorithmic structure. Software designers are as much crafts-persons as they are engineers. His example shows that all of us, no matter our professions, design and build in some way.

Charlie March
San Jose, CA

Acknowledgements

THIS IS NOT just a book for men or for those working the carpentry trade. For one thing, there are many accomplished women who are building contractors, carpenters, millwrights, cabinetmakers, woodworkers, and artisans. And above all, *A Carpenter's View of the Bible* is for anyone who wants to know God. Most of us, at some point in our lives, must use our minds and hands to make, fix, design something, or comment on a style that appeals to our eye and sense of orientation. The result may be a beautiful patchwork quilt or an unstable doghouse that your pet refuses to enter because of his innate senses that have kept his breed from extinction. I base every printed word ahead of this sentence on this fact: we are blessed with the capability to design and fabricate things because we are made in the image of God, the ultimate fabricator/builder. We inherently possess this particular strain of his genetic material, and from this viewpoint we will have a look at ourselves in light of biblical truth.

All of us must have teachers to imitate, and I was fortunate to have a few who took the time to help me along the way. I would like to thank a few of them. First, I would like to posthumously thank my father, Harry March, for his example as a woodcarver. He was a pioneer in commercial aviation and spent many of his off-flight hours at the carving bench. If he had taken the effort to market himself, I believe his works could have sold in fine-art galleries. His attention to detail was magnificent, and his striving to reach perfection bore out in his results. He was especially gifted with manipulating cutting edges and working within the environment of "grains." His ability was simply a "God thing." Second, I would like to thank Roy Lambert, who, at the time I worked for him, was the owner/operator of Lambert Roofing in Monterey, California. Simply put, Roy taught me how to work. We might think the concept of work should come as part of our personal package at birth, but for me this sadly was not the case. Roy was the consummate tough teacher who instilled in me the concepts of preparation, organization of materials, focusing maximum effort while mentally preparing for the next task, and the minimum eighty-plus-hour work week. I directly applied these disciplines to earn a Master's and a PhD degree within seven years . . . and to write this book.

I would like to thank Pete Moffat of Pete Moffat Construction, Palo Alto, California, who was the most compassionate employer I ever knew. The attention he paid to his employees in providing the best medical, dental, and retirement plans was wonderful. His generosity is, at this moment, being paid back to him by his employees in their craftsmanship and loyalty.

The names of the carpenters who helped and taught me along the way are many, and it is sad that many of their names have faded from my memory. As I will relate later in this book, most of these guys were more gifted than I, and I tried to emulate them as best as I could. I recall some of the best: Bard Sherman, Brett Fowler, Gerrard Powers, Matt Lindsay, Mark Twisselman, and Ruben Lopez. I extend my best wishes to them.

This book is dedicated to my wife, Cathy, our daughter, Jennifer, and our son, Benjamin. They were by my side at every step of the journey that produced this work. I will always be grateful for their eternal and unconditional love, patience, and abiding friendships.

"Where were you when I laid the earth's foundation?
Tell me, if you understand.
Who marked off its dimensions? Surely you know!
Who stretched a measuring line across it?
On what were its footings set,
or who laid its cornerstone—
while the morning stars sang together
and all the angels shouted for joy?"

Job 38:4–7

INTRODUCTION

Wisdom has built her house;
she has set up its seven pillars.
PROVERBS 9:1

The name of the Lord is a fortified tower;
the righteous run to it and are safe.
PROVERBS 18:10

If a man is lazy, the rafters sag;
if his hands are idle, the house leaks.
ECCLESIASTES 10:18

THE BIBLICAL TEXT is saturated with building imagery. As we see in the three verses introduced above, King Solomon used building metaphors in his wisdom statements throughout the books of Proverbs and Ecclesiastes. Similarly, from the earliest chapters of Genesis we see folks stacking stone *to* the heavens, and in the last verses of the Book of Revelation we have the City of God descending *from* the heavens. There is an architectural bridge that spans the beginning and end of biblical time. We should pay attention to this important aspect of God and his scriptures.

A Carpenter's View of the Bible is a presentation of this bridge, a gathering of buildings, builders, and architectural metaphors analyzed through the lenses of archaeology, architectural theory, theology, and personal life-application. The table of contents depicts this procession running in a chronological-biblical order.

My comprehension of the biblical construction narrative did not come to me until I spent a number of years working as a carpenter in residential construction. In tandem with my carpentry, I taught adult Bible classes for several of those years at the church we were attending. During my studies, I often deviated from studying my lesson plan and found myself lingering over verses pertaining to buildings and builders and making associations with my daily job site experiences. The days spent forming and pouring concrete foundations and framing roof systems were becoming relational to scriptural passages. "A fortified tower," foundations over rock, sagging rafters, a leaking house, and a carpenter's son struck deep chords in my mind. There were certain truths behind timber dimension, rafter span, and distortion under tension, and how the depth and solidity of a foundation directly corresponds to a house's integrity. It was illuminating to see that all of this was imagery expressed by a divine architect very much caught up in his work.

A new dimension of truth was opening for me. Over the years I have nurtured a few insights along these lines yet was woefully inadequate in expressing them. I bounced ideas for a book pertaining to the Bible from a carpenter's perspective off a few close friends, family members, and school acquaintances over the years and received positive responses. Up until the present, I felt that I was not ready for the task, and even now it is daunting to write of these things.

Now that the economy has broken for recess along with my finish carpenter job (and perhaps career), I find myself in a "broken-enough" state to write on the things of God. At present, I have time to put down what has been germinating in my mind over the years, and it has become somewhat of a fascination. I do not know if I will find another topic like this, and as I am writing about almighty God, I do so with more than a bit of trembling. Though I write in a fairly relaxed prose (and a bit of humor), I am not being insolent or pedestrian. I am utterly in awe of the

Lord and his inspired Word.

This work focuses on the character of God as architect and builder. This perspective of God is not new; however, an in-depth study on what I consider a character trait of the Trinity has been missing in scholarship and thoughtful study. My intent is for this to be a reflective work, a starting place to think of God in a different perspective.

God has set architecture and the concept of "place" in our hearts just as he has injected in every heart a yearning to know him. This dimension of God is in our DNA and becomes another piece of evidence that we are from him and similar in nature so as to be called his children. We see this in the places where we find safe haven, raise ourselves and our families. Years later they become places of fond (or not-so-fond) memory, like our hometowns and the houses where we grew up and experienced personal change. They become poignant patches of earth. Our concept of place finds particular importance in the character of the natural or structural sanctuaries where we go to meditate on and worship God. We intuitively understand the differences among the types of places that fill our lives.

The perspective of the God who builds is so prevalent in the Scriptures and revealed in the natural world that I would add it to his list of traits alongside omniscience (all-knowing), omnipresence (always present), and omnipotence (all-powerful). God is the omni of architecture and built form. In this book we'll look at a handful of biblical examples where God demonstrates his power as a builder, and where he passes it on in limited ways to his servants who, in turn, become builders in his image.

We will also see the result of those who build outside of God's plan, who purposefully deviate from the designer's intent. Their structures are problematic, and their end is prophesied, then realized in catastrophe. Structural collapse reveals the motives behind their decisions, motives that have as much to do with relationship and obedience to God as they do with proper building methodologies and construction decisions. Jesus describes a building's foundation as the critical component that defines a building's sustainability and a person's integrity. It is an inescapable truth: just as a building should be firmly set in the ground, we must be "founded."

The Foundation as Metaphor

"Where were you when I laid the earth's foundation?
Tell me, if you understand.
Who marked off its dimensions? Surely you know!
Who stretched a measuring line across it?
On what were its footings set,
or who laid its cornerstone—
while the morning stars sang together
and all the angels shouted for joy?"

JOB 38:4–7

As far as I can tell, God is the first in recorded history to speak of foundations in spiritual terms. Through his prophet Isaiah he describes himself as a builder with a measuring line, setting foundation stones as a mason upon which all life rests. In Genesis, God lays the founding principles of architectural landscapes, building materials, and a natural world. This world exhibits engineering principles that humans later apply to their built forms with astonishing creativity. In Matthew, Jesus the Son of God sits on a mountainside overlooking Galilee, completing his sermon with an example of foundations and wise and foolish builders. The one who made the cosmos and the natural world is there in the flesh, offering insights into his creation.

The Bible treats the construction process as a metaphor for life. Working plans are drafted, by either righteous or immoral hands, and lives are built over a span of days to stand accordingly. Similarly, houses are founded on sand, situated on fault lines, and end in catastrophe, collapse, calamity (all the C words). Many of us can identify with a similar manifestation in ourselves and others. In chapter 9 we will see that the doomed cities on the plain of Sodom rest on a soft sedimentary layer, and beneath this lie deep fissures to an ocean of magma. Later, Jesus connects with this imagery in which houses built over unstable subsoils of truth are vulnerable to the destructive course of natural consequences. Knowing this, we see those we love living as structures teetering on the precipice, and we cry out warnings in the wind and rain, yet we may be blind to our own unstable situations. Our heedlessness is a stubborn rejection of the reason behind the natural forces that guide and—I hesitate to use this word—control our lives.

On the happier side of things, the positive response to life is to build in accordance with biblical truth. To build in truth is to release control of the architectural plans of our lives. This release gives us moral and spiritual stability. As our forms are sunk deep in the earth of God's truth, we allow infinite opportunities to add on to our lives, to increase their bounds, though not necessarily with material stuff. The struggle our natures have for this control over our circumstances is why, I think, there is such strong scriptural teaching on soils, rocks, and foundations.

Buildings founded on solid ground endure tremors. Those tremors symbolize the life experiences that shake us. It is as though two tectonic plates of the earth's crust grind together, and we helplessly hang on until things stop falling off the shelves. When the dust settles and the broken china we've lovingly collected over the years is swept into the bin, we inspect the structures of our lives, see them strong and viable, and are able to go on despite the losses. This is not a humanist proclamation; life stripped to its bare frame is a grounded structure shaped in biblical truth.

But foundations are tricky things. They are mostly hidden, as is the true nature of the soil that supports them. It's ironic that foundations are the most important element of the building, because they are largely ignored and definitely not pretty; they are not critiqued by designers as being proportionate or aesthetically pleasing. We don't have to be concerned with foundation colors clashing. Yet window treatments, custom paint hues, and designer cabinetry won't stop walls from cracking and beams from slipping when the foundation sinks an inch or breaks away altogether when floods come or clay soil dries, splits, and crumbles.

Our spiritual lives are like foundations in these ways. No one sees us in our deep relational times with the Lord, the hours we set our foundations with him. We are buried in seclusion. We receive no public acclaim or monetary gain there. The time may be filled with expressing frustration and disappointment rather than joy (though I need to express joy more often). The presentation of our self-images, that part of us that stands above ground, is a direct reflection of our spiritual lives. Our foundations determine whether we hang plumb or askew on walls standing over weak foundations.

The foundation is the hidden strength that lies beneath, the surety against calamity. Its construction is the first of a series of processes that ensure square and plumb walls, level floors, and ceilings. The geometric life of a building is birthed with the foundation. In the Sermon on the Mount, Jesus presents the capstone of his teaching by using a metaphor from what he knew during his trade days. The parable of the wise and foolish builders (Matt. 7:24–27) shows what will happen if we ignore God's truth. His metaphor was an unmistakable revelation to all of how spiritual truth operates within the natural world. Buildings stand or collapse according to certain principles, as do lives. A life founded on the Rock is the enduring truth of life.

My Biblical View

I should pause to explain my view of the biblical record. I accept Scripture as it is written within its literary and historical contexts. I believe there was an Adam and an Eve, an unfinished tower on the Plain of Shinar, a Noah and an ark, a nation of Israel that crossed the Red Sea and Pharaoh's chariots that did not. I believe there is a New Jerusalem under construction in heaven. I don't accept views that biblical stories are mythical metaphors for God's love and redemption—stories that reveal God's character but did not occur historically. Many who think along these lines argue their points from perspectives of rationalism, sarcasm, skepticism (all the "isms"), and by testing the things of God using scientific method. To understand the infinite Godhead in this manner is futile. Perhaps it is inherent in most of us to find ways to limit God, to make him smaller, more comprehendible and simplistic—more like us, so we may not be overwhelmed by his infinitude and be crushed. Perhaps we see this as a means of evening the relational divide so that we can be loved and accepted as his child. However, this is futile and unnecessary.

So, I take Scripture as it stands. I am not a literalist; words are often written in many sociohistorical contexts and literary forms, and the Bible is no exception. The Scriptures are a wonderful literary mosaic that must be appreciated as such, but it is something more as well. The Bible is an inspired text—inspired not by human intellect or literary cleverness but imbued with God's Spirit (Timothy called it "God-breathed," 2 Tim. 3:16), a living, abiding wisdom that enlivens the words, sentences, and paragraphs with a presence that cannot be explained other than that it is of God.

In this light, the issue of possessing good literary support is not a problem. The Bible is brimming with building projects, both visionary and material. It overflows with sacred landscapes: Mount Sinai, the land of Israel, the temple, Jerusalem. God called many of his servants to build things: an ark, pillars, altars, the tabernacle, Solomon's temple, Jerusalem's walls, and in a metaphorical sense, his church. Rock is the preferred foundation material for weathering life's storms; Peter is the rock on whose example Christ builds his church; Yahweh[1] himself is the Rock.

Introductory Thoughts on Jesus the Builder

Ultimately, I always return to the reality that when the Creator, the Son of God, came to earth and lived as we live, he elected to be brought up in the home of a tradesman-builder. Yet biblical evidence only hints at whether Jesus was a builder until he was thirty years of age (or if he had even built at all, for that matter). Two fleeting comments in two verses in the gospels mention Jesus and his earthly father having worked in that occupation (Matt. 13:54–57; Mark 6:2–3). This is enough for me to build a case on.

If we were running the show, it would have made sense to have him born into either a Levite or Pharisee family and be raised within Judaism's center of temple worship and administration. The process of establishing a kingdom would have been direct. Jesus' career path seems odd. If he began helping his father in the construction industry by the age of ten, he spent approximately eight times as many years in the trades as in ministry. I think this discrepancy deserves some attention.

The fragmentary evidence of Jesus' pre-ministerial work is discouraging. I would have loved to read about his leveling and plumbing walls without a bubble level and pronouncing his creation, as he had with his primordial work, "very good." I can imagine Joseph saying after a few months of Jesus' apprenticeship that "the boy excels me" and that "his construction decision-making is . . . well . . . perfect."

Most in the theology business consider Jesus' pre-ministerial period as unimportant—he was on hold in a blue-collar Egypt, a land of servitude, before the Father gave him the green light to proceed. Pastors' sermons have related Jesus' early years of humiliating work and calloused hands—the result of manual toil in a backwater town under a hot Galilean sun. I take a different view. In chapter II of this book, I take the perspective on Jesus' trade life based on the archaeology of Nazareth, the affluent city of Sepphoris only four miles away, and the family of Herod that orchestrated a vibrant civic construction effort throughout Palestine, particularly in the Galilee region.

Jesus could have picked any family—or created any family, for that matter—that would have expedited his messiahship. But God chose Jesus to be brought up in a family whose subsistence was derived from construction. If we follow what we know of the typical family business of that day, Jesus became an apprentice builder under his surrogate father. They would normally work together side by side for years, and eventually the apprentice son would assume the business. I have noticed over the years that carpenters who learned the trade from their fathers possesses a deeper intuition, a clearer anticipation. They carry the years of their fathers with them.

I believe Christ experienced this father-son apprenticeship, but in a more complex way. His dual nature gave him the experience of building with his earthly and heavenly fathers. Expanding upon this father-son imagery of Jesus and Joseph in Nazareth, one can imagine the Father and the Son before creation out in primordial space suffused in an environment of plans and designs, then executing these images into material forms. The universe was their design studio: endless angles, arcs, tangents, inexplicable freehand lines and millions of color swatches of brilliant blends were etched and splashed across an infinite sky. I wonder if Jesus reflected back to this while working with Joseph and making things in a human context. The Second Adam created again with a second father within a shop or out under the sun that he had formed, whose gaseous fire he had lit.

Until he became man, the Creator God had not created in human form. He spun the cosmos into being, created the physical forces and geometries from which humanity could build, and formed stone, forests, and plants whose by-products of timber and organic sinew would support vertical loads. Only God working as a tradesman-builder could complete the circle of re-creating things out of what he had created originally. The "hand of God" had been an anthropomorphism. In Nazareth, God's hands became reality. They worked in harmony with the natural forces that he had spoken into being. The Limitless built in limitation; he was restricted to the confines of his own laws.

I wonder if Jesus ever became frustrated when trying to get a wall straight and plumb while working with rough field stones and a stiff back. Did he ever feel the pressure of finishing a project on time for a demanding or complaining homeowner? Or when crunch time came, did he merely "speak it into being" in the way he calmed the storm or sent the swine into the Sea of Galilee? I think he suppressed his power, delaying it until the revelation of his ministry, and yet I think it must have given him great pleasure to work in "weakness." As incredible as it may seem, building as a man was perhaps sailing through uncharted seas. He had never built "in the flesh," and the feeling must have been exhilarating. For the Son of God to pick up a mallet and chisel and cut into wood grain might be have been like an inventor successfully testing his invention—times infinity. Likewise, I wonder whether the scriptural insight he expressed in the temple as a child was also manifested in his abilities with craftsman tools and insight into forming the elements of a house. We cannot go further with this line of questioning; we can only wonder at wonder.

We design from the cognitive processes of our minds: we use and arrange geometries, guide lines, and curvatures whose interconnections establish solid surfaces. A cursory scan of the creation-nature passages in Genesis, Job, and Psalms informs us that God works similarly; however, he designs well beyond the vanishing points of our lines of sight. He is the one who defines the inside and outside of interior and exterior spaces. In his omnipresence, he is present and imbued within the concepts of "in" and "out" in the unbounded sense of these terms. God does not limit himself to the design aspects of shaping forms; he fully involves himself in the task of fabrication and arrangement and mixture of colors, and the fabric of organics produced from his creative infinitude. We work similarly as apprentices to a master craftsman.

Next we begin at the beginning. Architecture is birthed at creation. God doesn't create buildings along with the natural world, but we will see how landscapes and elements in nature inform architecture in its materials, design concepts, and construction methods.

Devotional Questions

The purpose of the following questions is to orient ourselves as designers, makers, and builders in God's image. It is important that we identify with God in this way. These are foundational questions upon which the rest of the book will be built.

1. Name and describe a few specific things you have designed and/or made in your lifetime.

2. Think about the process it took to design and/or make your project. From where did you get its idea? Did you change it? How and why?

3. What were you feeling when you were working on your project? For example, frustration, concentration, joy, peace?

4. Why do you think Jesus of Nazareth worked as a carpenter before his ministry? Has this ever affected your image of him? If so, in what ways?

5. What connection can you make between Jesus building on earth and Jesus with his Father fabricating nature and humanity at creation? What could have been the purpose for Jesus to spend his early years in the building trade?

CHAPTER 1

CREATION
The Word of God and our Natural Landscapes

In the beginning God created the heavens and the earth. Now the earth was formless and empty, darkness was over the surface of the deep, and the Spirit of God was hovering over the waters.

GENESIS 1:1–2

BEFORE DARING to write a chapter about the genesis of the natural world, I found a quiet place and pondered as many mental images as I could reproduce of birds, bugs, fish, mammals, animals, microbes, planets, and stars. I tried to recall what I had seen on countless television programs, the BBC's Planet Earth video series, trips to the zoo, and NASA's Hubble space images. Hundreds of creatures and landscapes splashed across my consciousness as James Earl Jones's voice boomed the first verses of Genesis 1, the way I imagined God would want it properly narrated. Just as my mental circuit breakers began to pop, I awoke with a clear revelation. I decided that creation is too vast, too incomprehensible to package neatly in a theological box tied with a bow. Perhaps others of much greater intellect are capable, but I cannot. I cannot apprehend its wondrous, beautiful infinitude. Words cannot express it.

However, as I limit the perspective to thinking of God as a builder, I have a small piece of his identity with which to work. Scriptures that for years I superficially glossed over are highlighted as if by an unseen marking pen. God reveals himself to the author of Job as a God who set the string lines for eternity's foundations. As one who has worked similarly on the soil of this planet, I can relate to this metaphor and make some observations. I can wrap my mind around him in a new way.

I have broken the Genesis material into two chapters. Chapter 1 introduces the concept that when we build, we follow paradigms exhibited in nature, and accordingly we extract its elements to fabricate our world from its treasure trove of secrets. As such, we fall second in line within the creative process. We are creators in a limited sense. This means we don't create originally, in the sense the Creator does, though we may claim our edifices are innovative. We begin with an existing landscape, observing and relating to the world's geography as it has been since the Lord rested on the seventh day. The principles of how we work with the natural world have spiritual counterparts— hidden truths behind what we do and make.

In chapter 2 we'll see that God has put his creator image in our hearts and instilled his wisdom within nature. We'll consider the views of some ancient Mediterranean thinkers who believed that a personal God operated within nature. They saw this through the connectedness of all things: geometry, mathematics, astronomy, and philosophical reason. Thus they understood there was an intermediary at work within these interrelationships that led back to a creator God. The name they gave this intermediary was *logos*. They often personified the *logos* as a divine architect or master carpenter at work within the natural world. They didn't believe that nature is God, but rather that nature is imbued with the wisdom of God's character and intimately maintained by his Spirit. (Sing with me: "He's got the whole world, in his hands . . .") We see this concept in the Bible when we read of Old Testament Wisdom (a poetic personification of God's wisdom). We see it most fully in the *logos* made flesh, Jesus of Nazareth.

Chapters 1 and 2 (the physical and spiritual aspects of the natural world) will establish a starting point from which we may apply construction metaphors to the biblical narratives in the rest of this book. It is important to see that these metaphors are founded at the very beginning of Scripture and continue to its last pages.

God the Creator

Our knowledge of God as builder begins with the first verses in the book of Genesis where the components of architecture and built form have their origins. The concept of "original creation" begins with Genesis 1:1–2.

> *In the beginning God created the heavens and the earth. Now the earth was formless and empty, darkness was over the surface of the deep, and the Spirit of God was hovering over the waters.*

For comparison, I quote the same verses from a Jewish translation of the Torah:

> *When God began to create heaven and earth—the earth being unformed and void, with darkness over the surface of the deep and a wind from God sweeping over the water.*[2]

Here we have the Spirit of God moving over preexisting waters before he participated in the creation of the heavens and the earth. The verses present the possibility of a pre-biblical place (a liquid form void of earthly substance) before God established a landscape for the Bible's storyline: a created mass before the creation. The account seems to indicate that the deep had a face, an elemental mass that was substantial enough to be moved over. The scene was "unformed" and "void," thus lacking solidity (dirt). We sense the existence of a watery, dark, unlit environment. It is logical to think that God created this mass of water before making the rest; life on earth is fully dependent on its existence and continuance. The waters have been interpreted as some sort of a mist, "the chaos of the deep" or "the void of the deep," but I have never been content with its being nothing or somehow evil. Perhaps the waters should be seen as a preexisting, preparatory canvas or template over which the natural world was laid.

The creation narrative depicts the Godhead, in a series of days, generating all life and its natural and celestial settings. The biblical dispute over the number of days (whatever the length of a day was in primordial history when no clock hung on a wall . . . when there were no walls . . .) it took to get the job done is irrelevant. I think God mentioned the "day" business to keep our short attention spans locked in on the fact that this work was preconceived, executed, and finished—the same sequence of tasks we wrestle with to complete our ironing. Or perhaps his joy at doing this work was so intense that tracking time was irrelevant. But for us he used the tag of "days" to indicate it was a process that took a relative moment to consider and execute. God did not have a deadline; he did not squander his time thinking about how he was going to "do" his plan or get sidetracked with how to fit in the dinosaurs, Australopithecus, and the "Missing Link." God did not have to deal with the drama of running short on time (the six-day work week) and being forced to cram in the animals and humans to avoid having to pay a late fee or go to arbitration court. We do not see evidence of God leaving out time-consuming details and features like fingerprints, noses, and gills. God never left anything blank (as we do with the tough questions on multiple-choice tests) before moving on to the next easiest thing.

In Job 38:4–7 (quoted in the introduction), God describes himself as a master builder. He does not describe himself as Santa Claus, a warm fuzzy, or a supreme angel. I don't make light of this. Of all the possible anthropomorphic identities God could choose from, he explicitly describes himself as a builder applying his tools to the crafting of the universe. Clearly, this was purposeful on God's part. God reveals his mind as if on a therapist's couch: "I am a hands-on creator; I did not merely speak everything into being—I built it."

The foundation imagery follows exactly the same procedure builders use when laying out the foundations for any building that is intended to endure. The temple that represents the church in the book of Ephesians, and the City of God in the book of Revelation, will possess foundations similarly laid out. Humans build (literally and spiritually) with the precepts of the Master, holding seniority over the animal kingdom as the Lord's ordained building apprentices, so to speak.

Much of our relationship with the Father is non-physical when we meditate on his Word and pray. Yet we can associate with him physically in what we make without entering that nasty world of idolatry. Granted, our joining bits of wood together or erecting a stone wall looks pathetic next to, say, a giant sequoia redwood, Half Dome in Yosemite National Park, or the North Star—but no matter, we still feel that association despite our infinite divide. We are able to build to his glory. And this is no small miracle.

Tools and the Process of Making Something

"Look what I've made!" I could not help but make the exclamation as I finished an oak fireplace mantel and surround for a friend of mine. It was one of the most rewarding projects of my career. The project was a rare opportunity where I was free to design, choose materials, and build it as I saw fit. I explored molding profiles from past issues of Fine Woodworking magazine and applied a few of them in new ways. I cut two-inch sheets of sandstone, layered them with beautiful sediments, and laminated them over the cheap brick facing on the firebox. I joined the two ends of the lintel pieces (a connection similar to pieces on a jigsaw puzzle) over the fireplace box with a butterfly joint. I cut the butterfly key piece (shaped like a butterfly) so that there was no need for grout. This is a common joinery technique in woodworking, but I had not seen it done in stone. I thought I would give it a go. I spent much time on this. As I delicately cut and shaped the little pieces, my mind wandered to the amazing Inca stonemasons and imagined the methods they might have used to set their giant stones with perfect joinery. While I was doing this, time was not marked by hours, but only by occasional hunger pangs and the movement of the sun.

When I'm working from a well-thought-out plan, everything flows in progression, and there is a joy in the midst of it that is difficult to explain. It could be like that of an athlete who plays "in the zone." Unfortunately, it's a fleeting mental and physical state. But to have experienced it even once is worth noting its effects in a journal entry. When the mantel was finished, I put away my tools and cleaned up the debris. For the last time in my role as builder, I stood in front of my finished creation and viewed its broad form and details. If I were to do it again, I would do a few things differently, but I judged it as the best object I had ever made. I cringed at the tiny imperfections no one would notice (that I hoped no one would notice) and decided that if I were perfect, I wouldn't be here on earth.

Anyone who has made something, no matter how humble or exotic, is a creator. We are creators in the sense that what originated in our minds and was then transmitted to and executed by our hands did not previously exist. And in making something new, we discover something about ourselves and the materials with which we work. A task becomes, to various degrees, relational. We find the word "make" a mysterious symbiosis between inspiration, thought, eyes, hands, tools, and materials. The exclamation "Look what I've made!" identifies us with the Lord at the end of each creation day. I think the phrase, "and God saw that it was (very) good (Gen. 1:10, 12, 18, 21, 25, 31)" is similar to what we express when we complete something (hopefully good) born from a creative spark in our minds. God makes; we make. And in the process of making things we have another contact point in our relationship with the Lord.

The Allure of Tools

The allure of tools for the craftsperson is a complex thing to comprehend. For the aspiring builder the decision to buy vs. the bank account/credit card balance often becomes a bane on marital coexistence and a battleground for justifying guilt. Now and then I receive a tool catalogue in which I circle the item numbers of those (I tend to personify them) I would love to have in my collection. Then I file it away from direct eyesight, knowing I have neither the funds nor the profit-bearing projects to justify their purchase.

I once caught a ride from a London taxi driver, and as we drove toward Victoria Station our conversation shifted to woodworking. He, in strict confidence, admitted that he had not told his wife that he had charged on his Visa card a router and a number of carbide bits when he had not yet paid off his new table saw. He had breached a verbal agreement ("Thou shalt pay off one tool before thou dost purchase another") with a woman who apparently was more than a figurehead of authority in his life (can you say, The Queen?). I could cut the anxiety in his voice with a knife. Though we had never previously met and lived in different cultures many thousands of miles apart, we established a deep bond. I commiserated with my driver and suggested a marital counseling website for financially distraught woodworkers. I told him that though he was new to the craft, many have paved the way ahead through the stormy seas of marriage and woodworking.

We parted company at Kings Cross Station. It was ten days after the July-seventh bombings, and a mass of people were evacuating St. Pancras Station just adjacent to it. Someone had called in a bomb threat. Immediately our priorities shifted to a sterner reality.

Re-creators Applying Nature's Divine Designs

Translucent Cowfish by Chris Newbert, Minden Pictures.

From years of observing nature and subscribing to nature magazines, I find endless insights from the natural world. I was looking at photographs on the National Geographic website and noticed the geometric image of the hexagon: made by bees forming the cells of the honeycomb, shaping the scales of a boa constrictor, and adorning the translucent skin of a cowfish swimming along a reef off Kona, Hawaii.

This random observation was a joyful revelation. At the time, I was feeling a little sorry for myself (blood sugar was probably low and I needed some chocolate and exercise), but when I linked the three photographs, I could only laugh with incredulity. How can this not be from the unfathomable hand of God? I sensed by the expression on the little Round-belly Cowfish (or Transparent Boxfish), with its pouty mouth and wide eyes, that it was trying to communicate something to me like: "Oh no, you're not supposed to be down here!"

The hexagonal patterns that form its skin raise the question: why are there identical geometric patterns on the skin of a fish, a snake, and a bee's hive? They express a similar design intellect behind three vastly different species. I was astonished and confused; I thought geometry was solely a human tool to bridge the divide between the natural and human-built worlds. Yet here was a cowfish staring at me, looking like a lit-up billboard of hexagonal shapes professing, "Nope, I was made with this wallpaper long before any human drew this shape." Here we have God imprinting a geometric image on a sea animal during the events of Genesis 1, a deliberate act of divine decoration that would later help humans engineer their built world.

After meditating on the creation narrative and pondering the wonders of the world around us, we begin to grasp that when we design and create, we do not do so in an original sense. We stand second in line in this process. God has built the prototype, and we borrow its copyrights to fabricate whatever our minds devise.

As with the hexagon, much of what we use in our daily lives comes from ideas and examples found in the natural world. The design of the airfoil that lifts and maintains the flight of an aircraft imitates the shape and skeletal structure of bird's wings. The bird's ability to ascend, descend, and turn in the air was translated into ailerons and horizontal/vertical stabilizers. Tubes carrying electricity, oil, and hydraulic fluid run throughout the plane in much the same way nerves and veins carry power and blood supply to the extremities of the bird's body. The plane's metal skin and the fuel that propels it were extracted from the earth and applied according to their chemical natures.

Likewise, animal architecture (the science of animal-home construction and design), trees, and plants remain viable tutors today. The veining in tree leaves, the dome structures fabricated by beavers, the hollow-tube bone structure of the falcon that allows it to endure immense forces while flying at tremendous diving speed, the interweaving bands of fibers that allow a massive oak tree limb to extend horizontally from its trunk, and the hexagonal compartments in the honeycomb are applied to modern design and engineering applications. Our technologies may find new uses but in many ways mimic original source material.

At the very time I was writing this, my wife, Cathy, showed me an article in National Wildlife magazine called "Mimicking Mother Nature."[3] It mentions a number of cutting-edge advancements in design taken directly from nature. I did not tell Cathy that I was, exactly at that moment, writing on the same topic. God is the God of serendipity. The article tells how the scalloped edges on the humpback whale's flippers are being applied to a new generation of windmill blades to dramatically cut wind resistance. Mercedes Benz designed their Bionic Car after the aerodynamic shape and lightweight bone structure of the yellow boxfish found in the reefs of the Indian and Pacific Oceans. Zimbabwe's largest office complex was modeled after the passive-cooling ventilation system used by African termites in their great tower mounds. Throughout the tower's inner chambers and corridors, termites work to farm a fungus that demands a constant temperature. By plugging and opening apertures in a supremely complicated ventilation system that they incorporate in their mud towers, the termites adjust cool and warm air currents to keep the interior cavities within the mound at a precise 87 degrees, despite outside temperatures ranging from 35 to 104 degrees Fahrenheit. It is engineering genius. How is it possible to apply the term genius to termites?

The article goes on to say how the bat's echolocation system has been replicated in a product called the UltraCane, where ultrasonic sound bounces off objects, allowing the vision-impaired to safely pass by obstacles. Earlier in the 1940s, a Swiss scientist invented Velcro upon analyzing the cocklebur under a microscope, after struggling to pull a host of the burrs from his dog's fur.

Currently I am pondering in what form I might build our next house. I am thinking of something environmentally/aesthetically cool, possibly a giant termite mound, though I think it is unwise to build this type of structure in monsoon country. Cathy might also object to living in a house of dried mud.

Instead, I have turned my attention to an exceptional building I experienced at Savill Garden in the Windsor Great Park, County Surrey, England. It is the Visitor's Centre, known as the Savill Building. It is designed with an elliptical roof covered with plantings and a smart drainage system. I would like to imitate something like this, in miniature, for our place, especially if we end up in tornado country. Though it was patterned after a leaf, the roof reminds me of a relatively flat tortoise shell. What an "inspired" shape this is! If you think about it, where does the tortoise go when it is threatened or when great storms beat against its shell? Does it leave its shell and head for a fox's burrow or a hollow log? No, it drops the shell down to ground level and hunkers inside until danger passes. The shell's shape provides the perfect wind foil and, in comparison, it makes our pointy-sloped roofs look pretty stupid. It's fascinating to watch the telecasts when hurricanes send roofs sailing by in the wind. You never see a tortoise flying through the air.

Though our fabrications are inspired from the creative processes of our minds, we take what has already been made, with patterns exhibited in nature, and apply them in human settings. In this strictest sense, our creations are only re-creations or reapplications of what already exists. The fireplace mantel that I spoke of previously was a composite of ideas from woodworking magazine articles and observations, adapted and reformulated in my creative mind. I took a lot of pride in its pure originality, but it was a mosaic of the swirling ideas of others, tweaked to my preferences. Though what we might do may be considered contextually unique, it will always remain second in line behind the first creation. Only God creates originally.

Elie Wiesel, the Nobel Laureate and author of *Night* relates, "It is not given to man to begin. Beginning is God's privilege. But it is given to man to begin again—and he does so every time he chooses to defy death and side with the living."[4] Wiesel argues that we cannot start to build ex nihilo as the original Creator, but there is true freedom in beginning again as we enable ourselves to emerge from the holocausts of our pasts into new life of our own design. We can thus reconstruct our narrative of the world, even though we can never build the world within which we narrate. We do not build in an original sense; we create new applications to existing paradigms established by God. Strangely there is wonderful creative independence in building and designing things by taking what is already there and instilling our desires and preferences into our fabrications.

The idea that we are not first-source builders was expressed in the first century BC by the ancient Roman architect Vitruvius. He was struck by the way humans adopted the shapes used by animals in the construction of their homes. Animal architecture, in his opinion, was the primary source material for humans to build properly within their environments. It seems animals were the first earthly "intelligent" builders.

Vitruvius's Viewpoint on the First Home

Vitruvius was a Roman architect who worked a generation before Jesus' birth. Vitruvius is significant to our study because his book *On Architecture* is the only architectural treatise to survive antiquity, and it explains much of what we know of classical architecture with its Greek-style temples and beautiful fluted pillars. He was a professional architect during the reign of Augustus Caesar (he dedicated his book to Caesar), and today his writings are taught in every architecture school in the world.

Vitruvius tells us the first people to build used what was

exhibited in nature for their design and building techniques. Fire (which nature taught humans to make) became the catalyst that brought humanity together in social groups to create shelters.

> *Hence after meeting together, they began some to make shelters of leaves, some to dig caves under the hills, some to make mud and wattles places for shelter, imitating the nests of swallows and their methods of building.*[5]

Vitruvius placed the genesis of building at the very origins and heart of human society, just after humans first used fire, developed communication through spoken language, and became aware of their immediate environment and the cosmos above. He stated that the inspiration for the first freestanding homes came from imitating animal architecture in the way swallows constructed their nests by shaping clay and intertwining twigs and branches.[6] The leaf-shaped Savill House is a contemporary application of a classical architectural theory.

This evidence points to God integrating animal architecture within nature for us to imitate and thus pushing us along the intellectual highway. We learn from the living prototypes operating around us. We have the termite and sparrow as teaching professors demonstrating their architectural insights. In the humility of their brilliant examples we find solutions to our architectural and engineering problems and put the stamp of human expression on their divinely appointed behaviors and physical characteristics.

The First Standing Houses

Vitruvius thought the coming together of societies (around the communal fire) not only sparked a compulsion to build, but propelled societies to more advanced levels of living.

> *When, however, by daily work men had rendered their hands more hardened for building, and by practicing their clever talents they had by habit acquired craftsmanship, then also the industry, which rooted*

itself in their minds, caused those who were more eager herein to profess themselves craftsmen. When, therefore, these matters were so first ordained and Nature (natura) had not only equipped the human races with perceptions (sensibus) like other animals, but also had armed their minds with ideas and purposes, and had put the other animals under their power, then from the construction of buildings they progressed by degrees to other crafts and disciplines, and they led the way from a savage and rustic life to a peaceful civilization. Then, however, building up themselves in spirit, and looking out and forward with larger ideas born from the variety of their crafts, the began to build, not huts, but houses, on foundations, and with brick walls, or built of stone; and with roofs of wood and tiles. Then by the observations made in their studies they were led on from wandering and uncertain judgments to the assured method of symmetry. When they observed that Nature had brought forth profusely, and provided materials abounding in usefulness in building, they handled them with fostering care, and equipped with delights the refinement of life, increase as it was by their several crafts. [7]

Vitruvius taught what many modern theorists agree upon— that the mental processes involved in designing and building structures spawned an intellectual renaissance ten to twenty thousand years ago. The natural tendency to create things in more complexity prompted the development of the arts, the concept of aesthetics, and the sciences, thereby raising cultures to higher levels of sophistication.

One of the concepts Vitruvius mentioned was symmetry. Symmetry means an appropriate dimensional relationship between varied things in close proximity. It is synonymous with proportion: the dimensional and aesthetic harmony of different architectural parts. Symmetry that is proportional is relational in the way differences are preserved when they are combined in proper order. It is the act of melding different parts together so they make sense as a whole. A well-designed building is pleasing to the eye; it does not look like a jumble of unrelated parts but appears to flow.

The advancement in building also made people aware of the natural landscape. While God created a great variety of landscapes, humans eventually came to artistically express their identities (self-esteem) relative to the emotions they generated. So we come full circle back to our natural environments and the God who made them.

The Creation of Landscape

And God said, "Let the water under the sky be gathered to one place, and let dry ground appear." And it was so. God called the dry ground "land," and the gathered waters he called "seas." And God saw that it was good.
GEN. 1:9–10

When we read that the "waters" were separated by "land," we have the generation of the first landscapes. Fortunately, we are not stuck with a lunar landscape but one as diverse as nature's palette. Though the word landscape is very common, an exact scientific definition of it is elusive. Its use is relatively new, having come from the eighteenth and nineteenth centuries when European landscape painting reached its zenith and surpassed the popularity of human portraiture. Paintings, once dominated with the human figure (with subdued natural backdrops), transitioned into immense landscapes with tiny human forms seemingly swallowed up in nature. The concept of landscape likewise developed its definition and philosophy during this time. I will briefly present some of its important ideas.

The geographical nature of landscape is obvious as it refers to the regions of the earth: plains, hills, valleys, desserts, mountains, rivers, lakes, and seas. Thus, the study of landscapes is related to the scientific discipline of classification, mapping, and analysis.

Yet a more accurate definition lies within the word itself. The root words of landscape associate people together with place.[8] Danish lanskab, German landschaft, Dutch landschap, and Old English landscipe all combine two roots. Land means both a place and the people living there. Skabe and schaffen mean "to shape." Suffixes skab and schaft, as in the English suffix ship, also mean a collective group, association, or partnership. Though no longer used in ordinary speech, the Dutch schappen conveys a magisterial sense of shaping, as in the biblical creation. To dwell means to make and care for a place.

To shape a place, according to the early twentieth-century German philosopher Martin Heidegger, is to define personhood. To arrive at this, Heidegger traced the verb in High German and Old English; in both cases the root for "to dwell" means "to build."[9] In German, the roots for building and dwelling and "I am" are the same. I am because I dwell; I dwell because I build. Bauen—building, dwelling, and being—means "to build," "to construct," but also to "cherish and protect, to preserve and care for, specifically to till the soil, to cultivate the mind." Thus, early in the twentieth century, Heidegger initiated the concept of applying the essence of humanity, what he termed simply as "being," to the landscapes of place and built form.

Notions of landscapes are, by definition, human creations, and the cognitive and physical act of building on a landscape is essential to the act of being human, according to modern philosophers.[10] Thus we can say Jesus' identity and work as a carpenter was a confirmation of his full humanity. He stood upon the Palestine landscape within townscapes and cityscapes, on fields, orchards, hills, and sea. His body was fully integrated with his world. This must have been an amazing feeling for Jesus. He could take in, with all his senses, what he had designed and fabricated before time began.

The spiritual side of me would like to add that my humanness in respect to where I am in the world involves my place before the Godhead as a product of his divine will. But the idea here is how we perceive our place in the world, how we interpret what is around us and establish ourselves within it. Thus, it could be said that landscapes were the first human texts; our ancestors "read" the lay of the land—before the invention of other signs and symbols. Landscapes were defined as humans formed impressions of them by immersing themselves within them.

Fortunately, we are not left with an orbiting mass of life and landscapes rotating for its own sake. If it were so, this book would end here. However, there is something much more going on within the natural world. There is a curious spark to its workings; many of us sense there is an enlivening that operates within it, keeps the ball spinning, so to speak. We'll look next at some ancient thinkers who, without the aid of direct revelation from God, perceived this "hidden intellect," this abiding presence, as divine. We'll see their perceptions meld with biblical truth to reveal a God who is architect and craftsman.

Devotional Questions

Our frame of reference in this chapter relates to the building and design insights we take from the natural world. God created a world for us to live in, but also he integrated it with teaching examples in nature to help us create our own worlds. In this way, we follow behind him as apprentice creators or re-creators. We apply what exists.

1. What are your favorite examples of animal architecture? (For example, bird nests, beaver dens, bee hives.)

2. What methods do these creatures use to make their homes? How do we do the same with the things people make?

3. In addition to the examples in this chapter, what has humanity borrowed from nature and applied to modernize civilization?

4. What is the best thing you ever made (not necessarily a material thing)?

5. What is your favorite tool? (This can be any hand tool or electronic device used to create something.) What ability does it have that makes it your favorite? How does it feel in your hand?

6. What is your favorite landscape? Why do you think you are drawn to certain places over others?

7. Think of your favorite landscape in terms of architecture. Does your landscape have great verticality or flat expanse?

8. Why do you think God has oriented us personally to particular places?

CHAPTER 2

CREATION II
The Word of God as Architect and Builder

In the beginning was the Word, and the Word was with God, and the Word was God. He was with God in the beginning. Through him all things were made; without him nothing was made that has been made. In him was life, and that life was the light of all mankind. The light shines in the darkness, and the darkness has not overcome it.

JOHN 1:1–5

I WAS TEN YEARS OLD when I was first confronted with the opening verses of John's gospel. My Sunday school teachers were encouraging us to memorize a select list of Bible verses. For each one we could recite from memory we earned a gold star that we pasted to a cutout cross labeled with our names. The crosses were posted on a bulletin board in the classroom. The more stars on one's cross, the more ecclesiastical affirmation one would receive; conversely, the fewer stars on one's cross . . . well, you get the point. Peer pressure in a Christian setting can be a tough blessing. Needless to say, among some of the more troubled of us, there was a black market in gold stars.

Then came the week I had to memorize the first five verses of John 1. I got as far as "In the beginning was the Word." My star achievement came to a screeching halt. I had no idea what this verse and those following it meant when they used the word *Word*. What was this *Word* business all about?

Nancy Pelosi, the former Speaker of the House of Representatives, seemed to struggle with the concept of the *Word* when she said the following at a Catholic Community Conference on Capitol Hill. These are her exact words without edit:

> *They ask me all the time, "What is your favorite this? What is your favorite that? What is your favorite that?" And one time, "What is your favorite word?" And I said, "My favorite word? That is really easy. My favorite word is the Word, is the Word." And that is everything. It says it all for us. And you know the biblical reference, you know the Gospel reference of the Word. And that Word is, we have to give voice to what that means in terms of public policy that would be in keeping with the values of the Word. The Word. Isn't it a beautiful word when you think of it? It just covers everything. The Word. Fill it in with anything you want. But, of course, we know it means: "The Word was made flesh and dwelt amongst us." And that's the great mystery of our faith. He will come again. He will come again. So, we have to make sure we're prepared to answer in this life, or otherwise, as to how we have measured up.*[11]

Despite her Zen/politico-like confusion, I could understand where she was trying to go with this. The *Word* is tough to comprehend in the brain much less coherently verbalize in front of learned people. Give it a try and you'll end up like Nancy by throwing the whole kitchen sink at it too. Maybe the task is better left to the Holy Spirit who can express a spiritual truth like this in spiritual words (1 Cor. 2:13).

My mother and miscellaneous church people told me it was Jesus Christ, but why did they use *Word* for him instead? Why did I have to memorize something that didn't make sense? But I was young, and as such I blindly accepted what I could not fully comprehend and moved on to the next star.

The Logos

Ironically, forty-three years later I was confronted with the *Word* while researching for my PhD thesis, a project outside the realm of Christianity. I discovered that the word *Word* comes from the Greek *logos*. Its earliest use was by a Greek philosopher named Heraclitus who lived between 535 and 475 BC. He used it to describe the source and fundamental order of the cosmos. A century later, Greek philosophers including Aristotle (384 to 322 BC), went further in calling it the "discourse" or "rational discourse." *Logos* was not used in the grammatical sense but for the act of speaking and the inward intention behind the speech act. In this chapter we will briefly track the use of this very important and interesting word (*logos*) through ancient Greek and Roman thinkers, and then connect it with the biblical creation narrative—and ultimately to the person of Jesus Christ. We'll do this because the *logos* has a lot to do with building and architectural design. This philosophical stuff will lead us to the realm of our God as builder.

While studying ancient Roman architecture, I discovered that much of its theory came from Greek philosophical thought. This is still true; philosophy remains at the heart of architectural design. This is important for us because the Greek perspective of proportion and design—the first ever to be formulated and documented—came out of concepts of the divine. Today we separate religion from the arts and sciences, but the Greeks considered them to be fully interrelated. For some philosophical schools, mathematics had as much to do with music, religion, and dance as it did with architecture, geometry, and physics. The Roman architect Vitruvius related the principle of symmetry, the proper proportion of a building's individual elements, to its overall structure. The spacing of windows or decorations across a wall's face, for instance, was analogous to the ideas of musical cadence and dancers moving across a stage. A building's architecture was seen as a composition of music and rhythmic movement over a landscape.

Since Greek philosophy developed an exact language to describe how God (their perception of a supreme God and a family of lesser gods) operated in the heavenly and earthly worlds, it should come as no surprise that philosophers touched on things close to the Christian theological doorstep. As a Christian reading this genre for the first time, I was amazed at how close ancient pagan theorists' insights were to biblical concepts. Many said an abiding "rationale," an intelligent divine nature, was infused within the elements and operation of the natural world.

Early Christian theologians modified Greek philosophical concepts and borrowed some key words to describe the person of Christ and the Trinity in exact terms. One of these was the Greek word *ousia*, meaning "essence." In the fourth through sixth centuries AD, these theologians used forms of *ousia* to battle over the fullness of Christ's humanity and divinity. Some said Christ was similar in nature (*homoiousios*) to the Father; others said Christ had exactly the same nature (*homoousios*) as the Father.

The Ancient Thinkers Who Will Help Us Understand What Is Behind It All

To connect all of this with the biblical view of God as builder-craftsman, we'll need to look at the writings of several ancient philosophers—Plato, Philo of Alexandria, Sextus Empiricus, Proclus—as well as the Roman architect Vitruvius. Plato lived in Athens about five hundred years before Jesus began his ministry. Philo of Alexandria was a Jewish philosopher and contemporary of Jesus who died nearly twenty years after the crucifixion. Sextus Empiricus lived about one hundred years after the last apostle. Proclus, a follower and commentator on Plato, lived four hundred years after Christ. The spread of years between them is important because it establishes a consistent, progressive stream of thought for nearly nine hundred years.

These ancient thinkers came to understand, through reasoning and observation, that a divine element permeated the natural world. Though their opinions were not by any means unanimous, many saw the connectedness of all things. They understood there was reason imbued within existence, a rationale, a ratio of similarity that could only be directed by a single creator-God (likely not equivalent to the biblical God). Though they wrote as believers in a single all-powerful God, most of them also believed in a number of lesser deities who handled specific life concerns, relationships, and all that crazy baggage behind the word *fate*. But they matter because their insights came long before the revelation of Christ, the letters of the apostle Paul, the gospel of John, and the others who wrote the New Testament canon under the inspiration of the Holy Spirit. (However, Philo was a Jew and a learned man of the Torah.)

The Meaning of Logos in Respect to Creation, Architecture, and the Divine

In a work called the *Timaeus*, Plato described God creating the earth with certain base elements that were imbued with a reason that allowed them to exist and operate together in agreement:

> *Thus it was that in the midst between fire and earth God set water and air, and having bestowed upon them so far as possible a like ratio (logos) one towards another . . .* [12]

Plato's use of the word *logos* speaks of something "agreeable" at work within (what he believed were) the four main elements of creation (fire, earth, water, and air). Likewise, the inspiration for the architectural concept of symmetry came from what the Greeks called *analogia* or mathematical proportion. *Analogia* comes from the base word *logos* (principle, calculation).

God made the cosmos and established a relational proportion within its main elements: an even ratio between the building blocks of life. The meaning of the word *logos* expanded from its core meaning of *word* or *number* to include *theory, calculation, principle, reason, ratio,* and *definition.* I find it fascinating to see these abstract words, very early on, associated with God and the divine effects in nature.

Thus, it is critical for us to see that one of the earliest concepts of the word *logos* was of God spanning the physical and metaphysical (beyond physical into the spiritual) worlds—or more accurately, infusing himself in it. Specifically, the *logos* is God's active nature in the world—the operator, so to speak, who does the work.

Proclus, writing nearly nine hundred years later, commented

on Plato's ideas on the *logos*. Plato wrote in his *Timaeus* that "man is a microcosm of everything that is in the cosmos, in a divine and complete way."[13] Proclus emphasized and extended Plato's ideas to say that the human person is a composite of what consists of the earth and heavens. He understood that, in addition to the physical stuff of our bodies, there was also a divine element to our makeup. To this element he applied the term *logos*—a phenomenon he saw operating within humanity as well as in nature.

The creation of Adam in the book of Genesis clarifies Proclus's impressions from a biblical perspective.

> *Then God said, "Let us make mankind in our image, in our likeness, so that they may rule over the fish in the sea and the birds in the sky, over the livestock and all the wild animals, and over all the creatures that move along the ground." . . . Then the LORD God formed a man from the dust of the ground and breathed into his nostrils the breath of life, and the man became a living being.*
>
> GEN. 1:26; 2:7

Adam is formed of the earth and made alive with the breath of God, thereby inextricably linking us to the soil of our landscapes and to the nature and image of God. This might explain how, while our feet are grounded on the earth, humanity so often looks to the heavens for salvation.

The idea of *logos* runs in architecture. Vitruvius, who likely studied Plato's philosophy during his architectural schooling, said there is a common discourse, a *ratio*, in regard to what is made and the theory or principles that guide the mind and hands of the maker. (*Ratio* was his Latin equivalent of *logos*.) Vitruvius went further to use symmetry as an example. The symmetry of a building and the placement of its architectural components (windows, doors, roof eaves, ornamentation) establish a rhythm made from a continuous setting of (let's say) temple columns and the spaces between them.

Vitruvius explained,

Inexperienced men might find it astonishing that a person, as a matter of course, should be able to master so many subjects and contain them in his memory. But they will easily believe it possible once they realize that all disciplines are joined to each other by the things they have in common. For the whole of learning is put together just like a single body, from its members . . . Every art is made up of two things: the work and its ratio. The first of these belongs to those who are trained in particular things: that is, the execution of a work. The second is common to all learned men: that is, ratio. For instance, the ratio concerning the rhythm of the pulse and movement of the feet is common to both musicians and doctors. . . . Similarly, between astrologers and musicians there is common discourse concerning the sympathy of the stars and musical harmonies . . . and in all the other subjects, many, even all things are held in common for the purposes of discussion.[14]

Vitruvius' use of metaphor in describing how many disciplines find commonality is similar to how Paul described the church as a single body with many parts (Rom. 12:4–8). Building is not simply designers and craft people making things for their own sake; there is a deep, living undercurrent at work in the creative act. Vitruvius's ideas of rhythm, movement, pulse, music, astronomy, medicine—the abiding, mutual things existing in the heavens and on earth—are what the philosopher Sextus Empiricus expanded upon two hundred years later.

Sextus Empiricus and the Sympathetic Bond

The second-century-AD philosopher Sextus Empiricus advanced the term "sympathy" (*sympatheia*) as a unifying principle, very much in the same way the *logos* and *ratio* worked:

Of bodies, some are unified; some made up of things joined together, some of separate things. Unified bodies are ruled by a single "attraction" bond, such as plants and animals; those made of things that are joined are put together of adjacent elements which tend to combine in a single principal entity such as chains and buildings and ships; those formed of separate things, like armies, flocks and choruses, are the sum of parts which are disjoined, and isolated and which exist by themselves. . . . Seeing, then, that the universe is a unified body . . . it is neither of conjoined nor of separate parts, as we can prove from the sympathies it exhibits.[15]

Sextus went on to suggest that the entire cosmos (the earth and planets) is a unified whole comprising the entirety of all bodies combined into a "single bond." They effectively operate in "sympathy" with each other (the way the moon operates on ocean tides). Greek *sympatheia* (not to be confused with symmetry, which means an aesthetically pleasing or harmonious balance and proportion) means separate entities within a system working together without conflict. Their agreeable relationships (no matter how insignificant they might seem to the overall picture) mean success for the overall organization.

Things working in sympathy speak of selfless team play where each alternately allows the other with the greater skill to apply itself in the particular instance to which it is best suited. The result glorifies the whole; it is the way to win. In successive weeks I once watched the Navy Midshipmen and then the University of Connecticut Huskies beat Notre Dame on nationally televised football games. Notre Dame's athletes were highly recruited out of high school, whereas neither Navy nor Connecticut had attracted players with as much fame. Yet, despite their disadvantages, they defeated a more powerful foe with what I would call the principle of sympathy. There were no obvious stars, though everyone seemed to be one. The announcers calling the games mentioned an inordinate number of names. Everyone was making plays; great blocks were matched by great runs, throws, receptions, and vice versa. It was a master's course in victory as inspired greatness was generated from the principle of a group working in sympathy.

Connecticut was emotionally galvanized by dedicating their play to the family of one of their players who had been senselessly murdered that season. And I heard the Navy coach (on the radio) speak of his players who, in order to survive the rigors of the academy, constantly and selflessly attended to the scholastic and emotional needs of their teammates. These examples show that the strength of sympathy arises from humility, the setting aside of individual glory for the elevation of the group. Sympathy in architecture is similar—all of a building's architectural elements, no matter their individual beauty, are used to draw the eye to appreciate a building in its entirety.

Late antique theorists (living between AD 200 and 600) also related sympathy to *philia,* meaning friendship, in the sense of a relational bond between separate things or people.[16] They would have loved watching Navy and Connecticut play. This bond was applied to the relationship between certain physical materials and their essences. From an architectural standpoint, sympathy is the harmonious relationship of its parts working together to embellish the whole. Sympathy is generated from the essence of a design.

All of these ancient writers sought words to clarify the difficult task of explaining the relationship between the person and God, to make the impossible connection between God and human by means of a third element. Concepts taken from the words *sympathy* and *logos* were combined with the Greek word for essence. Recall that the Greek word for essence (not to be confused with Emeril's cooking seasoning—see the Food Channel)) is *ousia. Ousia* is the meaning or essence of someone or something condensed down to its base principle. This essence could take on a life of its own and be an abiding reality—like a person. The idea was developed by philosophers to include the sympathetic *essence* between a person and thing or a person and the divine to achieve a connection or relationship. In this way a person may have an abiding, unbroken relationship with something inherently unobtainable (say, God) through something or someone existentially connected to it (say, Christ). Thus, *ousia* became a linguistic tool for early Christian theologians to explain how Jesus of Nazareth could have been simultaneously fully man and fully God, sympathetically related to humanity.

This at once raises and answers a question: How can the infinite be united with the finite, the sacred with the profane? This dual relationship is inherently unsuitable, like mixing water- and oil-based paints, which are composed of disparate elements. The two parts never unite, no matter how vigorously you stir the paint.

To solve this eternal dilemma, there must be a bonding agent—a third element or person (consisting of both parts) to enter and sympathetically operate within this relationship. Before Christ, this bonding was typically accomplished by laying an animal upon an altar. In Christ the principle of sympathy was activated so that we may achieve an impermeable bond with God. Incredibly, we can become his friend. Still, there is more to add in support of this line of thought. We will see how these spiritual terms became joined with architecture.

The Logos as Architect and Craftsman

The Jewish philosopher Philo of Alexandria, writing his *Commentary on Genesis* during the time of the apostle Paul, describes God as architect and builder, designing and building from perfect models, paradigms, and wax imprints in his soul:

> *God, understood in advance that a beautiful copy would not come into existence apart from a beautiful model, and that none of the objects of sense-perception would be without fault, unless it was modeled on the archetypal and intelligible idea. Therefore, when he had decided to construct this visible cosmos, he first marked out the intelligible cosmos, so that he could use it as an incorporeal and most god-like paradigm and so produce the corporeal cosmos, a younger likeness of an older model. . . . [I]t may happen that a trained architect comes forward. Having observed both the favourable climate and location of the site, he first designs within himself a plan of virtually all the parts of the city that is to be completed— temples, gymnasia, public offices, market-places, harbours. . . . Then taking up the imprints of each object in his own soul like wax, he carries around the intelligible city as an image in his head. Summoning up the representations by means of his innate power of memory and engraving their features even more distinctly [on his mind], he begins, as a good builder, to construct the city out of stones and timber, looking at the*

model and ensuring that the corporeal objects correspond to each of the incorporeal ideas. . . . Just as the city that was marked out beforehand in the architect had no location outside, but had been engraved in the soul of the craftsman, in the same way the cosmos composed of the ideas would have no other place than the divine Logos who gives the [ideas] their ordered disposition. . . .

If you would wish to use a formulation that has been stripped down to essentials, you might say that the intelligible cosmos is nothing else than the Logos of God as he is actually engaged in making the cosmos. For the intelligible city too is nothing else than the reasoning of the architect as he is actually engaged in the planning of the foundation of the city.[17]

Philo drew upon the metaphor of the architect as designer and builder to help provide an explanation for the creation of the cosmos. Philo related his Jewish doctrine to Greek philosophical thought (as did many Christian theologians) and clearly made the connection with the *logos* as the active "reasoning" or wisdom of God that is fully integrated within creation. The *logos* of God is not merely an idea but an abiding reality.

There is almost a divine act described in short phrases: "summoning up," "innate power of memory," "engraving distinct images," a "good builder" who, in each case, "ensures correspondence" between what is in the soul to what is being built in real space. After much double-checking and attention to detail, what was drawn in the mind and impressed on the soul as "wax" has its exact representation transmitted to earth.[18] This type of imagery will be used again in chapter 6, where we have the Spirit of God setting exact patterns and forms in the minds of Moses and David for the tabernacle and temple.

Proclus and the Logos as a Carpenter

Nearly 350 years after Philo, the philosopher Proclus spoke of Nature (in the feminine, as did the writer of Proverbs 8) as the active creating element operating under the reason principles of the One who created all things. He said there has to be someone with the ideas from which Nature can create—an original, sovereign source of all things. You have to admit, this is an amazingly logical conclusion. Proclus used the image of the carpenter to describe how Nature infuses the *logos* (wisdom principles) within the natural world:

> But if nature has the reason-principles, there must be some other cause prior to it that contains the Ideas. For Nature, when she enters into bodies, acts as you might imagine a carpenter descending into his pieces of wood, hollowing them out inside, straightening, drilling, and shaping them. Such is the way of Nature, infusing herself into bodies, dwelling in their solid masses, and breathing her movement and her reason-principles into them from inside. [19]

It is interesting that two prominent Alexandrian philosophers of the first and fifth century AD (Proclus trained in Alexandria before going to Athens) used analogies from the building profession to describe how nature is imbued with the *logos*. Proclus expressed an appreciation for the art of woodcraft, a skill he may have taken part in. He saw the essential act of a carpenter as descending into wood. The methods of hollowing, straightening, drilling, and shaping are determined by the characteristics of the material. This is not merely cutting into a piece by exerting brute force to bring about conformity, but a careful sensitivity in shaping the craftsman's purpose within an object in sympathy with its natural attributes. The carpenter and the worked material create a sympathetic friendship by "running with the grain."

Proclus went on to say:

> Every creative agent works upon what is by nature susceptible to its action, that is, upon what is capable of receiving its action . . . by its very aptitude presents itself as a collaborator with the agent that can create . . . so the thing that comes to be is a likeness of its creator . . . hence as he thinks he makes, and as he makes he thinks, and he is always doing both. [20]

What I believe he was saying is that the creator and created are in cooperation, working in concert for a desired end, for the one bears the essence of the other. The imprint of the creator's thought and personality has been infused within the object. This is equally true of the natural world as it is with the children of God. We are his spiritual imprint, a living expression, an echo of his personality in the process of being shaped toward a finished form.

As a pagan, Proclus did not apply his insight to the example of Jesus of Nazareth. However, I find Proclus's words very comparable with the way the Savior works within his believers. Though Christ's children become converted during the initial act of belief, Christlikeness is a honing process of personal spiritual transformation (the Christian has willingly made himself or herself susceptible to the influence of Christ). This happens as Christ shapes the believer to his image along the long road toward sanctification. Through the indwelling of the Holy Spirit at conversion, believers are capable of receiving this action; they are spiritually susceptible. As a carpenter works a piece of wood, Jesus works to shape the believer into a "new creation." Redemption is a matter of shaping.

We now take what we have developed to this point and apply it to the Old Testament and the person of Wisdom.

Proverbs and the Role of Wisdom in Nature

Within Old Testament Wisdom literature, the following section in Proverbs relates God's Wisdom closely to what Plato, Vitruvius, and Sextus wrote of sympathy, bond, reason, and harmony. God's Wisdom is the interactive element over all creation and speaks here in the first person:

> "The Lord possessed me at the beginning of His way,
> Before His works of old.
> I have been established from everlasting,
> From the beginning, before there was ever an earth.
> When there were no depths I was brought forth,

When there were no fountains abounding with water.
Before the mountains were settled,
Before the hills, I was brought forth;
While as yet He had not made the earth or the fields,
Or the primal dust of the world.
When He prepared the heavens, I was there,
When He drew a circle on the face of the deep,
When He established the clouds above,
When He strengthened the fountains of the deep,
When He assigned to the sea its limit,
So that the waters would not transgress His command,
When He marked out the foundations of the earth,
Then I was beside Him as a master **craftsman;**
And I was daily His delight,
Rejoicing always before Him,
Rejoicing in His inhabited world,
And my delight was with the sons of men."

PROV. 8:22–31 NKJV, EMPHASIS MINE

Wisdom is personified as the craftsman working in conjunction with the Creator when the world was formed, the cosmos spun, and the seas and land divided. I have emphasized "craftsman" because I love the term here. It intimates a hands-on, skilled workmanship. Wisdom was not an idea or passive observer but was a co-participant or co-fabricator infusing his or her attributes into every element and the ceaseless workings of the cosmos, atmosphere, and earthly planet. Personhood here is not literal but is used to emphasize wisdom's active, animate nature.

The following verses clarify that nature is not God or inundated with gods lurking within all things, such as animals, trees, forests, and landscapes (pantheism, animism). Proverbs supports Genesis and the thoughts of Plato, Proclus, and Philo: nature was created by and operates under the abiding wisdom of God.

How do birds and butterflies know how to migrate thousands of miles to the same trees in the same forest? How do salmon know how to leave their freshwater stream, swim thousands of miles out into the Atlantic, then return back to the same stream to spawn and die? The migratory network of birds, fish, whales, and butterflies, if drawn in lines over a flat world atlas, is staggeringly complex; countless living strands link oceans and continents like light fibers strung within communication cables. The answer lies in Proverbs 8 and other passages that credit Wisdom as the paradigm under which all creation exists:

> *How many are your works, LORD!*
> *In wisdom you made them all;*
> *the earth is full of your creatures.*
>
> Ps.104:24

> *By wisdom the LORD laid the earth's foundations,*
> *by understanding he set the heavens in place.*
>
> PROV. 3:19

For Vitruvius, the third element that connects two disparate things (which I relate to biblical Wisdom) involved a "common discourse" of language that he used to describe correct methods of design. We see God has set proportion, sympathy, symmetry, and the essence—the *ousia*—of his wisdom within the workings of his nature and cosmos. Next we will see how this third element became incarnate in the *logos* of Jesus of Nazareth.

The Logos in the Gospel of John

In the opening verses of the gospel of John, the *logos* (Word) is personified as Jesus Christ. I was told this when I was ten, but not how or why. This was wise on my teacher's part; I would not have understood the answers anyway, and it would have only added to the confusion of the Word business.

John's defining Jesus of Nazareth as the *logos* of God carries deep significance. His gospel begins with a philosophical treatise adopted not from Jewish theology, but from pagan Greek logic.

Thus we become joined in thought with Plato, Proclus, Sextus, and Philo. God put insight about the *logos* into the hearts of men who stood far apart from biblical truth. However, this concept became an inspiration to a first-century fisherman working on a lake in the Galilee region of Israel, to be used as a deep paradigm for Christ's nature.

> *In the beginning was the Word, and the Word was with God, and the*
> *Word was God. He was with God in the beginning. Through him all*
> *things were made; without him nothing was made that has been made. In*
> *him was life, and that life was the light of all mankind.*
>
> John 1:1–4

The apostle John sees Christ as the rationale, the active principle saturating all life—in essence, life itself. He transcends verb tense; He forever was, is, and will be. In the beginning he was simultaneously "with" and "was" God—the co-participant and director over the creation event. He is simultaneously in and over life—the abiding, sympathetic essence unifying humanity with salvation. Only the word *logos* could express this difficult reality. No wonder I could not understand this as a ten-year-old.

Christ as Craftsman: At Work within His Believers

Christ as *logos* infuses life within creation. It can just as easily be said that he works as a carpenter (see chapter 10, "A Carpenter's View of Jesus") in shaping and honing his believers to his desired end. He works in us and we are his "workmanship." Christ knows the grain of his children and runs his chisels accordingly. The following New Testament verses relate directly to this:

> *He who began a good work in you will carry it on*
> *to completion until the day of Christ Jesus.*
>
> Phil. 1:6

For it is God who works in you to will and to act
in order to fulfill his good purpose.

PHIL. 2:13

For we are God's handiwork, created in Christ Jesus to do good works,
which God prepared in advance for us to do.

EPH. 2:10

Christians are metaphorical blocks of wood, being shaped and worked according to the purpose set by the Craftsman, God. After the chisel work, drilling, and cutting is completed, our final shape will be revealed to us at the "day of his appearing." Our individuality, exhibited in the patterns of our grains—unique cell fibers forming rings, rays, fletching, and ribbons—is highlighted and glorified through the abiding wisdom in the hands of the Creator. We are made in sympathy with the rest of creation. He knows our individual personalities, deepest personal intricacies, and set patterns as he goes about redeeming our rough features while keeping us in harmony with his ultimate will. We are God's workmanship, and through his craft we are redeemed.

Concluding Thoughts

God has infused his character within life; the nature of his wisdom saturates every pore. Through systematic observations, the great pagan philosophers could not help but arrive at startling theories of a third active element operating within nature. Plato, Sextus, Proclus, and Vitruvius called it *logos, ratio, hexis,* and Nature. Philo, working out of the Torah, called Yahweh an architect, whereas Proclus applied the persona of a carpenter to his vision of a creator God. They, to a man, abstractly applied these relational words to how we build in proper sync with creation. Old Testament writers called it Wisdom; the apostle John used *logos*, pushing the word into a new realm to describe Christ, the ultimate intermediary, the sympathetic bond who operates on our behalf. However, what pertains to this work is how these words are connected, in metaphor and in reality, with architects, architectural design, construction, and carpentry. The ultimate earthly example will be Jesus of Nazareth. The simple truth is this: God loves building and design. As we will see, the Scriptures are saturated with building projects where God is always, somehow, present.

Devotional Questions

These questions are designed to help you wrap your mind around the Word, the logos of God. In the first verses of his gospel, the apostle John cryptically describes Christ as the Word. We have seen this term used as the governing principle, the rationale within the workings of nature. Before the time of Christ, the Word was beginning to be used by pagan and Jewish thinkers as embodying an architect and a builder who is God. By definition, the Word conducts proper order, rhythm, and symmetry in life. Wisdom in Proverbs 8 is connected to the carpenter, Jesus of Nazareth. I believe the Word influences our perception of space and the things we design and build.

1. "In the beginning was the Word. . . ." What do you understand this verse to mean? If you start sounding like Nancy Pelosi, try again!

2. Why do you think the apostle John chose to use "the Word" to describe Christ?

3. What did the Greek philosophers believe the *logos* was?

4. To what professional did Philo of Alexandria relate the *logos* of God in laying out the plan for a city? Why?

5. What craftsman did the pagan philosopher Proclus relate to the way Nature infuses her principles into the world? Why?

6. In what ways does the world around us have a repetition or rhythm?

7. How do buildings have rhythm in the way doors, windows,

and décor relate to each other? Have you seen houses that seem out of sync, disjointed, out of alignment? What was your reaction to them?

8. Who was the "craftsman" at God's side during creation in Proverbs 8:22–31?

9. Since we know Christ is the *logos*, write a definition of him.

10. How has this chapter increased your knowledge of Christ as the God who builds?

CHAPTER 3

THE ARKS OF NOAH AND MOSES
The Passing Over of Chaos

[God said to Noah] "So make yourself an ark of cypress wood; make rooms in it and coat it with pitch inside and out. This is how you are to build it . . ."

GENESIS 6:14–15

IN THE FIRST WORDS of the Bible, Yahweh converts the formless watery deep into malleable and ordered space by creating earth and sky (the horizontal and the vertical), and dividing the land from the water. In this new place, defined against the heavens and the seas, God establishes his creation. God is the generator of space, place, topography, and sacred landscape. However, in the Noah narrative we have God destroying it. At first glance this seems very odd. It seems as if it was only yesterday when he went to the trouble of making it. What went wrong? Is this a story about a mad scientist whose creation takes on a life of its own and becomes something other than he intended? Can you say "Frankenstein"? We will see that God, as creator-artisan, destroys what is detrimental and keeps what is substantial, and what is of substance is the righteousness existing within a single man.

Although we have an early passing reference to Cain building a city (Gen. 4:17), the first documented construction project engaged the principles of land and water—the base elements in creation. We will now look at a man commissioned by the Lord to build, of all things, an ark.

There lived a righteous man named Noah who found favor in

the sight of the Lord—which is to say he honored his relationship with God with prayer and sacrifices and carried himself with dignity expressed in proper moral behavior. He cared for and loved his family and stayed true to his wife. He lived a life in contrast to the cesspool of immorality that surrounded him (Gen. 6:9), and this, as we know, is not easy, especially when acute immorality defines one's civilization. I imagine Noah and his family living in the country, far from city life where one is compelled to fall to the lowest common denominator. Plus he needed plenty of room to build an ark.

When God Kills:
Crossing the Line and Wiping the Slate Clean

Now the earth was corrupt in God's sight and was full of violence. God saw how corrupt the earth had become, for all the people on earth had corrupted their ways. So God said to Noah, "I am going to put an end to all people, for the earth is filled with violence because of them. I am surely going to destroy both them and the earth.

GEN. 6:11–13

You have searched me, LORD,
and you know me.
You know when I sit and when I rise;
you perceive my thoughts from afar.
You discern my going out and my lying down;
you are familiar with all my ways.
Before a word is on my tongue
you, LORD, know it completely.
You hem me in behind and before,
and you lay your hand upon me. . . .
Where can I go from your Spirit?
Where can I flee from your presence?

Ps. 139:1–5, 7

At this point I have to stop and leave the topic of construction.

It is time for a tangent. I will come back to Noah and the ark shortly, but something extremely important must be said about the judgment of God and his deliberate annihilation of creation.

In the movie *The Bible, In the Beginning* (1966), a little boy with big, innocent eyes is told that no one survived the destruction of Sodom. He asks Abraham (played by George C. Scott), "Were even the children killed?" The little guy has a point. Complete annihilation at the hand of God is pretty much overkill for someone we consider all-loving. George C. Scott's portrayal of Abraham is of an emotionally tortured man pushed to the brink as he stares at the smoke of burning Sodom on the horizon. His anguish is palpable as he questions, even hates, God for his deed (Hollywood loves to present biblical heroes doubting and even rejecting God).

This issue has caused much tension in Sunday school classes, and it is tempting for those who teach to gloss it over with, "That was before the New Dispensation in which we live" or "It was *really* bad back then" or "This only makes me feel even more grateful for what Jesus did for us on the cross." Intelligent audiences know deflecting statements when they hear them, and the teacher's stock immediately takes a nosedive. Though we will revisit this issue when we talk about the cities of Sodom and Lachish (chapter 9), we must say a few words about the human casualties caused by the flood.

God is watching us. His interest in us is not passing; he is intimately aware of our deepest selves. Yikes. Psalm 139 reflects the poetic epitome of this. Actually, the reality of this doesn't bother me a bit. In fact, I have come to strongly appreciate God's constant surveillance. This is so because I have become increasingly aware of it in the little (and great) serendipitous, nuanced life occurrences that seem unnatural yet somehow planned. And this is coming from a pretty rational person. I am not a space cadet. But I know that God is working in and around me.

The fact that he is present is a comfort. Somehow he puts up with me and does not seek vengeance when I make a wrong choice. I don't fret the possibility of rising water reaching my lower lip when I lie in bed, like that elderly couple in a scene from the movie *Titanic*. Through the intercession of Christ, I can talk to God anytime, anywhere, about anything; even the most intimate stuff can be set on the table without fear of retribution. Even when I am mad at God, I don't have to dodge and weave like a boxer as he sends a right cross out of heaven for doubting his love. I know for a fact that if the worst were to happen (like a giant croc slipping into the pool while I'm lap swimming, or a great white shark thinking I am the most beautiful seal he ever saw), he would walk beside me all the way to my heavenly home. No matter the worst, things are eternally fine.

So knowing God as I do, it is difficult imagining him in full destruction mode (FDM). I wonder what the last straw was that broke the camel's back, compelling God to flush the ecological system. But then again, when I read Revelation and the final judgment, I discover that I am missing (or ignoring) a very important attribute of God. It is sobering to think that his last judgment will far outdo the flood. The events leading up to the judgment at the great white throne are enough to wish this a literary allegory rather than prophetic reality (Rev. 20:11–15).

We read in Genesis 6 that God's response to humanity's depraved behavior had run too deep for too long. Occasionally we glimpse true evil: mass murderers, Adolph Hitler, Pol Pot, terrorists, child abductors, and so on. I get the sense that the earth then was full of these people; it was out of control, and God was forced to act.

For those new to the Bible, this flood story comes as a bit of a shock. Actually, it causes some to shut the book and walk away to find a kinder, gentler God. And if they don't walk away here, they probably will in the book of Joshua when Yahweh commands Israel to annihilate most of the nations (all the "-ite" peoples) between the Jordan River and the Mediterranean Sea. The very God who is supposed to love and save is also a killer. God goes postal; why does he do this to those he made in his image?

However, if we keep our cool and stay with the following verses, we learn something pretty sobering about God. His vengeance is calculated against a framework of laws. This is a bit scary. A disciplining, account-taking, vengeful God is not what we want out of him. A quick survey of people on the street would likely prefer a Santa who gives but does not bother us.

We have several choices here:

- We may recognize his discipline as necessary; the evil of this people must have been beyond our comprehension. It seems as though there was no restraint, no possibility of redemption, conversion, repentant hearts, or spiritual revival.

- We may consider this something God had to do a long time ago, but he has now softened with the advent of Jesus. The God of the New Testament is different from that of the Old. He is now a God of love and forgiveness.

- We can ignore this part of him or ultimately reject this paradigm of God altogether. I have Christian friends who will, selectively, not read these pages of the Bible and are satisfied to consider it fable.

- In conjunction with #1, we can say God is a sovereign king. He does what he wants, when he wants. God chooses. Paul used craftsman analogy in illustrating the problem in questioning God's dominion:

    Shall what is formed say to him who formed it, "Why did you make me like this?" Does not the potter have the right to make out of the same lump of clay some pottery for noble purposes and some for common use?

    Rom. 9:20–21

Paul's teaching on God's sovereignty is particularly hard to swallow when we believe we have certain inalienable rights regarding our identity as a child of God. The relationship with a God who cares, saves, and loves (the God who builds) is hard to pair with one who judges and destroys (a God of demolition). Our humanity struggles to accept the contradiction. We would rather associate with a God of love, a God who loves on our terms or at least within the realm of our comprehension. However, the flood tells us this mentality is in error; there is no contradiction. God's perfect justice and righteousness is defined by his treatment toward disobedience and immorality, for which the typical response is his corresponding punishment. He reacts harshly against *sin*—the word for any violation of God's commands. He simply won't have it.

Perhaps we should see that God sending his Son to earth to die for us was a radically more extreme response/solution than the one he used to deal with the flood. It is our human arrogance to never consider God's sacrifice out of his love for us. It is different when punishment is directed toward *us*, when discipline costs *us* something. These are hard things to accept. Yet we are working here toward comprehending God. Simply, he is not bound; he is free. God needs neither our sense of justice nor affirmation nor permission. Enough said.

Aliens, Asteroids, and Us: The Popular Choice for Earth's Destroyer

The business of earthly destruction is not confined to Scripture; the secular world is quite taken up with it as well. I am trying to recall the movies that have come out of Hollywood depicting aliens and natural/cosmic disasters that threaten to destroy the earth. There have been so many of them over the years (such as 2012), it is as if we are subconsciously begging for something (that is not God) to come down from the sky and put us out of our misery. Can you say, "vampires"?

What I particularly like about the genre is there is always a heroic human remnant, led by a dynamic visionary, who believes we will survive even the worst catastrophe. Hope in humanity lies in the right person, or a special wisdom lies in the sovereignty of Mother Nature. What is key is even the most irreligious understands the earth is not right with itself. Something is missing; life is not the way it should be.

I must respond to this nonbiblical Armageddon-Apocalypse phenomenon. (I will get back to Noah!) Personally, there are times when I am so fed up with society that I would welcome a good asteroid to come winging toward us from the depths of space and give us a good whack—a good glancing blow that kicks the planet off-kilter and blows a chunk of land mass and ocean off into space.

Instead of the asteroid, I think quite a few Americans would prefer aliens attacking in awesome *War of the World* spacecrafts, creating havoc like blowing up Jim-Bob's double-wide outside of Hogopolis, Arkansas. Before the pieces of aluminum and R-11 insulation hit the ground, we would get the green light, and the shooting would immediately commence. Even the antigun crowd would don paramilitary gear and blast away. We would have some wonderful adversaries to pit ourselves against, like the creature in the movie *Predator*. Though, to be politically correct, our battles would only come after we first try to reach out to have a conversation and apologize for marginalizing them somehow.

All this leads me to consider that people would rather accept an alien invasion or environmental disaster than the Lord's discipline. Perhaps this genre is an unconscious self-admission of world guilt, a quiet knowing of a secular society that believes we deserve destruction and saving. We never see movies of humans going to other worlds and saving other peoples from themselves.

Yet living a life outside God's control is a delusion. We are free, but we constantly bump into boundaries we did not create. Our control over our circumstances is illusory when we encounter fate and the unpredictable tossing of the cosmic dice. We can "self-actualize" our lives, but not ultimately. A new diet may improve the quality of our years, but we have no say as to our length of days. We can surgically enhance ourselves, but only artificially. We can be happy, but only for a moment. An atheist takes God's name in vain and, in the same breath, argues against his existence. All things considered, one must know him well enough to hate him. Knowledge that we are ultimately impotent in our self-determination is a strong source for the considerable latent frustration and anger within society. Perhaps in Noah's time, society had taken this to the ultimate degree. Rage and hate had saturated life.

The subterranean spring and sea waters were not enough to do the job, so God collapsed the entire vapor of the sky and did not hand out umbrellas and water wings. Everyone died except for Noah, his family, and the two-by-two pairings of the animal kingdom sheltered within the ark.

Against this backdrop, the inscrutable ways of God take its course. It is amazing to think that just before the sky was to fall and everything that could be seen would be no more, God told a righteous man to build something. You've got to love it. "Go build an ark!" My editor reminds me that just as we are near the end of the biblical timeline, Christ tells us to go and build his church. It seems that when humanity is close to a historical precipice, God has his children build something.

God Reacts to Noah's Righteousness

Perhaps perfect justice dictates that one type of chaos deserves another. The catastrophe of sin must be recapitulated by a righteous catastrophe from the Creator. Since a single familial thread of humanity chose to live in righteousness, God likewise responded in perfect righteousness. Just when we think we have him figured out, God changes course. His perfect attributes seem to be fluid, not rigid categories segmented by lines on a graph or by charts and narrow columns. That would be like calling the Bible a list of dos and don'ts. God allowed grace to enter the waters; disaster brought redemption and renewal.

Noah and God: Co-participants in the Ark Job

The Noah's ark story is a divinely inspired building project. God instructs Noah not only to construct an ark, but in the specifics of how to build. God, as architect and building consultant, verbally drew dimensional plans with specified materials. Simply, the ark was a wooden bubble containing nature and humanity: a divinely inspired physical form enclosing and protecting divine creation. Instruction and planning came from God; obedience in imitation and physical effort was from human endeavor.

This reinforces the idea that God loves to design and is particularly taken with the details. He did not say, "Go build a really big barge-like thing that can float on water. Oh, and don't forget to seal it with pitch and tar, otherwise you will experience another physical principle of mine called sinking." He is not vague, and he knows humans need precise instructions or else they will find some way to get themselves into trouble . . . like installing a window in the hull just below water level.

God demonstrated to Noah, in a micro sense, how to build in the precepts of his image in accordance with the physical forces operating within the natural world. This was the first (known) transfer of logistical knowledge between God and humanity and it, of all things, pertained to the architectural design and construction methodology . . . for a seacraft. We will later see this interrelationship and specification of materials in the construction of the tabernacle and Solomon's temple.

Figuratively and chronologically, the ark and the life it contained participated in the reenactment of the original creation. As the Spirit of God had once moved over the waters, the ark floated over the deep. The ark contained the essence of that first creation, while God once more separated the land from the water and ordered the primeval chaos. The parallels between the creation and flood became more distinct as the waters subsided, revealing new landscapes that once again separated the seas. Noah and his ark provided a matrix of a new creation, existing within the womb of a ship, with the chaotic, exterior world outside its walls. This passing over the terror of the deep, in built form, extended God's attributes of architect and builder to humanity in a most intimate way. The ark, a divine-human collaboration, was the vehicle that facilitated the redemptive act.

Out of this pattern, another ark was later carried by the Levitical priesthood of Israel as they, with Joshua, traversed the rough, chaotic seas of Canaan, redeeming the land from its idolatrous peoples. Even later, that ark rested in the tabernacle and then the temple, extending its lineage as an architectural representation for deliverance.

As far as construction methodology is concerned, God had given Noah the most difficult of woodworking projects. Building a watercraft is much more complicated and exacting than, say, a house on land. Not only must the ship be formed of processed materials that resist water intrusion, the craft must also be in balance and the builder cognizant of the load and placement of its contents (or whether the contents can move about—like, if the two elephants decide to run back and forth or dance the tango, will the ship flip over?). The survival of all life on board depended on being obedient to the physical tenets of balance, displacement, water intrusion, and stresses of structural loads. Noah could not deviate from God's instructions as he saw fit. The parallels between Noah's obedience as shipwright to the behavior of those facing pending judgment is marked.

The parallel between the laws of naval engineering and the laws under which we conduct our lives is clear. Jesus' Sermon on the Mount (Matt. 5–7) and the lifestyle teaching in the Epistles are a practical methodology for a balanced existence, not to mention the warnings against drilling holes in the hulls of our lives while navigating the seas of life. We must be cognizant of the loads we carry and how they affect the water we displace. If we carry burdens that exceed our design constraints, water will breach the gunnels, flood the decks, and penetrate to our lower, more intimate levels. We are designed with limitations and boundaries, while our keels and rudders allow us to navigate and not be tossed by the waves and blown about by any wind that happens to gust up (Eph. 4:14). A buoyant and directed life is only possible by following the Creator's blueprints, list of materials, and construction methods. Deviation from them posits the question made famous by Bill Cosby: "How long can you tread water?"

The Arks of Noah and Moses

When she saw that he was a fine child, she hid him for three months. But when she could hide him no longer, she got a papyrus basket for him and coated it with tar and pitch. Then she placed the child in it and put in among the reeds along the bank of the Nile. His sister stood at a distance to see what would happen to him.

Ex. 2:2–4

I think it is poignant that the Hebrew words for the ark (of Noah) and the basket (of baby Moses used on the Nile) are identical.[21] The lives of these two men are intimately linked by this curious type of watercraft. The two deliverers (Noah and Moses) faced the trial of passing over (or through) the deep, and it is a provocative thought that God often pairs water with his acts of deliverance. Baby Moses and the man Noah relied on the integrity of their craft for their survival. We will see that, for Moses, his relationship with rivers runs deep.

Though the basket of Moses is a minute example of biblical construction in comparison to Noah's ark, the ark of the covenant, the tabernacle, and Solomon's temple, it must stand in equal significance upon the landscape of faith. And as we make a comparison, it is interesting to note that all of the marine fabrication issues Noah faced—balance, water intrusion, weight, and buoyancy—Moses' parents also dealt with before sending their only son out on the waters.

I see in the "ark stories" of Noah and Moses the allegory of crossing over uncertain waters from one shore to another. The passing over the watery divide is clearly a faith issue. Similar to Noah and Moses, we eventually come to the place where there is no way out; rain clouds are gathering and Pharaoh's storm troopers are banging their sword butts on our front doors demanding our lives. To escape we embark in brokenness by sending the crafts of our lives out on the waters of faith in hope that we will reach the other side. The other side means a new start, a new beginning where we can be safe and restored to new life. We pray that the Spirit of God who hovers over the waters enables our safe passage, and it eventually dawns on us that the entire creation story could very well be about establishing a landscape for our passing through to salvation.

Moses: His First Redemption with Water

Sweat ran down the faces of Moses' parents, Jochebed and Amram, as they smeared the little basket with pitch in preparation for its voyage off the banks of the Nile. Perhaps Jochebed, still light-headed from her delivery of the child a few days before, sat down to rest and allowed her husband to finish the job. "From one womb to another" she whispered out loud to herself. "No dear, we have built an ark for our son." It had occurred to Amram that tar was the material Noah and his sons used to waterproof the ark, and this at least gave him some glimmer of optimism. "We must trust our Lord to deliver our little 'Noah of the Nile.' As he navigated Noah to a new land, he will also bring our son to a safe harbor. As our ancestors lived by faith, so must we."

The next day, as Amram was building for the Egyptians, Jochebed and daughter Miriam brought the ark down to the shore and set it adrift. Jochebed couldn't bear to watch the basket drift away; she asked Miriam to watch from a concealed position and report back the news, whether good or bad.

Deliverance came from the daughter of Pharaoh, who chose to defy her father's direct command to kill all Hebrew male babies by throwing them into the Nile. Instead, she took him for her son.

> *Then Pharaoh's daughter went down to the Nile to bathe, and her attendants were walking along the riverbank. She saw the basket among the reeds and sent her female slave to get it. She opened it and saw the baby. He was crying, and she felt sorry for him.*
>
> Ex. 2:5–6

A baby floating toward her on the Nile must have seemed

a gift from the river god. As she lifted him from the bobbing basket, a word common to Egypt—*moshe*—came to her. The Egyptian equivalent for Moses meant, "to be born," or as a noun, a "child" or "son." Moses, in Hebrew, means "the one drawn out" or "he who draws out." Pharaoh's daughter's statement: "I drew him out of the water" is a joining of Hebrew and Egyptian name meanings. The common name, unbeknown to her, had a dual meaning for her now and years later for the nation of Israel. The act of drawing out applied not only to being taken out of a watery cradle but also to the drawing out of a people from the waters of slavery—and a sea.

The physical sense of rebirth for the baby in Pharaoh's daughter's arms must have been palpable as she carried the child to the shore. The imagery of receiving new life within a wicker womb could not have been clearer: water drops falling from her while carrying the child symbolized the emergence of new life, with the Nile serving as midwife.

The significance of water in Moses' life began at birth. He entered the world through the breaking of his mother's waters into a hostile world. In a supreme act of faith and courage, he was placed in an ark to be "drawn out of the waters" by a princess who bestowed upon him a name relating to that event. Moses' very name signified one "who pulled his people out [*moshe*] of the depths" (see Isa. 63:11–13).

Now we will look at Moses endowed with the responsibility for the construction of another ark. While his parents had fabricated one out of a reed basket for his salvation, Moses is given precise instructions for one to house God's presence and symbols of his eternal promise.

The Ark of the Covenant (Testimony)

"Have them make an ark of acacia wood—two and a half cubits long, a cubit and a half wide, and a cubit and a half high. Overlay it with pure gold, both inside and out, and make a gold molding around it. Cast four gold rings for it and fasten them to its four feet, with two rings on one side

and two rings on the other. Then make poles of acacia wood and overlay them with gold. Insert the poles into the rings on the sides of the ark to carry it. The poles are to remain in the rings of this ark; they are not to be removed. Then put in the ark the tablets of the covenant law, which I will give you.

"Make an atonement cover of pure gold—two and a half cubits long and a cubit and a half wide. And make two cherubim out of hammered gold at the ends of the cover. Make one cherub on one end and the second cherub on the other; make the cherubim of one piece with the cover, at the two ends. The cherubim are to have their wings spread upward, overshadowing the cover with them. The cherubim are to face each other, looking toward the cover. Place the cover on top of the ark and put in the ark the tablets of the covenant law that I will give you. There, above the cover between the two cherubim that are over the ark of the covenant law, I will meet with you and give you all my commands for the Israelites."

Ex. 25:10–22

Behind the second curtain was a room called the Most Holy Place, which had the golden altar of incense and the gold-covered ark of the covenant. This ark contained the gold jar of manna, Aaron's staff that had budded, and the stone tablets of the covenant.

Heb. 9:3–4

Housed within its tabernacle enclosure, the ark was to be the place of communication with God, who would present himself between the two cherubim. This place on the top surface of the ark was called the mercy seat or the throne of God, while the ark itself was designated by God as his footstool (Ex. 25:10–22; 37:1–9). Until the tabernacle was permanently located in Israel, it was to be carried by members of the tribe of Levi by its poles. Exodus 25 says the ark was essentially a rectangular box made of acacia wood. The box was covered with a lid. Two angels were positioned at either end of the lid, facing each other with wings extended up and forward. Their faces looked down at the lid, which was called the mercy seat or atonement cover. The lid and the cherubim were crafted from a single piece of wood; only a master craftsman could execute this. His name was Bezalel, and he is credited with building the entire object (Ex. 37:1).

Thus, the ark was not huge like an armoire, and did not need a lot of very strong guys to carry it, though the weight of the gold required at least two men on each pole to support it. This was especially necessary when crossing the slippery bed of the Jordan River and circling the uneven ground around the city of Jericho and the many other cities Israel was required to take. The ark was covered entirely with gold plate, inside and out. Out in the sunlight it must have shone like a beacon, though it was likely covered with a veil.

Interestingly, the acacia tree was known to the Egyptians as the Tree of Life. In their mythology, the first human couple—Isis and Osiris—were said to have emerged from the acacia tree of Saosis, which the Egyptians afterward referred to as the "tree in which life and death are enclosed." Our study of New Jerusalem (chapter 15) will show the Tree of Life planted by the flowing water of life (Rev. 22:2). Perhaps it is a literal acacia tree. When we look at the tabernacle, we will see acacia wood prominently used in its construction. Its varied uses and symbolism as the Lord's preferred wood species in his worship architecture (along with cedar) attract our attention.

The Ark and the Golden Mean

The dimensions of the ark were 4.27 x 2.56 x 2.56 ft, which are geometrically symmetrical in their proportions. They fall within what is known as the golden mean—a geometrical calculation invented by ancient Greek geometers (probably Pythagoras) and used by Phidias in his design of the Parthenon in Athens. They found a perfect relationship or ratio between the dimensions of a structure's parts and their sum. Basically, the parts are in perfect mathematical agreement with the whole. Symmetry was found when the relationship between the longer of two sides was equal to their sum (being added together). Woodworkers often use this calculation when designing drawers of various sizes in furniture chests. The Greeks used it to calculate the height of a temple's columns in relation to its length and width.[22]

The depths of this calculation are still being explored today, but from a spiritual aspect, the concept of an equal ratio between the whole and its parts is striking. Our relationship with the Lord (when we become his child) is constant. Though we may change in many ways, we cannot alter our dimensional relationship with him. Our perfect ratio with the Lord is always preserved, though we may feel far from him or believe we have let him down in some way.

For the nation of Israel, a nation consisting of twelve tribes, the bonding of parts to the whole became critical when they crossed the Jordan River. Though they were not likely aware of its geometric connotations, the symbolism and functional use of the ark was deepening.

Crossing the Jordan

Early in the morning Joshua and all the Israelites set out from Shittim and went to the Jordan, where they camped before crossing over. After three days the officers went throughout the camp, giving orders to the people: "When you see the ark of the covenant of the LORD your God, and the Levitical priests carrying it, you are to move out from your positions and follow it. Then you will know which way to go, since you have never been this way before. But keep a distance of about two thousand cubits between you and the ark; do not go near it. . . .

"Tell the priests who carry the ark of the covenant: 'When you reach the edge of the Jordan's waters, go and stand in the river. . . .' See, the ark of the covenant of the Lord of all the earth will go into the Jordan ahead of you. Now then, choose twelve men from the tribes of Israel, one from each tribe. And as soon as the priests who carry the ark of the LORD—the Lord of all the earth—set foot in the Jordan, its waters flowing downstream will be cut off and stand up in a heap. . . .

"Now the Jordan is at flood stage all during harvest. Yet as soon as the priests who carried the ark reached the Jordan and their feet touched the water's edge, the water from upstream stopped flowing. It piled up in a heap a great distance away, at a town called Adam in the vicinity

of Zarethan, while the water flowing down to the Sea of the Arabah (that is, the Dead Sea) was completely cut off. So the people crossed over opposite Jericho. The priests who carried the ark of the covenant of the LORD stopped in the middle of the Jordan and stood on dry ground, while all Israel passed by until the whole nation had completed the crossing on dry ground. . . .

"Choose twelve men from among the people, one from each tribe, and tell them to take up twelve stones from the middle of the Jordan, from right where the priests are standing, and carry them over with you and put them down at the place where you stay tonight."

JOSHUA. 3:1–4, 8, 11–13, 15–17; 4:2–3

The crossing of the Jordan River is one of those underrated miracles. The crossing of the Red Sea has for certain gotten more Hollywood movie time. I have come to appreciate the crossing of the Jordan, and I feel bad that I have neglected it over the years. The crossing of the Red Sea seems as though it was done in a panic. You can imagine feeling the hot breath of all those chariot horses on the back of your neck, and just as the archer behind the driver is about to release an arrow into your spine, you plant your foot where deep water has just been. No time to observe the hallway of water, to pick up some interesting shells, or throw some stranded fish into the walls of water and hope they make it back in. There's a lot of destruction, bodies of the bad guys floating face down after it's all over, and a big party afterward.

The crossing of the Jordan with Joshua seems much mellower. There must have been lots of time to check things out, like sticking your finger into the standing waters and hanging out with friends to laugh in incredulity at what you were experiencing. The crossing was a celebration, a triumphal entry into a new land that had been anticipated for more than a generation. Select members of each tribe had plenty of time to stop in the middle of the riverbed and pick up one of the twelve stones to set up at Gilgal. This was done to commemorate God drying up the Jordan so "that all the peoples of the earth might know that the hand of the LORD is powerful and so that you might always fear the LORD your God" (Joshua. 4:24).

We'll delve further into the meaning of standing stones and altars in chapter 5. The focal point of the crossing was the ark of the covenant, which the Levites held stationary and through which the power of the Lord held back the waters. It must have been an awesome experience to pass by it, keeping a healthy distance away from it. Joy must have been tempered with holy fear and wonder.

Comparing Arks

I find the arks fascinating. First of all, why did the Lord institute them? We see a growing lineage of arks. There was Noah's ark, Moses' ark that carried him as an infant, and then the ark[23] Moses built to contain elements representing God's faithful presence with his chosen people. To complete this chapter, I would like to explore what symbolic meaning can be determined between the three arks, especially since the ark of the covenant was carried across the Jordan River.

As we have seen, Noah's ark carried the microcosm of the animal ecosystem along with a single family over the floodwaters of judgment until the waters receded and life could resume after they exited the craft. The ark that carried Moses in his infancy and the ark of the covenant, each in their distinct manner, involved passing through water. Noah and baby Moses floated over water by means of an ark, and the nation of Israel carried an ark through the floodwaters of the Jordan River (via the Lord's hand). Perhaps this is a sign of growing maturity in the Lord— those of a later lineage now carry the craft instead of being carried by one.

In all these cases, the means of deliverance is paired with a symbolic baptism of water. As Christians we carry God in us, for we are living temples (see chapter 10), and are commanded to pass through the waters of baptism as a public testimony of our faith in Christ. Whether the vessels are fabricated from raw materials or consist of our fleshly bodies, we see a symbolic architectural thread linking God's means of salvation with his people. God as builder instructs us to build literal and symbolic structures to expedite his deliverance for us. We in turn become living representations of that built form; we stand sanctified before him, seated forever at his table. We are saturated with his architectural symbolism.

> *Then God's temple in heaven was opened, and within his temple was seen the ark of his covenant. And there came flashes of lightning, rumblings, peals of thunder, an earthquake and a severe hailstorm.*
>
> REV. 11:19

The ark of the covenant was not a temporal, disposable instrument. Revelation 11:19 shows that it currently resides, in symbolic form, within the temple in the City of Heaven. The ark is in the vicinity of the River of Life and the Tree of Life—the natural elements that have always been intimately connected to it.

Next, we will look at something a bit more depressing yet very insightful. We'll examine a construction failure—the first ever documented in history. It is called the Tower of Babel.

Devotional Questions

1. What construction methods do Noah's ark and Moses' basket have in common? How is this significant?

2. The Hebrew word for the ark of Noah and the basket of Moses is the same. What symbolic connections can we make between the two craft? What were their uses in their stories?

3. What connections can you make between God's use of water and spiritual redemption?

4. What reasons does the Bible give for God's wrath on his creation? Do you accept this vengeful aspect of God as true? How does this affect the way you understand him?

5. How good are you at following instructions? Building an ark by exactly following God's instructions is symbolic of how we should build our lives. Read Ephesians 4:17—5:21. What does this passage say about how we can have a balanced and righteous life while sailing through life's seas?

6. How does the ark of the covenant crossing the Jordan relate to the redemption stories of Noah and Moses? What symbolic role does water play in the three narratives?

The ark of the covenant possesses symmetry in its dimensions. The Greek roots of the word symmetry mean "to measure together." In English, the word has two basic meanings. First, something symmetrical has harmony in its shape and dimensions. It is aesthetically pleasing in its proportions. It has balance. The object is subjectively pleasing to our eyes. It embodies a sense of perfection.

Second, symmetry is precise in its measurements. It has what geometers and mathematicians call a "patterned self-similarity." If you cut a symmetrical object in half and let the parts lie flat, each should be a mirrored reflection of the other. In this sense, symmetry can also be related to time, the transformation of something, architectural space, music, language, and knowledge.

7. The dimensions for the ark of the covenant came from God. What is God teaching us about himself through its symmetry?

CHAPTER 4

THE BABEL JOB
Miscommunication and Building the Wrong Vision

Now the whole world had one language and a common speech. As people moved eastward, they found a plain in Shinar and settled there.

They said to each other, "Come, let's make bricks and bake them thoroughly." They used brick instead of stone, and tar for mortar. Then they said, "Come, let us build ourselves a city, with a tower that reaches to the heavens, so that we may make a name for ourselves; otherwise we will be scattered over the face of the whole earth."

But the LORD came down to see the city and the tower the people were building. The LORD said, "If as one people speaking the same language they have begun to do this, then nothing they plan to do will be impossible for them. Come, let us go down and confuse their language so they will not understand each other."

So the LORD scattered them from there over all the earth, and they stopped building the city. That is why it was called Babel—because there the LORD confused the language of the whole world. From there the LORD scattered them over the face of the whole earth.

GENESIS 11:1–9

ASIDE FROM NOAH'S ARK, the Tower of Babel was the first documented land-based construction project in history. Instead of a project involving a single family, it was a coordinated effort of an entire society, and it was not a success. Ironically, it ended in failure when language (of all things) broke down. Many are surprised at this, thinking societal upheaval, war, plague, or finances would have halted construction. But if I told guys I knew in the trades that communication was the reason for the Tower's end, they would not be shocked. Communication is always the Achilles' heel on a job. Even when things are plainly said, in necessary detail and by the best communicator, instructions are often interpreted incorrectly and workmanship mimics interpretation.

It reminds me of the contractor in Carmel Valley who told his Mexican laborers to dig the footings of a house up to the inside of the white perimeter chalk line. Unfortunately, his simple Spanglish, sign language, and simulated digging pantomime were misunderstood. When he took off in his truck (mistake), they proceeded to dig to the outside of the line, thinking that, in this way, you can have a bigger house (a good thing). After they dug the footings twice their required width, the house had an immense foundation (a good thing) but at twice the cost (a bad thing). New plans had to be drawn and resubmitted to the county building department (a nightmare), and fees were paid a second time (start the violin music). You know the communication dilemma has entered the twenty-first century when you hear that, very recently, a home demolition company received wrong GPS coordinates and sent their wrecking crew to the wrong address.[24]

Beyond issues of communication lies the motivation behind intent. We must see the Babel project as a case study in which human self-determination expressed in a monumental vertical structure failed—not from weaknesses in engineering or construction, but from the psychological and ideological factors driving the project. The Lord observed this society's industrial capabilities when allied with a common tongue and seemed "startled" (an interesting choice of words) by their progress. But our interest is in the intent behind building in extreme verticality. It lies within the phrase "so we can make a name for ourselves and not be scattered."

The ancient Jewish historian Flavius Josephus, in his *Antiquities of the Jews*, elaborates on the first-century Jewish understanding of the intent behind the construction of the Tower of Babel:

Now it was Nimrod who excited them to such an affront and contempt

of God. He was the grandson of Ham, the son of Noah—a bold man,
and of great strength of hand. He persuaded them not to ascribe it to
God as if it was through his means they were happy, but to believe that it
was their own courage that procured that happiness. He also gradually
changed the government into tyranny—seeing no other way of turning
men from the fear of God, but to bring them into a constant dependence
upon his power. He also said he would be revenged on God, if he should
have a mind to drown the world again; for that he would build a tower
too high for the waters to be able to reach! And that he would avenge
himself on God for destroying their forefathers! Now the multitude were
very ready to follow the determination of Nimrod, and to esteem it a piece
of cowardice to submit to God: and they built a tower, neither sparing
any pains nor being in any degree negligent about the work. . . . It was
built of burnt brick cemented together with mortar, made of bitumen,
that it might not be liable to admit water. When God saw that they acted
so madly he did not resolve to destroy them utterly, since they were not
growing wiser by the destruction of the former sinners.[25]

Josephus's narrative links pretty well with our Biblical passage.
Here we have a nemesis: Nimrod (mentioned in Gen. 10:8–9) as
the fascist dictator influencing the minds of the populace against
God. His doctrine sounds familiar: our freedom must be self-
determined and void of God. God's sovereignty is a threat to
human autonomy, so the battle lines are set. Only cowards need
God for a crutch. Thus, as Josephus relates, Nimrod encouraged
them to build upward to avenge God for the flood. There is
nothing like feeling capable of attacking God on his own turf to
get people motivated for physical work. "To the winner go the
spoils."

There is also a bit of humor here, as the rationale for building
high is protection from another flood if God chooses to go after
them again. Talk about an admission of guilt! This also assumes
rising water is the only weapon in God's disciplinary arsenal. I
suppose the builders were aware of the high-water line of the
flood (a dirty soap ring around the side of a mountain?), so
they needed to rise above that to have some sense of security—the
plateau of the thing broad enough to carry the entire populace.

Of course, if the thought line of this concept were extended, how would the people eat if the Lord decided to not recede the waters for, let's say, ten years, and the biggest folks on top decided to play King of the Mountain, and what about the sanitary facilities?

Though the mental state of those running the operation was one step away from climbing on board the Mother Ship, the construction of the tower was sound in their use of high-quality materials. Burnt brick would not dissolve in water, and the use of bitumen (tar) for mortar indicates that this was a water-resistant (emphasis on "resist") structure. Tar, the bonding agent of the tower's bricks, was the sealing agent Noah used on the planks of the ark and is synonymous with the pitch used on Moses' Nile basket—same technology for different applications. Tar was employed on the tower in defiance against God; it was used in the ark's fabrication in obedience to God's instruction.

Symbolically, the Tower of Babel becomes a countertype, a humanistic building that challenges God's law and threatens to provoke divine discipline. It is the architectural representation of sin: a neutral form (the building itself is not sinful) invested with the evil intent of its makers and morphed into the representation of the violation. Thus a building, an inanimate form, attains a measure of guilt through association. This paradigm is a common thread throughout Scripture: those who take on the appearance of sinful behavior, or associate with those who do likewise, risk becoming fully culpable (1 Thess. 5:22). Work done in sympathy with God's statutes endures. Those averse to his tenets are doomed to premature abandonment. If we consider Josephus's account, this was not meant so much to be a building as it was to be an island—the inverse conception of Noah's ark. As the ark floated over the waters of chaos in cooperation with God's commands, the tower was a human fist extending upward in defiance toward God.

This story concludes with the peoples dispersing across the earth, where they develop (by communicating the desire for functional and aesthetic buildings) varied forms of architecture to house their families and shape their cities. Yet here, the tower is abandoned—a magnificent, unfinished fragment of a distorted vision, the first of many representing the dreams of delusional megalomaniacs across the millennia.

Archaeological investigations of the region have not been able to determine the exact location of the tower's remains. Supposition has it later converted into a ziggurat, a stair-stepped stone structure for worshipping the moon and other solar deities, the remains of which are visible today in Iraq, near Babylon and ancient Ur. Another source mentioned by Philo has it destroyed by God through storms. Who knows?

It is unlikely the ultimate height of the tower would ever have reached the throne room of heaven to enable some sort of heavenly combat between humans and God. The scary part is that Nimrod may have convinced the people of its possibility. No matter the elevation at which they found themselves, the battle was already raging in their minds. It reminds me of the strong current of atheism in Western Europe and the United States. In conversations I have found the intense hatred toward God palpable. It is startling, actually. I can't help but think one would be wise if they could harness that hatred into constructing something. You can build quite high when energized by anger.

Yet symbolically, the concept of verticality and sacred space is a strong architectural constant across societies. It is in us to build on the heights. Temples are often found on elevated places on the landscape. Where structures do not literally rise to the heavens, prayers, communion cups lifted up by hands, and smoke from sacrifices and offerings complete the concept with ritual symbolism. In our deepest perception of orientation, up is where God is.

Babel Land and the Problem with Overconstruction

If we stop to think about it, the mentality behind building the Babel tower is pretty crazy. At what point did this really intelligent and industrious people completely lose their minds?

Or perhaps this is simply a matter of overbuilding, where the ego is greater than the means to establish an edifice for vainglory.

Many of us in the trades have worked on Babel residences. These are immense, beautiful places designed and built to the glory of the owner. They are statements of self-expression pointing to their professional success and the daring it took for them to amass their fortunes. For the carpenter, this is definitely not a bad thing. We certainly know how to ride an ego. Babel house designs are very challenging to construct, and to see your skills execute a gifted architect's imagination is extremely fulfilling. You often work with the finest materials, and there is nothing more fun than to shop for a new tool to fabricate something you have never previously made.

I have spent months of years on mountaintops overlooking the Pacific Ocean and the San Francisco Bay Area, in the grassland hills of Carmel Valley, along fairways on the Pebble Beach golf courses, and beside a sea inlet where at break times we watched otters play in the calm water. My surfer/carpenter friends call this "construction nirvana," and truly, it doesn't get better than this. You wish the work on these places could go on forever . . . and sometimes it comes close to doing so. On top of it all, every week there is another paycheck to support your family. I mention all of this to say that there is nothing wrong with wanting to build and live in a big house. I am a big fan of those that are uniquely designed, extremely efficient, and do not look like an assemblage of boxes.

In a few cases, the experience, from beginning to end, goes very well. In most cases it does not. They tend to become financial money pits and, for many reasons, the causes of intense marital friction. The husband and wife as owners are often stretched at the beginning, and the inevitable increases in time and expense push the envelope beyond their means. After many months, carpenters get to know the couple (and their children and animals) and call them by their first names, and if they are very wealthy, attempt adoption into this wonderful family unit. For many of the carpenters, this is the reasonable and merciful thing to do.

The following is a portion of an e-mail I received from a Greek friend named Anonymous nearly a year after we finished working on a Babel house that illustrates my point:

I gotta tell you, I really miss Bob [husband], Sara [wife], Mike [son], the rabbits, Dino [parrot], Brigitta [animal caregiver], you, Ruben [coworker], the property [huge piece of land on the coast range], the wildlife. I had another dream about the place last night . . .

Some carpenters long to go back to these places, and a few dream of them still.

Most construction problems come from the seemingly infinite things that are completely out of one's control. Off the top of my head I remember:

- Massive windows (14x6 feet and 8x8 feet, 1 1/4 inch thick) were not laminated correctly at the plant and under the right (wrong) conditions the panes fractured months after installation. Several orders of replacement windows shipped from Switzerland had tiny air bubbles captured in the glass panes and had to be disposed of. The third shipment was approved; it took a crane to remove the old and install the new window panes (we called them "pains").

- In a magnificent, newly installed kitchen, not one of its top-of-the-line appliances worked.

- The most expensive stainless-steel sliding doors in the world (seriously) leaked rain water like noodle strainers after they had been attached to the house under three layers of waterproofing. The water seeped under the exotic hardwood floors where sections had to be replaced. However, the new and old wood did not exactly match after staining and finishing with a clear coat, so the entire wood flooring in three rooms had to be removed, replaced, and finished. Lawsuits are pending.

- I heard this in 1990 from a subcontractor who came from another job: While an owner was inspecting work on his house, the carpenters high up on scaffolding accidently dropped a roof support beam that tragically killed his golden retriever, which he had let loose in the house. That was the worst thing I had ever heard. I barely finished the day.

- The owners arrived on the job with their moving vans on the day the contractor originally promised to hand over the keys. Unfortunately, the house was several weeks away from completion. The contractor thought they could stay at the hotel he jointly owned for free while he collected his completion bonus. Unfortunately, the owners decided to stay at the Lodge at Pebble Beach and play rounds of golf at his expense until the house was finished.

- A sheetrock screw missed a framing stud and went into a copper fire sprinkler line that created a tiny leak which, weeks later, ruined a new Berber wool carpet and hardwood floor. Repairs required tearing out the wall, repairing the leak, and putting in new carpets at the contractor's expense.

- Three coats of paint peeled away from the entire exterior of a five-thousand-square-foot house due to some mystery substance that leached out from the last stucco coat.

- A solder joint in the kitchen plumbing burst at night while under pressure.

- A bathroom was built an inch too small, and the unbelievably expensive, giant jet tub would not fit in its custom-designed space overlooking the ocean (this is where the wife started crying and the carpenter looked for an imaginary device called a wall-stretcher).

- Tragically, a carpenter made a mistake and drilled a lockset hole on the hinged side of a rare antique door (I have not done this but heard about it).

- A contractor who went too far in tearing out termite- and dry-rot-infested wood in a tiny rat-infested house deemed "historic" and was almost lynched by the city council (see the author's therapist).

- I remember another contractor (not me) who in a daze from hearing from a very wealthy owner's attorney (on retainer) that he would be losing his entire profit and thousands more simply because the client wished to not pay, went to another job and, with a chainsaw, accidently cut off a limb of an oak tree (wrong tree). The footprint of the house had been designed around this particular limb. Let me restate this again. The limb, this natural, living architectural element was (heavy accent on the past tense) purposed in the design of the entire south side of the house and sympathetically expressed in various ways throughout the building. This natural architectural element was created with the heavy applause and "encouragement" of the owners, city arborist, and city architectural design committee (enabling the permit to build). He went home to tell his wife that they might very well be sued by two different owners, one of which was justifiable.

- Another contractor I knew had a design change fail to be approved by the building department after weeks of fighting with the neighborhood design approval committee . . . and the list is endless.

With this partial running backlog of examples, I am led to an opinion of the Babel tower disaster as being (what the Lord must have instituted, for the first time) "construction meltdown syndrome (CMS)." It is where everything that could go wrong does go wrong, or Murphy's Law. Murphy's Law is not found in the book of Leviticus and usually does not come into play when the carpenters are working alone on the place. Everything is . . . nirvana. That is, until the subcontractors show up and all the many loose ends—all the previous construction decisions—become accountable. There are days when you can pause from the chaos at break time and wonder out loud, "What is going on?" The foreman on the job fights to keep control and puts out fires like one sticking fingers in holes on the face of the Hoover Dam.

With respect to Murphy's Law, I imagine the subcontractors on the Babel job couldn't get it together with the carpenters, job foreman, and contractor and vice versa. On a project that size, the construction process must have been difficult enough, but to not have the means to communicate properly . . . forget about it. The bigger the project, the more issues arise. The chaos of confusion threatens to disperse the workers across the reaches of the earth, and perhaps this is the merciful thing to do. The reality is: some jobs are a nightmare, and more often than not, the reason points to communication.

Language, Communication, and the Babel Job

We are led to the crux of the Babel story. The success or failure of the tower depended on coherent language. The Hebrew word used here for language (*safah*) is not a simple translation. Hebrew lexicons defines *safah* as "language," but it is different than the word used for "foreign tongue" (*law-az*). It is used twice, in Gen. 11:1: "The whole world had one *language* and common speech" and in Gen. 11:7: "Come let us go down and confuse their *language*" (emphasis added). Thus, this was not a matter of Uzbekistanis trying to communicate with the Maori natives of New Zealand or the British with Americans.

Safah pertains to natural boundaries and edges. It is associated with lip, band, brink, edge, vain words, and (sea) shore, intimating images of the human body and natural landscapes. Thus, *safah* has spatial meaning and can be construed in an architectural sense. It follows that the confusion of language was not only a confusion of spoken language but a breaking of enslavement involving the human body with architectural space and the natural landscape. The people on the Plain of Shinar were freed from construction bondage (not to mention futility). They can be compared to the Hebrew slaves making bricks without straw for Pharaoh's edifices. It's better to abandon futile projects and move on to something that communicates clear sense.

The Woodworker and the Mentality of Crafting False Images

As we see with the Tower of Babel, making something has as much to do with mental thought processes as it does with manipulating tools with one's hands. The prophet Isaiah writes of the spiritual nature operating within the fabrication of images for worship. The perception of an image is crucial to pagan idolatry:

The carpenter measures with a line
and makes an outline with a marker;
he roughs it out with chisels
and marks it with compasses.
He shapes it in human form,
human form in all its glory,
that it may dwell in a shrine.
He cut down cedars,
or perhaps took a cypress or oak.
He let it grow among the trees of the forest,
or planted a pine, and the rain made it grow.
It is used as fuel for burning;
some of it he takes and warms himself,
he kindles a fire and bakes bread.
But he also fashions a god and worships it;
he makes an idol and bows down to it.

Half of the wood he burns in the fire;
over it he prepares his meal,
he roasts his meat and eats his fill.
He also warms himself and says,
"Ah! I am warm; I see the fire."
From the rest he makes a god, his idol;
he bows down to it and worships.
He prays to it and says,
"Save me! You are my god!"
They know nothing, they understand nothing;
their eyes are plastered over so they cannot see,
and their minds closed so they cannot understand.
No one stops to think,
no one has the knowledge or understanding to say,
"Half of it I used for fuel;
I even baked bread over its coals,
I roasted meat and I ate.
Shall I make a detestable thing from what is left?
Shall I bow down to a block of wood?"
Such a person feeds on ashes; a deluded heart misleads him;
he cannot save himself, or say,
"Is not this thing in my right hand a lie?"

Isa. 44:13–20

In great detail, Isaiah describes the process of woodcraft, circa eighth century BC, and we discover that the tools used more than 2,700 years ago are still present in the modern craftsman's tool bag.

Idolatry was a major problem throughout the biblical period and continues to be so in the present. Today the terminology of idolatry is not used (definitely not politically correct), but its concepts (worship of things and lifestyle; worship of self) can be symbolically applied to our commercial advertising industry. The impulses of the heart remain constant; our willful natures are deeply affected by the physical images we believe will make us feel secure and fulfilled. We tend to look to stuff for our peace and redemption. Our natures impulsively move us toward worshipping the created rather than the Creator. Simply, things embody fleshly lust. Hence we have the misguided impulse to build the Babel tower.

Isaiah's words illustrate, step by step, the logic (or should we say illogic?) behind the mental process that injects the divine into mundane materials. The maker doesn't fully consider the rationale of morphing something temporal (that continues to be temporal) and powerless into something eternal and all-powerful. "Think about it," Isaiah says, "you burn the same stuff you fall prostrate before." We endow physical things with powers they obviously do not possess.

The classic construction question to someone working away is: "What are you doing?" Other than the obvious, the builder should know the question is aimed at understanding how his little project ties in with what surrounds him. No matter how insignificant, a single task has ramifications throughout the building. To build intelligently is to work in awareness of the macro aspect of what you do. If I am working too quickly and am too focused on making good cuts, I sometimes fail to step back and see what my work looks like, whether it is pleasing to the eye. Is not this the point?

I have two real-life examples pertaining to the need to step back and gain perspective on what we're doing. The first example is of an elder in our church who was helping his son build his house. They were at the stage of laying subfloor plywood over floor joists, and he was cutting the ends that extended past the lower basement walls. He was about eight feet off the ground when he snapped his chalk line and moved his body out onto the piece he was going to cut off. I am not making this up. Again, for the sake of clarity and belief, he was kneeling on a three-foot extension of a sheet of plywood out in space, eight feet off the ground. When his saw cut more than three-quarters through the sheet, what happened next was something out of the Road Runner cartoon when Wylie Coyote's Acme rocket-propelled roller skates ran out of fuel while jetting out over a deep chasm.

The second example happened during a church construction project. The pastor's vision was to have the congregation do most of the construction to help invest the people in the program and save much money. We were framing the walls of the administration building when I overheard the pastor and another young man talking as they were nailing the studs to the top and bottom wall plates. They were discussing how, if they were ever out of work, they could always do this type of thing. And I quote: "Yeah, there isn't much thinking in this." So, the two finished nailing together a ten-foot-long wall made of two-by-eights. It was the partition wall separating the men's and women's bathrooms, and they hauled it over and stood it in place. I lost track of them until I heard a loud crash and bang. They had forgotten to bolt the wall to the concrete floor and nail off its ends where it joined the other walls. I am not making this up. They stood the wall and walked away from it. I saw them look up from the next wall they were building and look back down as if to pretend it didn't happen. I remember saying something they could hear: "Yeah, you could always stoop to do this for a living . . . and kill somebody."

As I pointed out in the introduction, making something is as much a mental activity as it is an interaction between our hands and eyes. If our mentality is not focused properly on our task—either out of blown ego or simply due to being unaware of what we are doing—we can cause great harm to ourselves, or even worse, to others.

Likewise, I think Isaiah is asking, "What you are doing? Dude, how does this chunk of wood you harvested from the forest become a god?" In regard to fabricating an idol, the perspective of the overall process is ignored. There is a mental disconnection, a delusion that happens between the harvest of raw materials, milling, fabrication, and worship—like lopping off the piece of plywood upon which your body is suspended. We have seen this demonstrated with the false vision of the Babel tower project and later with Israel reneging on their spiritual heritage. Our perceptions affect our vision. And our hands work accordingly. Isaiah reveals that, like a wooden idol, we may have eyes to see but be blind.

Devotional Questions

1. Think of a recent time when someone didn't understand your request, complaint, suggestion, or instruction. What was the result of this miscommunication? How could it have been avoided?

2. Behind every project is a vision driving it. What was the vision behind the Tower of Babel?

3. Why do people become so angry at God? What character traits do these people generally possess? Chips on their shoulders?

4. When have you experienced over-construction, when something grew beyond its intended proportions? (It could be any type of project, not necessarily a building.) What was it? What was its cost?

5. How do things become people's gods? Consider Isaiah 44:13–20, which illustrates how a crafted image becomes a thing of worship. How does this relate to what we see advertised in the media?

6. How do we keep from falling into the trap of over-building, over-spending, and loving manufactured things?

CHAPTER 5

A MORE SUITABLE VERTICALITY
Altars, Heaps, and Standing Stones

THE PHYSICAL ACT of stacking stones, fire-hardened composite blocks of earth, and hay stubble, brings up the topic of altars, heaps, and standing stones often mentioned in the Old Testament. The people who built them composes a veritable *Who's Who* of Bible characters with Noah, Abraham, Jacob, Uncle Laban, Moses, the generic children of Israel, Joshua, Gideon, Saul, David, and Elijah—to name a few.

As architectural forms, altars, heaps, and standing stones are crude, seemingly uninspired things. They are the result of a single person or a group of people stacking stones on top of each other, or, in a few significant cases, raising a single one to a standing position. While unsophisticated, they carry deep significance within their scriptural narratives. Altars, heaps, and standing stones are highly symbolic and seem to be spontaneous creations. They typically come on the heels of the intervention of God in the course of one's life as a symbol of an agreement, promise, redemption, or salvation from earthly peril. Their construction often comes at God's command. It's interesting that God has people stack stone rather than write something honorific, paint a lovely picture, or sing a "happy-clappy" song[26] with someone banging away on a tambourine.

God knows we require physical markers in our lives to remind us of the passing of significant events. We tend to forget moments of our past, and our memories are stimulated when we encounter the environments we experienced many years earlier. Childhood memories of friendships, conversations, and sports competitions are activated when we walk the streets, school hallways, and playing fields of our youth.

I have a number of places that trigger feelings of nostalgia. I have written about one of these in my book *Your Voice Echoes Through: Gerasa of Jordan and the End of the Classical City*. The place is my grandmother Shepherd's house in Atherton, California. The house is long gone, a necessary victim to a property subdivision in the 1980s, but the street and most of the natural landmarks remain. Though I am in my fifties, I stand on the street and visualize myself riding my old bicycle and going off to play basketball at Menlo College forty years previous. The Lord applied this concept to Israel by requiring them to erect simple, vertical stone edifices.

If you count the altars, heaps, and standing stones from the pages of Scripture, you find there were so many of these things that you wonder if you could walk through Bronze Age Palestine without tripping over one. If you were informed as to their places and purposes, you could piece together an unbroken narrative of a chosen people in interaction with their God. As Joshua said,

> *"When your children ask you, 'What do these stones mean?' tell them that the flow of the Jordan was cut off before the ark of the covenant of the Lord."*
>
> Joshua. 4:6–7

As the Israelites crossed the Jordan River, representatives from each of the twelve tribes picked up a stone from the middle of the river while the Lord held back the waters. The stones were carried to the west bank and stacked in a heap. It was dedicated as a memorial to their dry crossing and the faithfulness of God. So from the first minute the nation of Israel entered the Promised Land, the habit of stacking memorial stones became a significant part of their heritage and religious identity.

The heap's function was similar to the phone devices you might listen to as you tour a museum. Tourist sites of Alcatraz Island in the San Francisco Bay and Stonehenge in Britain make these available where you stop at particular places marked by signs, hold the phone to your head, and listen to the recorded voice inform you as to the particulars of what, where, and when. Since technology of this type was not available two thousand years before Christ, we might look at these simple vertical forms as "recording" devices, storing the memory of an important moment in time. Since written Scripture was in the hands only of a few, the altars and pillars likely became integrated with an oral tradition that placed narrative with the form. Parents and grandparents recited the meaning of the stones to the next generations.

Examples of Altars in the Old Testament

I have selected several instances in Scripture I thought significant in our study of God within the context of building altars and stone memorials. God reveals important things about himself even in what we might consider our most plain and mundane tasks. The process of building from our spiritual and emotional motivations can be a transcendent experience. The ark and Babel jobs show the positive and negative sides of the same coin.

As soon as he was able to stand on dry land, Noah built an altar. I had always thought that the Lord simply decided that "once was enough" for his earthly destruction routine, but it was the smoke rising from animals sacrificed on an altar that changed his approach with human sin. Symbols of repentance and honor performed on top surfaces of altars affected the Lord's ultimate judgment with humankind.

> *Then Noah built an altar to the LORD and, taking some of all the clean animals and clean birds, he sacrificed burnt offerings on it. The LORD smelled the pleasing aroma and said in his heart: "Never again will I curse the ground because of humans, even though every inclination of the human heart is evil from childhood. And never again will I destroy all living creatures, as I have done."*
>
> GEN. 8:20–21

Abraham was a major figure in the lineage of altar builders; the act of building and sacrificing was integrated into Israel's perception of a Promised Land. They were indeed stones of promise; the land this altar sat on would one day be possessed by Abraham's (Abram's) descendents.

> Abram traveled through the land as far as the site of the great tree of Moreh at Shechem. . . . The LORD appeared to Abram and said, "To your offspring I will give this land." So he built an altar there to the Lord, who had appeared to him.
>
> GEN. 12:6–7

The following story of Abraham and Isaac's "altar incident" on Mt. Moriah may be seen as the first of a series of altars set up by the patriarchs on what was to become the site of the future temple of Jerusalem and eventually the ultimate sacrificial altar— the cross of Christ's crucifixion.

> Abraham took the wood for the burnt offering and placed it on his son Isaac, and he himself carried the fire and the knife. As the two of them went on together, Isaac spoke up and said to his father Abraham, "Father?"
> "Yes, my son?" Abraham replied.
> "The fire and wood are here," Isaac said, "but where is the lamb for the burnt offering?"
> Abraham answered, "God himself will provide the lamb for the burnt offering, my son." And the two of them went on together.
> When they reached the place God had told him about, Abraham built an altar there and arranged the wood on it. He bound his son Isaac and laid him on the altar, on top of the wood. Then he reached out his hand and took the knife to slay his son. But the angel of the LORD called out to him from heaven, "Abraham! Abraham!"
> "Here I am," he replied.
>
> GEN. 22:6–11

Jacob's altar construction, standing stone pillars, and stacking heaps of stones present some of the most fascinating occurrences in Scripture. Seemingly, they had as much to do with legality amidst family relationships as with worship. But then there is the Jacob's ladder revelation.

> *Jacob left Beersheba and set out for Harran. When he reached a certain place, he stopped for the night because the sun had set. Taking one of the stones there, he put it under his head and lay down to sleep. He had a dream in which he saw a stairway resting on the earth, with its top reaching to heaven, and the angels of God were ascending and descending on it. There above it stood the LORD, and he said: "I am the LORD, the God of your father Abraham and the God of Isaac. I will give you and your descendants the land on which you are lying. Your descendants will be like the dust of the earth, and you will spread out to the west and to the east, to the north and to the south."*
> *. . . When Jacob awoke from his sleep, he thought, "Surely the LORD is in this place, and I was not aware of it." He was afraid and said, "How awesome is this place! This is none other than the house of God; this is the gate of heaven."*
>
> GEN. 28:10–14, 16–17

Jacob's vision was of a stairway or ladder connecting the earth to the heavens. God bridges the divide while his angels emphasize the bond between heaven and earth by moving up and down its steps. Heaven and earth are linked, and the Lord establishes and maintains its principle. The name given to the place was *Beth-el*, literally "House of God," as it served as a symbolic gateway at the head of a concourse of ascent and descent. Though Bethel was to become a city on the landscape, the concept of God's house does not seem to be literal. Though Jacob honored God at the point on earth where the heavenly ladder was set, God is on earth and in heaven and all places between.

After waking, Jacob arose and was compelled to do something of architectural significance. He stood a stone that was once his pillow from the horizontal to the vertical position. He was in a sense creating sacred space by performing the architectural principle of raising a column to the standing position. Once a stone becomes a vertical linear element, it establishes a point on the ground plane and transforms space into a place of recorded memory. Against it, the sun casts its shadow and the pillar becomes a sundial allocating time to memory as its shadow line moves through the course of a day. In the morning the sun rises from the east, casting a western shadow; in the late afternoon it does so to the east. Ancient surveyors used a rod driven vertically into the ground to record both moments and draw a line connecting the east and west points. This east-west line was bisected at ninety degrees (making a right angle) to create a line running north-south. In this way they oriented the earth to the heavens and vice versa. Jacob's standing stone represents his response to revelation—using the most elementary architectural metaphor defining the permanent connection between God and humanity, the heavens and their angelic host with earth.

Later, in Genesis 31, Jacob again set up a single stone as a pillar, and then had family members construct a heap of stones close to the pillar. Jacob's adversarial uncle Laban announced that the two edifices—the pillar and heap—represented a two-party legal agreement (before God) that dictated neither family was to cross this territorial barrier and kill the other. I think more families should do this.

> So Jacob took a stone and set it up as a pillar. He said to his relatives, "Gather some stones." So they took stones and piled them in a heap, and they ate there by the heap. Laban called it Jegar Sahadutha, and Jacob called it Galeed.
> Laban said, "This heap is a witness between you and me today." That is why it was called Galeed. It was also called Mizpah, because he said, "May the LORD keep watch between you and me when we are away from each other. . . ."
> Laban also said to Jacob, "Here is this heap, and here is this pillar I have set up between you and me. This heap is a witness, and this pillar is a witness, that I will not go past this heap to your side to harm you and that you will not go past this heap and pillar to my side to harm me."
>
> GEN. 31:45–49, 51–52

After this, the Lord commanded Jacob to go back and reside

at Bethel. If I had been Jacob, I would have loved the idea of going back to Bethel (the House of God) to permanently reside. Talk about a sense of being "grounded"! Jacob set up a pillar (a more formal act than standing his stone pillow), poured a drink offering and oil over it, and built an altar. Jacob pouring an offering and oil over its rough, unfinished surface established that worship did not involve the stone as an intermediary. Decorative tooling would have drawn attention to its surfaces, where Babel-like pride might follow. Thus we have the grounding of sacred space—a commemoration stone and a sacrificial altar to the God who provides and delivers.

> Then God said to Jacob, "Go up to Bethel and settle there, and build an altar there to God, who appeared to you when you were fleeing from your brother Esau. . . ."
> Jacob and all the people with him came to Luz (that is, Bethel) in the land of Canaan. There he built an altar, and he called the place El Bethel, because it was there that God revealed himself to him when he was fleeing from his brother. . . .
> Jacob set up a stone pillar at the place where God had talked with him, and he poured out a drink offering on it; he also poured oil on it. Jacob called the place where God had talked with him Bethel.
>
> Gen. 35:1, 6–7, 14–15

There has been significant archaeological study pertaining to the presence of "standing stones" in Israel. They have been found from the Negev in the south to the ancient site of Gezer in north-central Israel, and their dating is estimated to go as far back as the late Stone Age. Based on this evidence, the act of standing stones as a base human movement toward the heavens transcends religion, society, and time. This is strong evidence to say this behavior is a part of our human nature.

Moses and Joshua each received instruction from the Lord to build altars—for Moses, at the base of Mount Sinai, and for Joshua, after crossing the Jordan to claim the Promised Land. At Sinai, God told Moses to tell the Israelites,

"'Make an altar of earth for me and sacrifice on it your burnt offerings and fellowship offerings, your sheep and goats and your cattle. Wherever I cause my name to be honored, I will come to you and bless you. If you make an altar of stones for me, do not build it with dressed stones, for you will defile it if you use a tool on it. And do not go up to my altar on steps, or your private parts may be exposed.'"

Ex. 20:24–26

Later, Moses and the elders of Israel told the people,

"When you have crossed the Jordan into the land the LORD your God is giving you, set up some large stones and coat them with plaster. Write on them all the words of this law when you have crossed over to enter the land the LORD your God is giving you, a land flowing with milk and honey, just as the LORD, the God of your ancestors, promised you. And when you have crossed the Jordan, set up these stones on Mount Ebal, as I command you today, and coat them with plaster. Build there an altar to the LORD your God, an altar of stones. Do not use any iron tool on them. Build the altar of the LORD your God with fieldstones and offer burnt offerings on it to the LORD your God. Sacrifice fellowship offerings there, eating them and rejoicing in the presence of the LORD your God. And you shall write very clearly all the words of this law on these stones you have set up."

DEUT. 27:2–8

In both cases the altars were to be of rough field stones, not touched by hand tools, but plastered with a chalky material. God revealed to Moses why his altar was not to be of dressed stones (refined and decorated with chisels) or to be elevated on a platform.

The last phrase of Ex. 20:26—"or your private parts may be exposed"—has been thought by commentators to have literal meaning: people below could look up the priest's robe and see his genitalia, which I think would certainly cause an attention problem among worshippers standing below. The revelation of this was astonishing for me. To make this assumption we would have to know how tight one wrapped his robes in 1400 BC. And the thought of the physical effort someone would have had to take to contort their body for an improper view is pretty ridiculous, if not really audacious. If I saw someone do that, it would give me a good excuse to pick up a nice field stone and brain that guy from thirty feet. Though this may very well be God's reason for restricting altar elevation, there could be something else at play here.

In respect to the idea of built form, particularly in respect to the Tower of Babel, there may be something more. Nakedness was the key issue in Genesis (chapter 3) when Adam and Eve sinned and for the first time became "self-aware." Awareness of the flesh, hiding from God, covering genitalia, and knowledge of "good and evil" are the result of the humanistic striving to become "like God." We saw this expressed above in architectural terms in the erecting of the tower and the desire to reach upward by means of a magnificent structure to battle God at the gates of heaven.

Architecture is created with intent. Reaching upward for the apple, and building upward to heaven are the human reflex for self-autonomy (not to be confused with "anatomy") and glorification. That same upward reach is directly related to building an altar on a raised surface. In climbing its steps Moses would, unavoidably, be glorified. The nakedness of pride of position is fully integrated within the human condition.

Altar design carried deeper connotations for human interaction than a mere assembly of stones. Raising the altar elevates one's intent with worship and magnifies the sacrifice and heartfelt thanks. But with the flesh there is a dark side to every good intention. God warns of its nakedness—whether it be an improper dress code or fleshly ego.

Altars also signified the turning away from idolatry and the repair of spiritual error: the serious mistake of offending God by straying from his commands and purposes. The writer of Judges tells us,

> *So Gideon built an altar to the LORD there and called it The LORD Is Peace. To this day it stands in Ophrah of the Abiezrites.*

That same night the LORD said to him, "Take the second bull from your
father's herd, the one seven years old. Tear down your father's altar to
Baal and cut down the Asherah pole beside it. Then build a proper kind
of altar to the LORD your God on the top of this height. Using the wood
of the Asherah pole that you cut down, offer the second bull as a burnt
offering."

JUDG. 6:24–26

This event with Gideon was one of a series of cycles for the nation of Israel, listed in the book of Judges. The cycle began when Israel fell into sin by adopting the lifestyle of the idolatrous societies surrounding her. Then God disciplined Israel with invading forces who stripped her resources. When the pain of affliction reached a certain level of agony, the people repented, and God, in his mercy, sent a judge or hero to act as a deliverer. In this case, the deliverer was Gideon and the affliction was the Midianites.

The angel of the Lord told Gideon to tear down his father's altar and build an entirely new and "proper" (British pronunciation: "propa") one on an elevated site. Again, elevation is a key word. In ancient Palestine and east of the Jordan River, pagan ritual sites were often set on prominent topography. For Gideon to build on one would not have seemed out of the ordinary. But in this time and place, it was a significant command.

The altar was not to be elevated on a human-made podium but on a natural height. Thus, those worshipping were not confronted with the issue of nakedness and the sinful pride that might occur with an altar constructed on an elevated platform. Height might be set in contrast to the place where the angel of God first found Gideon; he was threshing wheat in a winepress, essentially a pit in the ground. This behavior was not unique to Gideon, for Israel had resorted to living in caves and under-croppings of rock (Judg. 6:2). The persecution was so intense that Israel had gone covert—subterranean.

For Israel to sacrifice from a height was to make a statement relating to personal conversion and conviction. It was to say that from now on things would be different. Midian undoubtedly interpreted this as their enemy gaining confidence. They knew a serious confrontation was not far off in the future. However, God would not go into hiding; if it was his will, he would prompt his own to "go to guns" over his glory and enforce the Abrahamic promise of sacred topography. To break the final straw, Gideon destroyed the Asherah pole—a tree symbol used in pagan ritual—and used it to fuel the altar fire for his first sacrifice. An altar site on the skyline without poles and other paraphernalia made it dissimilar and thus noticeable.

An association I can make with this is when, while in college, I broke a pattern of lifestyle that affected my peer group relations. I was compelled to set up my "altar on a height" to make subtle statements and physical movements away from "going and doing" in one place to "going and doing" in another. Objects that I once thought were cool I happily threw on a symbolic pyre. The smoke's vertical finger rose to the sky, pointing in the direction of my convictions. A black line on a blue sky was definitive, a necessary artistic symbol set against forces seeking an ambiguous, indecisive mindset to work its destructive course. Granted, my life was not on the line as Gideon's was, but standing in the wisdom of the present, many years later, I can see that the course of my life was indeed at stake.

Several generations later, Saul was the Israelites' deliverer from their latest affliction, the Philistines. "You have broken faith," he told his men when they ate meat that hadn't been treated according to God's law. Saul commanded,

> "Roll a large stone over here at once." Then he said, "Go out among the men and tell them, 'Each of you bring me your cattle and sheep, and slaughter them here and eat them. Do not sin against the LORD by eating meat with blood still in it.'"
>
> So everyone brought his ox that night and slaughtered it there. Then Saul built an altar to the LORD; it was the first time he had done this.
>
> 1 SAM. 14:33–35

So often in reading the narrative of Saul's life I get this queasy feeling, like when you have done something really wrong and you are waiting for the hammer to fall. Saul had disobeyed God by allowing his men to eat the slaughtered meat of his enemies' flocks. We see several learning points in the account above. First, a severed relationship through disobedience against God must be repaired immediately. Repentance does not need to be fancy; make it immediate and heartfelt. I really like the idea of Saul and "the boys" rolling a rough field stone into position to do the sacrificial job. Then a rough altar was built nearby. The essence of repentance here is organic. In its most unrefined state we see a repentant heart moving stones into positions of worship. Stones become the platform upon which communion with God is reset. We do not see them being "tooled" or engraved with ritual images or enhanced with geometric forms. The materials are literally out of the earth from whence they came. The focus was on the sacrificial act and nothing more.

Elijah and the Priests of Baal

The following takes place on the summit of Mount Carmel in a confrontation between the prophet Elijah and the priests of Baal:

> Then Elijah said to all the people, "Come here to me." They came to him, and he repaired the altar of the LORD, which had been torn down. Elijah took twelve stones, one for each of the tribes descended from Jacob, to whom the word of the LORD had come, saying, "Your name shall be Israel." With the stones he built an altar in the name of the LORD, and he dug a trench around it large enough to hold two seahs of seed. He arranged the wood, cut the bull into pieces and laid it on the wood. Then he said to them, "Fill four large jars with water and pour it on the offering and on the wood."
>
> 1 KINGS 18:30–33

I have included Elijah's altar construction and sacrifice because of the role it played in the competitive face-to-face, "no holds barred" fight against the priests of Baal. It was a key player in the reestablishment of Israel's identity—an identity that had nearly been lost during the idolatrous milieu of Israel's kings. This evil was exemplified by King Ahab, who reigned in Samaria with his problematic wife, Jezebel, the daughter of a Sidonian king and pagan priest.

The forces of evil composed around this husband-and-wife team seem overwhelming. But again we find ourselves on a topographical height. In contrast with Gideon, Elijah is not tearing down an altar to a false deity but restoring a ruined one that had been active in a previous era in sacrificial service to Yahweh. It was ruined, which tells us something about the spiritual state of Israel; it had reached critical mass.

Elijah fixes twelve stones representing the twelve tribes of Israel to the altar base as a symbol reasserting unity and identity. Earlier in this chapter we saw how the Lord commanded Joshua to have his people pull twelve stones out of the middle of the Jordan River bed and make a memorial. In the book of Revelation, the New Jerusalem's foundation(s) are of twelve stones or twelve levels of them. The use of twelve is significant. I take from this that in the forthcoming conflict no one will be left behind. God's original intent for his people will be carried out. There will be no "missing in action" statistics. Throughout the biblical narrative, the Lord wants us to know that we who accept him as Savior will not be abandoned or forgotten when we reach the end of our lives. No one will be standing at the gate wondering if they missed their flight.

Our tour of altars ends with one that David built a generation after Saul's and several centuries before Elijah's. In chapter 8 we will discuss the architecture of Solomon's temple, but the preparation for the temple's construction began long before its foundations were dug. It began with the construction of an altar and the purchase of land from a Jubusite named Araunah, where five hundred years previously, Abraham had built an altar for the sacrifice of his son.

On that day Gad went to David and said to him, "Go up and build an altar to the LORD on the threshing floor of Araunah the Jebusite."

2 Sam. 24:18

Then Solomon began to build the temple of the LORD in Jerusalem on Mount Moriah, where the LORD had appeared to his father David. It was on the threshing floor of Araunah the Jebusite, the place provided by David.

2 CHRON. 3:1

This place possessed a lineage of altars. Abraham, David, and Solomon had built theirs there. The threshing floor, where the wheat kernel is separated from the chaff, had particular significance in the pairing of the relational terms: altars and threshing, sacrifice and winnowing. The altar equally emphasizes separation (as chaff) and restoration through the shedding of blood. It is the fulcrum balancing the winnowing away of sin and spiritual renewal: the means and the end. On one side is the joyful blessing of repentance and forgiveness through sacrifice; the other is much more painful. The hard superficial shell constricting our lives is broken down, separated, and blown away. Oftentimes the term *beating* is a very appropriate word to explain our coming clean before the Lord. Brokenness in repentance is a brutal process.

If I had lived then, I would have seen the life that had to die—a little animal lies lifeless over the stones, its blood running on my behalf. Somberness is mixed with the joy of my forgiveness. It is too hard yet to participate in the "happy-clappy" music. The garment that is my relationship with the Lord is now made with a much heavier fabric; I no longer wear it lightly. Though I am free, I know at what cost. Propitiation is a bloody word. This explains the rough organic nature of the stone altar; there is nothing to soften the sacrificial process, nowhere to hide, and no decorative imagery to distract one's mind from the cold reality of its great power.

Summary

The essence of this chapter is that sacred space does not necessarily demand four walls and a roof. An altar set on simple floor used for agricultural purposes stands as tall as any great temple of pillars. Rough stones in a field, gathered together and stacked to create a raised flat surface to conduct sacrifices to God, was the first and enduring form of worship for God's people. As this book moves forward, we will see places of worship become more involved, more complex and symbolic, yet with certain constants. Always there is a priority on obedience, heartfelt relationship, and humility within the simplicity of design, décor, and ritual.

Devotional Questions

1. Do you have any physical markers (standing stones) in your life? Is there a particular place that is special to you?

Several trees have special meaning to me. They mark the passing of time and places where I spent formative periods of life. They were standing, silent witnesses, companions to specific life events. The trees were younger and less tall then. Somehow we've grown up while apart from each other.

2. Why did God instruct the Israelites to stand stones? Should we do something similar when God moves in our lives, when significant changes happen? If so, what?

3. Rough stones in altars and memorials are humble things. Why doesn't God require fancy buildings and altars in order to worship him?

4. Who in this chapter built altars? Why was it important that they did this?

5. It seems that a requirement for God's chosen leaders was to build something or stand a stone. Why do you think God had them perform architectural tasks rather than do anything else? What does this reveal about God?

6. What are some other ways we can relate standing stones and altar building to our spirituality?

CHAPTER 6

JERICHO AND RAHAB
The Issue of Walls

Now the gates of Jericho were securely barred because of the Israelites. No one went out and no one came in.

Then the LORD said to Joshua, "See, I have delivered Jericho into your hands, along with its king and its fighting men. March around the city once with all the armed men. Do this for six days. Have seven priests carry trumpets of rams' horns in front of the ark. On the seventh day, march around the city seven times, with the priests blowing the trumpets. When you hear them sound a long blast on the trumpets, have the whole army give a loud shout; then the wall of the city will collapse and the army will go up, everyone straight in."

JOSHUA 6:1–5

I HAVE KNOWN about the battle of Jericho as far back as I can remember. The story was taught to me innumerable times, and I sang "Joshua Fit the Battle of Jericho" throughout my childhood Sunday school years and Young Life meetings. I likewise completed the circle when I taught through its verses in my Bible classes. Yet it did not occur to me that after all this time, I had missed a vital element to this story.

I have come to the conclusion that the battle of Jericho is primarily a story about walls. Wait! Before you bend over in hysterics and turn the knob all the way open on your oxygen respirator, try to get through the next few paragraphs, and hopefully this will make a little more sense.

Jericho's walls should be given a voice to this story. Why not? Walls certainly play a dominant role in the Jericho narrative

(Joshua. 2:6). Most of us can recall from memory: Jericho was "tightly shut up" behind its walls, the spies climbed out a window and down them to freedom, the Israelites ritually circled them for seven days, Rahab's home was structurally incorporated within them, a red cord hung down them from Rahab's window, the Lord supernaturally collapsed them, the Israelites likely ran up their fallen debris to capture the city, and the walls of Rahab's home stood when others fell. Amidst the many dynamics of this story, walls are a key participant. Walls seem to be everywhere.

Walls were as important to this story and, in particular, to Rahab the harlot as they are to us today. The walls around us set the place where most, if not all, of our actions and relationships take place. We often take them for granted and forget they are there with us. They are, like the floor and ceiling, unconscious participants in our lives. But walls in their architectural, historical, and sacred contexts play a vital role in the biblical narrative. The saying, "If only these walls could talk," is a light-hearted admission of a fundamental truth.

The intent of this chapter is to portray the Jericho narrative in light of a symbolic relationship between Rahab, the wall architecture that surrounded her, and the Lord of Hosts who stormed the walls of her heart. This is a fairly narrow focus that requires an intentional neglect of the story's other wonderful dimensions. However, understanding Jericho's walled environment requires much background information that will expand this into the longest chapter of this book.

Though walls cannot speak orally, they do in a metaphorical sense. Indeed they play a seminal role in defining Rahab's faith. I believe they were subtle, indirect participants in her coming to faith. The Bible is straightforward in describing how the destruction of Jericho's walls resulted from Israel's obedience to the Lord's instructions. However, in relation to Rahab and her faith in God, the walls carry another dimension that, as far as I am aware, has not been discussed.

Walls orient our lives just as walls ordered Rahab's world and affected her sensory-perception ranges with the awareness of: inside, outside, near, far, enclosure, seclusion, security, openness, public, privacy, between, edges, and barriers. I contend that while the Spirit of God penetrated deep into Rahab's heart, he also used Jericho's architectural forms as a passive, ministering-sensory influence during her process to salvation.

This is of course conjecture on my part. The Bible does not describe what affect architecture played on Rahab's spiritual and emotional condition. However, the Bible does go out of its way to describe her architectural, societal, and spiritual predicaments. I simply attempt to connect the architectural and the spiritual with commonly understood architectural principles found in popular texts.[27] This chapter will culminate with some extensive thoughts along these lines.

The Plan of this Chapter

To show how walls as architectural elements illuminated Rahab's faith, I must take a circuitous route through a number of topics. I will describe the experience of building walls from my construction years, and then, for a bit of seed-of-truth-humor, talk about Hollywood's perspective of Jericho.

It is especially important that we know the basic archaeology of Jericho, a place that is fraught with interpretational difficulties of all sorts. An important issue that arises with Jericho's archaeology pertains to how we perceive physical evidence, what we believe it says. We apply this more broadly in how we orient what we see with our eyes to how we "see" things in our minds in light of our emotional responses, personal perspectives, and principles.

The difficulty with the Jericho story is that it boils down to accepting, by faith, unseen and miraculous events which are not often compatible with scientific method. This is very similar to the problem Rahab confronted in her day: at what point does our confidence in the physical world end and our faith in the unseen Lord of Hosts extend beyond the stuff we passionately grasp with our hands?

Here we meet with Rahab on the same ground. Jericho, then

as a substantial city and now as a mound of built-up civilizations, presents the epitome of accepting, in faith, the unseen hand of God over the strength of contemporary opinion and societal status quo. After the dust settles we see Rahab walk away from the collapsed debris of her past into new life.

An Application from the World of Construction

During my years working on residential construction projects, the stage of erecting walls was one of the most enjoyable. The wall-building phase was highly anticipated because, for those who were with the house from the very beginning, it was a reward for a lot of hard preliminary work.

You find out pretty quickly that walls stand on floors, and floors rest on foundations. You have to do all the underneath part before you have a floor on which a wall will stand. Yes, I know, this is a ridiculously obvious statement, but to most outside the trades, the under-floor construction phase seems an afterthought. A home's focus generally rests on its more glorious upper structural attributes like siding and trim-work. However, a carpenter knows the effort it takes to build up to floor level; often it seems equivalent to constructing an entire home.

I remember weeks of heavy slogging in the foundation trenches. My job was to ensure the trenches' correct width, depth, and agreeable orientation to the taut string lines that outlined the house's perimeter and interior supports. Not every job existed on a flat surface. Setting a foundation on a thirty-degree slope added a tremendous physical requirement. No matter the situation, concrete form boards had to be set vertically to the string lines by fixing them to the ground. It took immense effort to ready all the needed elements for the concrete pour.

Pour days were often tense affairs. Some on the crew would resort to speaking words that sounded like a variant French dialect. The expense of flowing concrete was the equivalent of watching dollar signs pour out of a concrete pumper's hose. As the pumped concrete flowed onto the ground and rose up within the straining, groaning forms, there was no better quality control examiner of one's form work.

After the concrete set, we pulled the forms away, and depending on the house and the topography of its lot, wood walls were framed to support an elevated ground floor level. The crew then laid floor joists over the walls and glued and nailed plywood sheathing down over the joists, creating a floor surface.

The slang term for this entire process was "getting out of the dirt." This idiom was often uttered in terms of a future hope, while in the moment, a carpenter was covered in sweat-soaked dirt, nursed poison oak rashes, and swatted at tiny flies and gnats hovering around his ears and eyes. Having good drinking water on hand was an important necessity because the city/county Building Department seemed to have the propensity to push the start of projects to midsummer due to any one of a thousand "red tape" issues.

If I remember correctly, my experiences with foundations occurred either in the heat of summer or in the wet of late winter/ early spring. In the case of late winter/early spring, instead of heat and flies we faced flooded trenches, mud-caked boots, and treacherous footing. By the time the sub-floor of the ground floor was finished, the anticipation to sink nails into wall studs was unbearable.

The first morning we walked onto the clean subfloor to snap a wall layout with a chalk-line was like waking up to Christmas day. The red-and-blue chalk wall outlines imprinted on the flooring revealed a coming three-dimensional reality. We could see where the walls would stand, and somehow our intuitions made us walk around their linear-rectangular shapes as if they were already in solid form. Oddly there was a sensation of enclosure in a barrier-free environment. By the end of the first week of wall framing, we grasped a sense of the house's character—how its exterior openings framed elements of the natural landscape, and how interior walls partitioned and organized space.

Later, after the utilities were installed, sheet rock was fixed to the wall framing. An audible sense was added to the building's atmosphere. Working in the bedrooms, bathrooms, and closets

I experienced the sensation of depth and solitude, feelings I did not have when in the living-entertainment rooms, kitchen, and heavily traffic areas. I could somehow sense how air, light, sound, depth, and elevation played upon the overall perception, particularly on the interiority of a house.

Certain places in a house made me feel different than others. I came to love some houses and feel ambivalent toward others. I did not intentionally strive to judge these places, but they affected me in ways that made expressing opinion irresistible. I came to accept that buildings hold an influence, a passive, ambient power within their forms, which causes us to respond, physically and emotionally, in various ways. Often I find myself inhaling a deep breath in places of great expanse. Or I find myself anxious to find exits in meandering, constricting spaces.

Perceptions vary for each person. This is also a societal phenomenon; folks from western cultures with their straight grid-like street patterns have struggled to make sense of the narrow winding lanes in Near Eastern towns and villages. Systems of order are culturally relative.

While working on my doctorate, I began studying modern architectural theory with the aim of applying its principles to ancient Classical and early Christian architecture. I found the (typically boring) theoretical stuff to be a revelation. What I had felt, years before, on the jobsite was substantiated by the principles inherent in structural design. I could see the possibility of melding the experiential with the theoretical. I could apply it to new things.

In light of this, the story of Rahab and the walls of Jericho epitomize the interaction of the human-spiritual experience within built form. We will look next to see how Hollywood, an influential power in depicting the Bible to the world, views this story.

Hollywood and Jericho

Hollywood, from its earliest years, has extended itself into the biblical realm with some lively attempts at portraying—or I should say interpreting—scriptural narrative. The earliest I remember are: *The Greatest Story Ever Told* (1965), *The Ten Commandments* (1956), *Ben Hur* (1959), *The Robe* (1953), *Quo Vadis* (1951), *The Bible: In the Beginning* (1966), and maybe my all-time favorite: *Barabbas* (1961) with Anthony Quinn as Barabbas.

Unfortunately there has not been much done on Joshua and the battle of Jericho. Just think of what Spielberg could do with the collapsing walls sequence! I know of only two television programs that presented the Jericho story: a TV miniseries called *Heroes of the Bible* (1978), and a weekly show I watched as a child called *The Time Tunnel* that aired for two seasons during the years 1966–1967. (I have to interrupt here to say I can not believe, after 43 years, I can remember this show, when I can't remember what I had for lunch two days ago.)

Overall, *The Time Tunnel* was a wonderful program where two scientists from the modern era were cast back into time and inadvertently became participants in a number of well-known historical events. So it is not a reach to say the episode pertaining to Joshua and the battle of Jericho (twentieth episode) did not exactly follow the biblical storyline. Perhaps you too can spot the difference after reading this synopsis taken directly from the show's Wikipedia page:

> *The travelers arrive outside of the tent of Joshua during the night, two days before the end of the Israelite siege of Jericho. Joshua comes to believe they are who they say they are—time travellers—and sends them to spy inside the city. Doug and Tony save a young virgin from being sacrificed to the Levantine deity Chemosh by the high priest of Jericho. Doug is captured and sent to the dungeon to be tortured as an Israelite spy. Tony escapes into a house with an unlocked door. When the resident arrives, he calls her (Rahab) because, from the Biblical account, she is the one who sheltered the two Israelite spies. (Rahab is the sister of the almost-sacrificed virgin.)*
>
> *After Tony rescues Doug from the dungeon, they take refuge on the roof of Rahab's house, but are betrayed by her servant woman Azah, who desires the reward of 1,000 talents of silver. Doug escapes to tell Joshua*

the information that he seeks. Tony and Rahab are about to be stoned to death, but when the Israelites complete their march, blow their trumpets and shout, the walls of the city fall down as what appears to be a tornado traces the destruction. Ann, a skeptic, decides that since a tornado is a natural phenomenon, that the fall of the walls was not a supernatural event, while Ray is convinced it was supernatural (perhaps because tornadoes are not known to strike in the Holy Lands). The travellers are transported to a new era after telling Rahab she'll be safe.[28]

I know . . . the Bible doesn't get any better than this. Yet let's not throw rocks and relegate this episode from *The Time Tunnel* to the rubbish bin without considering several of its contemporary insights. In order to do this, I must take a few pages to discuss Jericho's archaeological history.

The Archaeological Remains of Jericho

The best aerial photograph I have seen of the ancient site of Jericho (*'Ain es-Sultan*) is of a raised oval hill that looks as though it could have been the practice site for our military's "Shock and Awe" bombing raids of Saddam Hussein's palaces in Baghdad. The holes and trenches that pock and gouge the hill are from sporadic archaeological digs spanning a hundred years from the mid-nineteenth century. The earliest excavation methods were, compared to today's methodology, somewhat crude if not brutal. The lasting affect of their work, plus the natural effects of wind and erosion, have nearly obliterated the possibility of piecing together a coherent understanding of Jericho's last years of occupation. And unfortunately, this is of the time of Joshua.

Geographically, Jericho sat on an important crossroads into Palestine. Considering the size of the hill upon which Jericho sat, it was a relatively small city. It was certainly smaller than others Israel was to face in their invasion of Palestine, like the cities of Megiddo, Hazor, and Lachish. However, it was a strategic necessity to take Jericho. It was the cork in the topographical bottleneck, and releasing this cork would allow Israel to acquire

Salem (Jerusalem) and gain access both to the north-south spine of Palestine's hill country and down onto the fertile rich plains of Canaan.

The ancient mound of Jericho is in the shape of an elongated north-south oval (150 x 550 meters). It was and is to this day fed by a perennial fresh water source called Elisha's Spring, named from the prophet who purified it (2 Kings 2:19–22).

The abundance of water flowing from the eastern foot of the tel determined Jericho's continuity. That water, with other local springs, provided irrigation for its agricultural produce. Though it was a trade city, it could self-sustain its populace. The spring on the hillside was eventually encompassed by Jericho's (late Bronze Age) lower retaining walls, enabling the city to endure long sieges by invading forces.

The earliest known human settlement at Jericho was by the Mesolithic people sometime between 10,500 and 8,300 BC. This places Jericho on the prestigious short-list of the world's earliest cities. Evidence of this settlement exists within the lowest strata of Jericho's sixty-five-foot-high mound. The hill is not merely an accumulation of soils. It consists of layers upon layers of human settlements, a sedimentary build up of crushed and inundated building materials, and miscellaneous human debris accumulated over a period of 9,000 years. This is the classic description of a *tel*.

British archaeologist Kathleen Kenyon[29] discovered twenty different architectural phases, each defined by its own layer, some lasting much longer than others. During the span of these twenty phases, Jericho incurred three major and twelve minor destruction events. The Israelite destruction was (in my opinion) its last, when ancient Jericho proper was finally abandoned. A later, "modern" Jericho was built by Jews and Greek Hellenists in the wake of Alexander the Great. Much later Herod the Great built several incredibly beautiful getaway-from-Jerusalem palaces nearby.

An important occupational transition occurred at Jericho between 8,300 and 6,300 BC during what is called the "Pre-Pottery Neolithic A" age. It was the time of the first farmers, when a relatively dry climate coincided with a development in agricultural methodology which refined grass seed cultivation and water irrigation.

At this level on the western side of the tel (facing the Palestine hills), Kenyon's workers uncovered stone and mud construction of an unprecedented scope (dating to the Pre-Pottery Neolithic A period). The remains were of a wall twelve feet high, six feet wide at the base, and a round tower over twenty-six feet high by thirty feet wide at the base with in internal staircase of twenty-two steps. Kenyon dated this great work to 8000 BC.

The revelation of the wall and tower indicates that very early in Jericho's societal history people were creating architecture on a scale archaeologists have never seen or thought possible in this era. A civic leadership organized mass quantities of materials and manpower to build upward in 8000 BC. The project reminds us of the Tower of Babel. This revelation in the lower strata of Jericho marked a new phase of human history. These walls built 10,000 years ago were the earliest generation of those that fell 6,800 years later at the time of Joshua. They were the great architectural forebears of the walls Rahab knew.

The Problem with Pottery

In the 1930s, British archaeologist John Garstang used improved excavation techniques to unearth a residential area near the ancient perennial spring that fed the city.[30] Near the surface Garstang found discolored building stones that suggested a fiery destruction and strong pottery evidence that led him to put the final destruction date of Jericho around 1400 BC, a time frame agreeable with the Jericho narrative in the book of Joshua.

Kathleen Kenyon, Garstang's successor, arrived at Jericho in 1954 to begin her careful and systematic methods of excavation analysis. She determined that Jericho fell much earlier than Garstang thought, possibly in the Middle Bronze Age by Egyptian forces, according to her analysis of the pottery fragments (sherds) found in her area. In 1954 this was a world-shaking statement.

What Kenyon was saying, in effect, was that the archaeology that supported the accuracy of the biblical account was incorrect. The physical evidence told her that it was the wrong time and quite possibly the wrong place for the biblical account to have occurred (if it did at all). From that point on, scholars have leaned heavily on Kenyon's opinion to support the premise that the Joshua saga is biblical myth, completely unsupportable by physical evidence.

Recently, a scholar named Bryant Wood wrote an important paper where he reviewed Kenyon's evidence and found significant problems with her conclusions. Wood, an ancient pottery expert, studied Kenyon's site reports and discovered that she ignored examples of common, locally made pottery and based her opinions on the absence of expensive imported stone ware from Cyprus (Cypriote ware).[31] Cypriote pottery existed throughout the Bronze Age periods (including the time of the Israelite invasion) and is a common indicator in dating occupation levels. Much locally fired pottery made for common use had been excavated before Kenyon arrived and had also been dated to the Late Bronze I period. The fact that she did not use it for dating remains a mystery. In her opinion, since this Cypriote ware was missing in the areas she excavated, it likely meant Jericho did not live as a city past 1550 BC. It was perhaps inhabited, but could have been no more than a small village with ruined walls at the time of Joshua.

Wood was astonished to discover that Garstang found a great quantity of Cypriote ware where he dug twenty years earlier on the other side of the tel. It is not known why Kenyon ignored or rejected Garstang's materials, on which he based his Israelite destruction date. Up until Wood's analysis of Kenyon's work, no one was aware of this discrepancy. Or if they were aware, they never bothered to comment on it. Through the reassessment of the physical evidence, Wood believes Jericho was a viable city during the biblical account. However, his study has not changed much of the archaeological community's viewpoint. We will discuss the reason for this shortly.

When Israel arrived on the scene (and I am asserting an Israelite destruction somewhere between 1400 and 1200

BC), Jericho had developed an advanced system of defense. Archaeological remains uncovered by Garstang and Kenyon indicate there were in fact two concentric walls around the mound, and both concluded they collapsed (to a great extent) during the last destruction event at Jericho.

So if ever you hear the stanza "Joshua fought the battle of Jericho . . . and the wall(s) came tumbling down" you might visualize two of them made of baked bricks. The uppermost wall surrounded the summit of the tel, the second was a lower revetment (or retaining) wall which established Jericho's first line of defense. Though the Hebrew word for *wall* in every case is singular, there is no reason to take this in a literal sense. It is likely a matter of linguistic transliteration from the Hebrew, or perhaps the writer did not count the lower revetment wall as *the* city wall since it supported, and was made up of, the continuous exterior walls of suburban houses.

The large stones built into the revetment wall's foundation on the lower slope held back (retained) the hard-packed earthen hillside, preventing slippage and erosion. The raised foundation provided a horizontal surface for a vertical wall, built to an estimated height of fifteen feet. This initial defensive measure made it extremely difficult for attackers to gain elevation and momentum to batter through the lower wall.

On the sloped area, between the lower and upper walls, stood a residential zone made of walls only one brick thick. We might relate these to modern minimum-standard residential tract housing. The houses rested on a steep, plaster-covered slope, called a *glacis* or *rampart*. If an attacking force succeeded in penetrating into the residential area, the slippery slope would have impeded them from gaining traction against the uppermost wall.

This inner housing district made an interesting system of defense. If the invaders somehow breached the lower wall, they would have been immediately forced into a maze of suburban alleys and enclosures. Contained between the upper and lower walls amidst narrow lanes, soldiers would have been forced to contend with blind corners and obstructions, while Jericho's defenders killed from above. Victory would have come at a high cost. In the case of Joshua and the Israelites, the Lord saw fit to circumvent these difficulties with a miracle.

In this suburbia between the two walls is where we might find Rahab's home. Scripture hints that it butted into or was incorporated with the lower revetment wall—an exterior window on the wall's side was the means for the spies' escape.

Kathleen Kenyon investigated Jericho's city wall ramparts by cutting three trenches into the tel's north, west, and south ramparts from the top down to the lower revetment wall. On the west side, she had her workers dig farther, extending the trench past the lower revetment wall beyond the city proper. Kenyon discovered a great quantity of fallen red brick debris which she determined, from the character of its fallen state, had cascaded down from the upper and lower walls. I must interrupt here to say that all of this analysis took a tremendous amount of work under difficult conditions, and Kenyon's painstaking analysis and conclusion is intellectually brilliant. We must never take the archaeologist's hard work for granted, nor critically or flippantly dismiss her findings.

The red brick color is important because it shows that the debris of the upper wall did not suffer discoloration from a conflagration. The upper walls were likely shaken and dislodged by an earthquake, and came crashing down into the lower revetment wall. Their combined mass spilled out beyond the bounds of Jericho. Evidently this field of fallen bricks was enough to provide a ramp for the Israelites to ascend through Jericho's defenses (neutralizing the suburban killing field) into the heart of the city. Yet, as with the curious treatment of the pottery remains, the evidence of fallen brick heaped outside Jericho's walls was noted in excavation journals and summarily ignored.

In an area thought to be the administration center, Kenyon's site workers found substantial grain reserves in storage jars in rooms whose brick walls had collapsed and were discolored by fire. Here Kenyon found agreement with Garstang's findings. The grain dates to the late Bronze Age, and its type and great abundance indicates it had been recently harvested and endured the heat from the destruction fires. This coincides with the biblical account of Israel crossing the Jordan River at flood stage during harvest season (Joshua. 3:15) and harvesting grain the day after celebrating Passover (5:11). It also fits with Rahab hiding the spies under freshly harvested stalks of flax (2:6).

Typically, when a victorious army (such as the Egyptians) sacked a city, they removed its food stores to feed themselves, like pulling up to a fast food window in your chariot, *circa* 1400 BC. Thus, folks who favor the historical viability of Joshua 6 accept the existence of the great quantities of grain *insitu* (in its original position or state) as proof of Israel's obedience to the Lord's command about not touching the "devoted things," the things given over or dedicated (consecrated) to the Lord for destruction (Joshua. 6:17–21).

But First a Word about Earthquakes . . .

When the trumpets sounded, the army shouted, and at the sound of the trumpet, when the men gave a loud shout, the wall collapsed; so everyone charged straight in, and they took the city. They devoted the city to the LORD *and destroyed with the sword every living thing in it—men and women, young and old, cattle, sheep and donkeys.*

JOSHUA. 6:20–21

The possibility of two separate earthquakes (the first causing a collapsing hillside to block the Jordan River, so that it backed up and enabled a dry crossing of the riverbed; and a second quake causing Jericho's walls to fall) is a popular assumption often kicked around in scholarly communities.

A geological map of the vicinity of tel Jericho, to an untrained eye like mine, shows enough fault lines for me to jump on the earthquake bandwagon; the landscape is intensely scarred with them.[32] One of the faults, called the East Fault, runs precisely along the east flank of the tel through the Spring of Elisha and then curves away to the northeast. Two major slip faults called the *Wadi Nu'eima* Faults (where two tectonic plates of the earth's crust rub together) run in close parallel to each other a few miles north of the tel; both of these slip or shift east to west during seismic activity. Another fault lying just west of the city, called (you guessed it) the West Fault, runs parallel to and in the same arc as the East Fault.

Applying this seismic business to a biblical context, the Lord may have very well used an earthquake to drop the walls at Jericho. It would not have been the first (or the last) time he used the natural forces of his creation to act on his command.

Difficulties in Dating Jericho and Back To The Time Tunnel

Bryant Wood's critical reassessment of Kenyon's findings and a more optimistic view of a Late Bronze Age destruction of Jericho by Israel is not a popular position within the archaeological community. Much of this has to do with the dissenters' view of the Bible as a primary interpretive source document. Since this is very important to our consideration of Scripture in its entirety, I feel it is necessary to take a good bit of time talking about it here.

A strong contingent of early biblical archaeologists (between the two world wars) were foremost American Protestant Old Testament scholars and ministers (led by William Foxwell Albright) who were bent on proving the historical accuracy of the Bible through the evidence of archaeology. Envision riding around Palestine on a donkey with a spade in one hand and a Bible in the other. The rush to substantiate the Bible was in part due to the serious inroads German higher criticism and other popular secular philosophical theories were making to reduce (discredit) Scripture to a mythical document.

Often, the Christian contingents' problems were self-inflicted. Though responsible for tremendous advances in Palestine archaeology, some of their work had an embarrassing biblical bias that often caused them to misidentify and misdate places and artifacts. Evidence was forced into a narrow interpretive framework based on an uncertain biblical historical timeline and narrow theological viewpoints.

Unfortunately, Jericho was viewed in this light. Fallen wall debris and burnt brick were immediately and literally attributed to Joshua 6, while afterward they were, through careful site analysis, dated to much earlier periods. This school of biblical archaeology lost significant credibility in the academic community.

The fact remains that exciting signs of wall collapse do exist at Jericho. However, there is no way to attribute them to exactly Joshua's time. As mentioned above, the depredations of erosion, rough treatment by nineteenth-century excavators, and a modern road cut through almost the entire eastern flank of the tel hinder us from piecing together this critical period.

Despite the story's enduring popularity in Jewish and Christian circles, there is no consensus as to whether it was an actual historical event. In fact many Jewish, Christian, and certainly most secular archaeologists and Near Eastern historians believe it is the stuff of fantasy within religious tradition. So facing this business of Jericho's falling walls is, to quote what Billy Crystal said in the movie *The Princess Bride*, "going to take a miracle." And the acceptance of miracles in scholarship is not likely.

Fundamentally, archaeologists are materialists in that they perceive history in light of the entire range of the physical artifact and contemporary textual-inscriptional sources. However this is not as simple as it might seem. The load of information found in an archaeological site does not exist for the sake of itself, just as a library does not merely exist so that we might inhale words between book covers. There is a "positivist" side (what archaeologists call "processual archaeology") where empirical information is tested by scientific method to determine what life was like for an ancient culture.

During the last half of the twentieth century the science of archaeology expanded from architecture, pottery, mosaics, glassware, and small handmade artifacts, into the study of animal and plant remains and the relationships of the sites to their surrounding natural environments. The ancient place was no longer considered an isolated thing behind walls but was interpreted through widening spheres of its ecological landscapes. The cultures that once lived there were approached from the perspectives of what can be known of their natural habitat, technology, economic strategies (trade routes, manufacturing), and social, political, and religious systems.

Recently archaeologists have expanded their focus to the small communities of the countryside where new settlement theories are considered. Some now see the Israelite invasion of Palestine in light of "settlement archaeology." They suggest the Israelites' takeover of the Promised Land was gradual rather than an immediate destructive conquest. This study looks at the landscapes of everyday life and ethnic social histories rather than the old school method of studying the great deeds by great men in great cities.

Out in the countryside strong parallels are being drawn between ancient and modern patterns of settlement, subsistence economy, and social organization. In many of these places people live today very much as they did 3,000 years ago—same environment with very little technological change.

The technical name for this is "ethno-archaeology." It is the idea that the early Israelite farmer in Manasseh, Ephraim, and Judah may have been influenced by the same environmental constraints as the native Arab or Israeli experiences living there today. An ancient culture can be better understood by observing a modern native society living in the same place and conditions where time has, for the most part, stood still.

The direction of these advances moves toward comprehending more clearly how ancient societies lived and goes further to attempt to understand what the artifact may have meant (in terms of symbolic meaning, power, and influence) to the person. Archaeologists term this "post-processual archaeology."

This chapter, if not this book its entirety, is an example of this. I meld construction insights and architectural theory to biblical narrative. I am not creating a new doctrine or theology, but I'm working toward illuminating a perspective of God within his Word.

Growing numbers of those working in the fields of

settlement and ethno-archaeology are taking a contrary view of an immediate, catastrophic Israelite invasion by Joshua. Instead they see a gradual influence of Hebrew culture over the old Canaanite peoples. In fact, rather than a separate, distinct Israel flooding in and destroying the old to possess the Promised Land, some assert a new Israel emerged *out of* the Canaanite peoples.

You can imagine how the Bible compares to these modern archaeological developments with stories about marching around walls and their collapse on the seventh day when the trumpets blew and the Israelites shouted. Most might buy the earthquake(s) motif, but to coordinate that with an entire nation doing "Walk for Destruction" celebration laps around a city, with all the blaring horns, and shouting business . . . ? This is not how the physical world works.

This leads us back to the last sentences of *The Time Tunnel* TV show synopsis, where we have two perspectives on the reason for Jericho's wall collapse. To help give a rational explanation, Hollywood created a hurricane to take out the walls, erasing their outline around the city as a child could do on an Etch-a-Sketch board.

The characters in *Time Tunnel* have two opinions about this event: Ann holds true to her profession and sees this as a purely scientific event, but Ray considers the destructive force a divine act. On our TVs we observe two very intelligent people simultaneously witnessing the same incident, yet possessing two opposite perceptions as to its cause. They see the same thing but perceive it differently.

This makes me believe that even if archaeologists had dug up collapsed walls with confirmed dating to Joshua's time and documentation from eye-witnesses recording the event in real time, there would still be two camps—acceptance and doubt. One side would accept what is seen; the other would dispute the accounts as influenced by religious superstition and physiological trauma.

At the end of the day I am left thinking that if this story is merely fantasy, *The Time Tunnel* storyline has as much value, as much historical integrity, as Joshua 6. Hey, why not let Mel Brooks throw in some Nazis?

Here is where I must leave the world of categories and enter the spiritual realm. I stake my tent in the camp that claims the physical artifact is critically important; however, it is not the endgame to comprehending life and especially the things of God. I believe life does not consist merely of the physical. There is no doubt in my mind that a spiritual, unseen part of life pervades our world.

I did not make this stuff up. This spiritual business is not something I took home after a visit to The Mother Ship. As we saw in chapters 1 and 2, God saturates the spaces of the natural world, and we are made in his image. There is more to life than stuff and our narrow interpretation of it. So we can take the biblical account (with its historical/spiritual messages) and compare it to the physical artifact and come to some conclusions. We understand that we do not know the entire story, but we can walk away with some possibilities, knowing that God holds the cards, and though he works unseen, his effects are visible, like falling walls and changed hearts (see Rahab below).

Rahab the Harlot and Life on the Walls

Then Joshua son of Nun secretly sent two spies from Shittim. "Go, look over the land," he said, "especially Jericho." So they went and entered the house of a prostitute named Rahab and stayed there.

The king of Jericho was told, "Look, some of the Israelites have come here tonight to spy out the land." So the king of Jericho sent this message to Rahab: "Bring out the men who came to you and entered your house, because they have come to spy out the whole land."

But the woman had taken the two men and hidden them. She said, "Yes, the men came to me, but I did not know where they had come from. At dusk, when it was time to close the city gate, they left. I don't know which way they went. Go after them quickly. You may catch up with them." (But she had taken them up to the roof and hidden them under the stalks of flax she had laid out on the roof.) So the men set out in pursuit of the spies on the road that leads to the fords of the Jordan, and as soon as the pursuers had gone out, the gate was shut.

JOSHUA. 2:1–7

I was out hiking yesterday, and while I was toiling up a steep, hot section of trail, a thought came to me concerning Rahab. It dawned on me that she is where the gold lies in this story. I know all the standard reasons why Israel had to destroy Jericho, and we can ponder why the Lord made them do all that marching around carrying the ark and blowing horns for a week.

Yet regarding Rahab I must consider that the reason the Lord commanded Joshua to take Jericho was merely so they could pull Rahab out of there. Her testimony is so rich and powerful that I think God, who planted a little mustard seed of faith within the heart of this Canaanite harlot's heart, moved heaven and earth so that this seed would grow into a giant Sequoia Redwood tree. Why is this not possible? Rahab became a direct forebear of Israel's King David, Solomon, and Jesus of Nazareth, the Son of God (Matt. 1:5), who, by the way, built his share of walls while living in Nazareth. Not a bad progeny.

I know this sounds crazy, but when we read of Jericho, we see a bunch of guy heroes rescuing a damsel in distress (and her family), walls coming down, a lot of hacking and hewing, and putting the place to the torch. No question these things were carried out at the Lord's command, but I sense there was something else much more compelling behind it all. At the end of the day I am coming to grips with the idea that this was a not-so-simple destruction sequence and rescue operation.

Again, I believe everything the Lord had Israel do after leaving the desert was in preparation to rescue the little lamb who was caught up in a thicket—the one that the Lord would leave his flock to find and bring back into the fold. Only a sanctified people acting on the Lord's behalf could participate in such a sacred task. I love this idea, because if the Lord would do this for Rahab, he would similarly divert the course of history for you and me. This is wonderful news, especially because Iran has enough plutonium to make several nuclear warheads and North Korea has an itchy trigger finger.

Cleaning Up Rahab for Church

Rahab's profession has kicked up some dust of debate in Christian circles. Sunday school teachers must sometimes lace up their dancing shoes for some fancy footwork when presenting a Bible hero with the "harlot" moniker. There is a righteous impetus to clear away not only the prostitution business but also the "white lie" Rahab tells for a higher good. Wow, is this woman scrutinized or what?

The first-century Jewish historian Flavius Josephus described Rahab as an innkeeper:

> . . . but at even they retired to a certain inn that was near to the wall, whither they went to eat their supper; which supper when they had done, and were considering how to get away, information was given to the king as he was at supper, that there were some persons come from the Hebrews' camp to view the city as spies, and that they were in the inn kept by Rahab, and were very solicitous that they might not be discovered.[33]

The Hebrew text does not say Rahab was an innkeeper, yet I believe Josephus' description of her has influenced writers over the centuries so that we now consider this aspect of her profession as fact.[34] This uncertainty about Rahab as innkeeper prompts me to take a second look at her profession.

The connection between inns and taverns with prostitution throughout ancient times is strong. Much of our knowledge of it comes from the much later Greek and Roman periods. Women typically "serviced" inns and taverns, but rarely owned them. A brothel (*lupanaria*, from the word *lupa*, she-wolf), or house of prostitution was a common sight and was often regulated by law. Prostitutes were usually relegated to the lower echelons of society, but not always. There were some who rose up to become influential within the ruling aristocracy. The Roman emperor Sulla willed most of his fortune to his concubine and in the sixth century AD, the emperor Justinian's wife, Theodora, came out of prostitution as a young girl.

Prostitutes were often used with religious cult; however, this does not seem to be the case with Rahab. She is presented clearly as a businesswoman, and she either personally provided this service or employed other women or both.

At best, the relationship between ancient societies and prostitutes was ambivalent acceptance.

The possibility that Rahab was an innkeeper is plausible. The placement of her home in the outer walls of the city would have made it a convenient stopping place for travelers who preferred to stay outside the congested city center and be in close proximity to their caravans and livestock. Sitting on the periphery of Jericho, Rahab's house gave the Hebrew spies good cover; they would not have stood out like elephants crashing a mouse convention.

The 1984 NIV Bible has "prostitute" in 2:1 footnoted with "Or possibly *an innkeeper*." Yet the Hebrew lexicon does not broaden the meaning of harlot in this way, and the 2011 NIV lacks the footnote. The Hebrew text clearly describes Rahab as a *zanah* (*zona*), a prostitute. The word has no connotation of innkeeper or tavern owner. Rahab's profession of faith to the spies has many thinking she would not have continued to work as a prostitute. She could not possibly have given such a great testimony while simultaneously playing the harlot.

Personally I do not pick up a devious, two-faced side to her. Rahab was not delusional. Her life was at stake, and her actions bore out her commitment in her profession of faith. When she enters the scriptural narrative I believe she is at the threshold of being a committed saint. I will build my case as we go on. However, after all this time the *harlot* label remains stuck to Rahab; this hero of the faith remains a dichotomy.

In these days of contemporary Christianity I suppose there is a strong impulse in us to purify Rahab before she is adopted into the nation of Israel, before a harlot is injected into the line of Christ—as *we* are in the line of Christ?

I know we are more comfortable with rehabilitated people around us. How would we react if a whore were to enter our church Sunday school class or Bible study group? The group leader says: "Okay, let's start by introducing ourselves: What is your name and what do you do for a living? Let's begin with the first person to my right." "Ah, yah, I'm Flower and I'm a hooker." Truly, the next sound we could hear would be someone choking on their breath mint and an echelon of folding chairs reshuffling in panic for the invisible Brontosaurus standing in the room.

I think our first impulse is to justify Rahab: "Nah, there has to be something in the Hebrew original that clarifies her profession, like . . . innkeeper, owner of The Outer Wall B&B." But no, I lean against trying to morally sanitize her with Christianity-approved, "Whore-be-gone." Must we make her acceptable so we can carry her in our Bibles to church?

Several weeks ago I listened to a sermon in which the pastor said Rahab was a linen worker because of the flax stored on her rooftop (raw materials for linen). The red cord she hung out her window was one she dyed herself. What I gathered was that by the time the spies came to her home, Rahab had turned to another profession. This is interesting, but pretty tenuous.

We simply have to face the fact that, for an earlier time in her life, even up to the instant her name appears in Scripture, she gave herself over for profit. If not for the same grace of God, are not we cut from the same piece of cloth? Are we not faced with the same chasm when we face eternity at our conversion?

We also should consider her faith in light of the number of theologians who question Rahab's relationship with the spies—whether she slept with them or not. They make linguistic comparisons between those who "went in" to harlots (see Samson and Delilah, Judges 16:1) and when Rahab "went up" to the spies on her roof.

Let me pause again to sigh. I struggle with how poorly women have been treated over the centuries by Christianity, how they tend to be the first suspect, how they have paid the heavier societal price for immorality or for an irreconcilable divorce because of a cheating husband. I hope the following words on Rahab's righteous behavior will dispense with this notion.

We cannot miss the parallels between Israel's processes of purification and the purity of Rahab's confession of faith. Concurrent with Rahab's verbal confession, Israel was making theirs, in a physical sense, at Gilgal. The red cord hanging from Rahab's window, identifying her home from all others, is parallel to the time when, just before the escape from Egypt, red blood was painted over the Israelite's doorposts before the Angel of Death passed over. In both cases, those who found refuge behind these red-marked walls were spared.

The circumcision of Israelite flesh metaphorically occurred within Rehab's heart of faith. The circular movement the people of God made around Jericho's walls is comparable to the affirmation of belief Rahab made by moving to provide safe sanctuary and a way out for the spies. The Hebrew word for the "kindness" (hesed) she showed the spies is packed with theological meaning (2:12). The word is also translated as mercy, steadfast love, loyalty, faithfulness. It is more frequently used within divine–human contexts. We should take it similarly here. She clearly saw the spies as extensions of the Lord's will, so just as she treats the spies, she treats the Lord. Clearly a sexual liaison with them was out of the question.

A big deal has also been made about Rahab's lying to the king's men concerning the whereabouts of the spies, as if it would have been a more righteous thing to honestly give them up to torture and a slow death. Rahab's lie is similar to when the Christian Corrie ten Boom lied to the Nazi SS about the Jewish family that was hiding behind a false wall in her house.[35] Again, along with the sexual innuendo business, to criticize this lie is ridiculous. I am not justifying lying, but this is a matter of moral priority. In these few extreme cases, deception against evil may be necessary to save lives. A tough moral compromise may be necessary to preserve life.

"Our lives for your lives!" the men assured her. "If you don't tell what we are doing, we will treat you kindly and faithfully when the LORD gives us the land."

JOSHUA 2:14

I wonder what Rahab thought as she saw the spies exit her window and descend the rope to the safety of open ground and the cover of night. Their last words sound a little unsure of the deal they made: "Remember, we die, you die; deviating from our agreement means all is null and void." This is not exactly like, "Really great to meet you and see you after all the dust settles!"

Knowing the end of this story, we might think this was easy, straightforward stuff for everyone involved. Yet I get the impression there were a few sweaty palms among these three. And I think this is so true to life. Though we might have great faith and expect the Lord's provision, that nagging human part of us remains. We don't necessarily doubt, but we definitely, with some anxiety, double-check the fine print and lock our doors at night. This is the tough part of obedience. We only know enough to trust that the Lord will work out the method of his promises through the skills and flaws of his human intermediaries.

When it was all over, the walls of her house stood as vertical testimonies to her belief. We have reached the important culminating section of this chapter where we look at Rahab from the architectural perspective of walls.

Rahab and Life on the Walls

She [Rahab] let them down by a rope through the window—for her dwelling was at the outer side of the city wall and she lived in the actual wall.

JOSHUA. 2:15, *Hebrew-English Tanakh*

As the archaeological evidence, the Jericho storyline, and the above verse from the *Tanakh* strongly alludes, Rahab's home was likely located within the suburban "demilitarized zone" between the upper and lower walls of Jericho. Attached to the lower revetment wall, she was a mere brick's thickness away from the wilderness. This stands in contrast to the greater distance she would travel through the residential district to confront another wall—the upper wall on the city's summit, which protected the neighborhood of the elite and ruling class.

Spatially speaking, Rahab lived in a dual world of "in between" and "on the edge." Locating her between the two walls, integrated within the lower, exterior wall might stand as a metaphor for her life.

I wonder whether being situated between Jericho's walls made her feel trapped between the two worlds of the suburban working class and the world of the elites. Her harlotry profession would certainly have helped delineate her separation. She likely belonged to neither class, though she lived among them. Perhaps before the spies came to her door, she was already a displaced resident.

Life on the wall is the epitome of living on the edge—it is the very line determining the actual inside and outside of Rahab's existence as to whether she was a planted citizen of the city or a wandering pilgrim of the outer world. I cannot help but imagine that life on the wall may have compelled Rahab to gaze over the vast reaches of the primordial landscape in the hope that her "place" in the world would come to her out its expanse.

Hope would not come from the upper reaches of Jericho; they were walled off to her. If an invading force were to assail the city, she would be the first sacrificed if the walls were breached. Perhaps in a Jerichoan world she saw herself as nothing more than a disposable entity. Undoubtedly, her life on the walls was a mere hand-breadth from the wilderness.

The difficult reality of being "placed" on the wall would have moved Rahab to open her heart to the Lord, who she had heard was working miracles and military victories for his people. She had not seen these things firsthand, but she recognized them as true when those carrying the news of the Israelites crossed her threshold. The metaphorical imagery of Rahab's architectural space extended itself to the Israelite spies when she opened her door to them and allowed them access to her home.

The Significance of Rahab's Front Door Threshold

Our front doors, just as the front door to Rahab's home, are our most direct exterior portals to the world. Through her door Rahab allowed the spies entry while it seems she barred the king's men access (a deviation from *The Time Tunnel* episode). In this light, Rahab's front door becomes a critical passive element to the Jericho story. The front door, in most cultures and throughout history, has always been a demarcation zone of acceptance and rejection. A visitor may or may not be given permission to travel inside a dwelling, into its more intimate spaces.

Studies in spatial architecture (uses and meaning of open spaces in architectural design) show that the farther a guest is allowed into a home, the higher the level of acceptance and consent the owner is granting him or her. As such an "outsider" becomes an "insider" as they walk the length and breadth of one's home as if through a veil of permission (verbal or assumed).

Allowing complete access to our home has its difficulties. It inadvertently exposes us to a certain amount of personal vulnerability. The guest can see every costly aesthetic treatment, every possession and ornament, while they form a mental estimate of overall life-priorities, wealth, and status. The same occurs if a visitor observes us in our poverty.

Sometimes, within the nasty realm of Christian legalism, allowing the "wrong" person inside our home is like handing a loaded Glock 9 ml. semi-automatic handgun to a child with the safety in the off position. It only takes one judgmental person to abuse the privilege of passage for the piercing rounds of gossip to wound the host terribly.

To prevent wounding (and lower the vulnerability level), a period of time is necessary to build trust in prospective guests. Observing a particular guest's behavior when they're invited in (see Bible study group) can build confidence. If there is some unease in this relationship, the guest should not go further into a host's home than the parlor or formal living room. That is the intent of these places—they are polite holding tanks to give someone tea and crumpets and have a nice chat before sending them on their way.

Similarly, it would seem Joshua's spies were given complete access to Rahab's house, from the ground floor to their hiding place on the roof. Their last exit was through a window that was likely not in a "common" room.

Again, Rahab clearly knew whom the spies ultimately represented. Obviously she knew they came to Jericho at the orders of Joshua, but she was deeply aware of their direct connection with the Lord of Hosts, the God who is simultaneously in heaven and on earth. And she likewise knew him well enough to risk everything to change her citizenship status, from Jerichoan to Israelite. The tenets of architectural space tell us that to give the spies complete access to the bounds of Rahab's home was the equivalent of inviting the Lord to enter her abode and inhabit it entirely.

The risk Rahab opened herself up to with this entry business is telling. When Rahab opened her front door to the Lord, she effectively collapsed the walls that defined her past life and utterly exposed her most intimate spaces to the eyes of the Lord. Through this symbol of access, the Lord entered to fill every pore of her being. This was no small feat. Ironically the immense inner strength it took to make her stand came out of a position of vulnerability, a place of brokenness. For Rahab (as well as for us) brokenness came when she saw there was no other place to turn, when all hope was gone.

To defeat the king's surveillance, Rahab let the spies out through a window incorporated into the outer defensive wall of the city. It is astonishing she possessed such an aperture, a natural breach in her city's fortifications. And indeed it was to be the breakout point for her life.

The view from this window must have looked out over an open wilderness landscape, and from what we can ascertain of Late Bronze Age Jericho, it stood as a solitary form upon its topography. Rahab could look through this window and envision a similar wilderness through which the Lord relentlessly guided his people. She must have sensed Israel would eventually cross her front door's threshold. The arrival of the spies confirmed her intuition and emboldened her to take a deeper step of faith. Perhaps her conversion to the God of Israel was a variant of a wilderness conversion. Through this window in the wall, she could look out over the landscape and see into the very wilderness of her soul, meditate on the heavily veiled, vast untamed stretches of her life, and seek solution to her unfathomable yearnings.

She would have wondered whether the answer to her life would come from the immeasurable reaches of this same wilderness (it certainly was not forthcoming from the wealthy upper city). It was a rational act for her to send the spies out through this portal (this natural breach in her heart) into the wilderness of her spirit to negotiate a settlement for her (and her family's) salvation.

Accurately defined as an architectural node fixed on its landscape, Jericho exerted concentric circles that pinged like sonar off the Israelites emerging from the desert. The collapsing walls symbolize the nullification of Jericho's power; it simply no longer existed. Conversely, Rahab's house stood—its walls remained vertical as a brick monument to the righteousness of an upright life. The standing walls of Rahab's home also testify to the Lord honoring Rahab lowering the walls of her heart—a confirmation of the Lord blessing her faithful commitment to him.

The essence of brokenness is strength, which is the defining element of grace. Truly all of this is a wonderful enigma. Again, Rahab's home stood because of her brokenness, stone scales fell from her heart and broke upon the ground, just as the bricks cascaded beyond the lower revetment wall and allowed the Israelite warriors to ascend Jericho's heights. What characterized Jericho's physical destruction metaphorically occurred in Rahab's life as a harlot morphed into a redeemed saint. Brokenness enabled the generation of new life.

Last Thoughts

The design of Rahab's home, its placement on Jericho's wall, and her movements within their bounds was a definitive statement of a sanctified life that, to this day, remains a potent force after 4,200 years. Rahab's faith is similar to a quote from the great American architect, Louis Kahn, who once said:

A wall is built in hope that a light once observed may strike it even for but a rare moment in time.[36]

Rahab's example teaches us that faith is not faith until its light is cast against the hard surface of one's life. We have been put on earth to respond and act according to our calling. I hear James speaking:

You see that a person is considered righteous by what they do and not by faith alone. In the same way, was not even Rahab the prostitute considered righteous for what she did when she gave lodging to the spies and sent them off in a different direction? As the body without the spirit is dead, so faith without deeds is dead.

JAMES 2:24–26

The light of belief must generate internal resolution expressed in physical action, and it is with this action that Rahab became a hero of the faith (Heb. 11:31). This lesson holds true for us.

Our faith in God is often defined by whom we let in, and equally, to whom we refuse entry. There are times we must shut the door to our hearts against the things that might cause ruinous collapse, while opening our portals to the things that propel us along Righteousness Road.

Rahab's example rises above the silent, confused layers of rubble on the Jericho tel. Archaeologists may squabble over dating its stones and pottery fragments, while deriding their role in a ridiculous myth. But Rahab knew. She was truly the brave one who looked through the window of her soul and found life.

Devotional Questions

1. Do you believe Jericho's walls fell as described in the Bible? Explain your view.

2. The issue of doubt is spread throughout this chapter. Name several instances where doubt plays a part in this story.

3. How important is it that the stories of the Bible are factual and occurred in real time? Why? Where do you draw the line between biblical myth and reality?

4. When was the first time you heard the story of Jericho's walls?

5. What do you think of Rahab's profession as a harlot? How have you heard her treated in sermons and other books? Was she described as an innkeeper, linen weaver, pub owner?

6. This chapter makes a connection between her life on the outer perimeter of Jericho's lower wall and her status in Jerichoan society. How important a role did her decision to reject her city play in her salvation? How do you think she came to this point in her life?

7. Was there a time in your life when you had to separate from others in order to come to the Lord as his child? How much courage did it take? What did the move entail?

CHAPTER 7

GOD WITHIN A TENT
The Fabric of Faith

*Whoever dwells in the shelter of the Most High
will rest in the shadow of the Almighty.
I will say of the LORD, "He is my refuge and my fortress,
my God, in whom I trust."*

PSALM 91:1–2

MUCH OF THE PROCESS of contemporary home building involves insulating the interior from the elements of the exterior world. The shell is waterproofed with various types of breathable synthetic fabrics and heavy paper saturated with petroleum. Developments in polyurethane caulking compounds enable them to resist drying and becoming brittle over time while maintaining the caulking's flexibility and bond while under structural movement. This high-grade caulking fastens to metals and plastic/vinyl "flashings" that tie windows, doors, and vent openings to "proof" the building. Doors and windows are insulated with double thicknesses and laminations of wood, plastics, metals, and composites. They are set within frames and jambs possessing strips of vinyl and rubber gaskets that compress and seal when fully closed and in the locked position.

There is a hidden battle waging between two environments within the energy-efficient home. Two worlds are set against each other as one incessantly works to enter enclosed space while the other seeks to escape its confines by finding any tiny aperture forgotten or lost in the mix by builders. The mechanics of how hot and cold air conditioning—by forced air and radiant systems—

affects air pressure is beyond me, but I know my eardrums tighten when the wind blows doors shut on a stormy day.

The environmentally efficient home must, however, breathe. A sealed interior space with hot showers, breathing people (and dogs, cats, birds, rabbits, etc.), clothes washers and dryers, and cooking ovens and stoves necessitates methods of circulating air and venting, like a body's pulmonary system. This was once a natural effect that our early hut dwellers enjoyed (perhaps too well) that now becomes lost during waterproofing. We discover, especially after mildew has formed in our closet walls, that natural air circulation had its good points. Now we must create an artificial draft and escort the unwanted air back out the waterproofed walls by, ironically, cutting holes in them.

Personally, I like the idea expressed by those living in tornado country that suggests we open the windows to balance the air pressure when a twister is close by. I suppose it is better to have everything you own experience a 150-mile-per-hour blast of wind than to have your home explode into pieces across the countryside.

All of this is to say that I am a big fan of an efficiently heated and cooled home. After living and traveling through Britain, I fell in love with the concept of two-foot-thick stone walls of beautiful blue slate that my wife and I saw while touring the Lake District of northwest England. The concept of massive amounts of interlocking stone bonded by mortar brings to mind the word *fortress*. No paint is necessary on the interior/exterior faces; the beauty of the blue-grey hues of the slate identifies the home as a blood relative to its environment. Protection by a deep thickness of stone makes me wonder what it must have been like for the first cave-person (cave couple?) when he or she left the cave to move into the first standing home on the landscape.

A school within anthropology accepts there was a cognitive revolution (a major light bulb turn-on in the brain) in the pre-pottery Neolithic B period (10,000–8000 BC) that inspired humanity to build the first known open-air rectangular structures. The earliest have been found in eastern Turkey and northwest Syria. These evolved from earlier buildings that tended to be oval semi-subterranean housing.[37] It is generally accepted that circular structures, whether underground or on the surface, were the first shape of built human habitation. The rise of the square (more like a polygon) house embarked humanity on a radically new course of planting geometry upon topography and more clearly marked the breach between the natural landscape and the constructed landscape.

The "practice" of the house in its design, construction, and maintenance generated Neolithic (New Stone Age) societies by necessitating bonds, dependencies, and boundaries between people to carry out the process.[38] The Tower of Babel (chapter 3) was a test case for this theory. A further stage in the evolution of human building and society came with the move from more rounded, circular shapes to angular geometric forms that stood against the forces of nature.

Constructing, observing, and living in the first quadrangular houses must have inspired a completely new human geometry, a new system of possibilities in self-regulating one's world. The emergence of geometry in human behavior dates humanity's ability to count and translate number into spatial pattern. Abstract forms emanating from human initiative could connect standing walls at ninety degrees, or fashion a near-perfect cube or rectangle—forms not naturally manifest in stone or wood.

So, you decide to make a round house. Your roof, determined by the outline of the walls, is a circle, but it must have slope to shed water, so the center must be raised and supported somehow. What do we call this shape: convex or concave? I suppose either, depending on where one stands, inside or outside. Speaking of which, when does inside become outside? Does the windward side determine the entrance, and how does the doorway function? How does the smoke from the cooking fire vent through the roof? From this simple example, we begin to sense the engineering issues requiring new thought processes. Caves didn't require this much thinking! The term con-cave must have been some Neolithic guy's bad pun on his former home.

The mental and psychological forces involved in transitioning into this new environment and working out the processes in putting up free-standing structures must have been immense. Calculating the geometries of enclosure, the effects of wind and rain on wall and roof design, the placement of doors, and the use of available natural materials is, even today, a substantial mental challenge. This does not take into consideration the many societal differences in the use of space, architectural expression in design, and decorative elements that transcend functional purpose.

Introducing the Biblical Tent

While some societies were sedentary, there were groups who lived in constant migration or semi-permanence, at times living close to towns and cities, but primarily in the open spaces of field and desert. Sociologists may use the word *pastoralists* to define them. Instead of solid structures, their interior worlds are encapsulated in fabric and animal skins.

It has always fascinated me that God had his chosen people live as migratory pastoralists rather than settled city folk. And even more astonishing, God likewise chose a tent within which to dwell and be worshipped, a tent called the tabernacle. Genesis 9:21 tells us that humans descended from a tent-inhabiting ancestor. After the failure of the Tower of Babel, Noah lived in a tent after the flood. Unlike his brothers Ham and Japheth, Israel's ancestor Shem alone is said to have possessed tents (Gen. 9:27). So we see a rapid second-generation adaptation to city living among some siblings while there is an unbroken ancestral line with Israel as a tent society until the invasion of Palestine under Joshua, though it is highly likely the pattern continued with some families.

Tents were pitched in a variety of terrains and environs, ranging from isolated mountains (Gen. 12:8; 31:25) to urban outskirts (Gen. 33:18). The tent door twice proved an auspicious setting: once as a place for Abraham to seek refuge from the day's heat (Gen. 18:1) and once as a location for Sarah's eavesdropping (Gen. 18:10). After her death, Sarah's tent passed on as an inheritance to the newlyweds Isaac and Rebekah (Gen. 24:67).

The word *tent* as domicile in the Hebrew text has many linguistic forms that indicate its importance and varied nature in the Hebrew Bible. Hebrew tent meanings act as an umbrella covering both permanent and portable structures—as tent and house and palace. Judges 19:9 has been translated from the Hebrew, "go to your tent," to mean "go to your home." This is similar to 1 Kings 8:66; 1 Samuel 4:10; 13:2; 2 Samuel 18:17; 20:22; 19:9; and 2 Kings 14:12. Also, solid structures are frequently referred to by tent-related designations. Scholars believe this to be the result of the process of pastoralists gradually settling in permanent towns and cities. Though they abandoned their tents for solid walls, they did not abandon centuries-old designations for "home." The use of words is fluid despite changes in habitation.

A Tent of Refuge against the Storm

Very often in the Old Testament we see conflict between the urban and tent societies of Canaan and Israel. In Judges 4 and 5 we have Israel's extended relatives, the Kenite people, tangle with some Canaanites. The defeated Canaanite general Sisera fled for his life from the Israelite forces and sought refuge at the tent of Jael, the wife of Heber the Kenite. Sisera, representative of the Canaanite city-states, used Jael's tent to hide, and the layers of tent metaphor doubled when Jael covered him with a blanket (Judges 4:18–19). The tent and the blanket (representing desperate fear) became a refuge for a city-based enemy. Now metaphor turned to irony. Although Sisera intended the tent to be his salvation, it proved to be his undoing. The tent became the tool for his demise, the murder weapon itself, as Jael hammered a tent peg into Sisera's head (Judges 4:22).

It was a woman's responsibility to drive the tent's pegs into the earth when securely fixing their abode upon the landscape, and it seems Jael was confident with those things. She transfixed an enemy to the earth as she would a tent. Staking a tent is a statement of determining residence, founding a structure so the walls may rise, and providing protection against high winds. Staking Sisera to the ground may be symbolic along similar lines: Jael was determined to take a stand against the enemies who came to shake her life. Perhaps this is spiritually symbolic of the way we must stake our temporal and eternal lives on the Word of truth and how, in doing so, we must kill off the fleshly things that try to overthrow us as with a gust of high wind.

The story of Sisera and Jael has always made me curl my toes a bit. I wonder if the last thought that ran through Sisera's mind (excuse the pun) was, "what's this sharp pointy thing coming through my cranium?" Or perhaps it was about wishing for a second chance at the fleeing business and discerning that he would have done better on open ground or within the walls of a city.

I have not spent a lot of time in tents. Most opportunities occurred during short backpacking trips; the longest period was over a summer in a twelve-man army tent while on an archaeological dig in Israel. My most vivid realization of how the Lord is my refuge, particularly in the way David prayed, was during the times I languished for hours in a tent under the conditions of stormy weather. The psalmists pray,

> *Keep me as the apple of your eye;*
> *hide me under the shadow of your wings.*
>
> Ps. 17:8

> *Have mercy on me, my God, have mercy on me,*
> *for in you I take refuge.*
> *I will take refuge in the shadow of your wings*
> *until the disaster has passed.*
>
> Ps. 57:1

Isaiah speaks in similar terms:

> *You have been a refuge for the poor,*
> *a refuge for the needy in their distress,*

a shelter from the storm
and a shade from the heat.
For the breath of the ruthless
is like a storm driving against a wall.

ISA. 25:4

I recall several times when inside the walls of a tent these verses quickly became my new best friends. The first experience began as a wonderful hike through the Los Padres National Forest just south and east of Carmel, California, and north of Big Sur State Park. The mountains that rise in that backcountry are deceptively rugged, and though I was in fairly good shape, I was not ready for the steep terrain and stormy weather ahead. I was falling apart mentally along with my cramping legs. It was so frustrating to make the final climb up a steep face, slipping in the mud, to a small plateau in a rectangular notch in the mountain's ridge known as the Window. My good friend, Norm, had reached the summit long before I did, had set up his tent, and was happily inside it. I was so unprepared; I had not brought serious weather protection, and he generously invited me into his pyramid-style tent. Inside I was able to recover and mellow out from the strain. I am remembering this after twenty years, and what is most vivid is Norm sharing his apple with me while we listened to the buffeting wind blow through the pine trees and the wet sleet hitting the tent fabric. Fortunately, Norm was not a Jael with a mallet and tent peg, though I can imagine how a Sisera could be frazzled enough psychologically to forget himself and think a great warrior in enemy territory could hide under a blanket inside a tent and believe all would end well.

The second stormy event was with Norm again, in the same forest, in the same tent, as high winds blew off the Big Sur coast and howled up the south fork of the Little Sur River to our camp at its headwaters, a place known as Torres Flats. I am not sure we slept a full hour, but what I do remember is that the lower half of me was in a sleeping bag while the upper half of my body was wrapped around the tent's center pole hanging on for dear life. The winds tore up the narrowing creek valley like a locomotive, the force of which threatened to rip the tent pegs out of the ground and bend the center pole in half. By morning the winds had abated, and we broke camp for home like elephants crashing through dense brush, sensing a prowling lion.

Not long ago I was caught in an early winter storm in the high Sierras, just south of Forrester Pass (the highest hiking trail elevation in North America) along the eastern approach to Shepherd's Pass. I was hiking alone and I could see billowing dark clouds approaching low over the crest of the pass. The night was Torres Flats all over again but with much heavier snowfall and thunder and lightning strikes that spontaneously made my body flinch in short spasms with every massive boom and searing flash. My tent design was a football-shaped dome, a much better design than a pointy pyramid to withstand high winds. Despite the worst the storm could throw at my shelter, it held up; not a drop of moisture penetrated the rain fly.

In these cases, though the thickness of the fabric between the elements was miniscule, it was enough to protect and provide refuge from the storm. As the fabric repelled the wet and stood up to the buffeting winds, I gained increasing confidence in its ability to protect while I intellectually grasped, full well, my frailty next to the outside forces. I was fully dependent on the tent's integrity.

I do not feel this way at home, inside my house. I do not hold my breath when great gusts of wind hit the walls of my building or check for leaks in fragile fabric during intense downpours. I take the refuge thing for granted, and I certainly do not pray during these times as I would in a tent. I wonder if God elected to have his chosen people live in tents because it is the environment of the constant reality check. It is the reality check of being aware of one's frailty and knowing full well that disaster may come with the next gust of wind. Every peaceful day is accentuated with joy and appreciation. If we lived in tents, we would feel and hear this relationship when the fabric vibrates and hums, when breezes turn into winds, when the sun radiates warmth, when the cold penetrates and the rain drums its staccato beat. I think if we lived for a time in tents out in the deserted places, we would write our own books of psalms like King David: pages of words dripping raw, honest emotion toward God.

The Tabernacle

"Then have them make a sanctuary for me, and I will dwell among them. Make this tabernacle and all its furnishings exactly like the pattern I will show you."

Ex. 25:8–9

Then the LORD said to Moses, "See, I have chosen Bezalel son of Uri, the son of Hur, of the tribe of Judah, and I have filled him with the Spirit of God, with wisdom, with understanding, with knowledge and with all kinds of skills—to make artistic designs for work in gold, silver and bronze, to cut and set stones, to work in wood, and to engage in all kinds of crafts. Moreover, I have appointed Oholiab son of Ahisamak, of the tribe of Dan, to help him. Also I have given ability to all the skilled workers to make everything I have commanded you."

Ex. 31:1–6

Then Moses said to the Israelites, "See, the LORD has chosen Bezalel son of Uri . . . and he has filled him with the Spirit of God, with wisdom, with understanding, with knowledge and with all kinds of skills . . . And he has given both him and Oholiab . . . the ability to teach others. He has filled them with skill to do all kinds of work."

Ex. 35:30–31, 34–35

All those who were skilled among the workers made the tabernacle with ten curtains of finely twisted linen and blue, purple and scarlet yarn, with cherubim woven into them by expert hands. All the curtains were the same size—twenty-eight cubits long and four cubits wide. . . . They made upright frames of acacia wood for the tabernacle. . . . They made twenty frames for the south side of the tabernacle. . . . For the other side, the north side of the tabernacle they made twenty frames. . . . They made six frames for the far end, that is, the west end of the tabernacle, and two frames were made for the corners of the tabernacle at the far end. . . .

They also made crossbars of acacia wood: five for the frames on one side of the tabernacle, five for those on the other side, and five for the frames on the west, at the far end of the tabernacle. The made the center crossbar so that it extended from end to end at the middle of the frames.

Ex. 36:8–9, 20, 23, 25, 27–28, 31–33

Bezalel made the ark of acacia wood.

Ex. 37:1

The Israelites had done all the work just as the LORD had commanded Moses. Moses inspected the work and saw that they had done it just as the LORD had commanded. So Moses blessed them.

Ex. 39:42–43

The tabernacle as a religious structure presents a simple relationship. It was a system of three spaces: the Holy of Holies (containing the ark of the covenant), the Holy Place (containing the table for the bread of the presence, the golden lamp stand, and the altar of incense), and the exterior court with the sacrificial altar and water basin. One passed through curtains to deepening interiority, with an increasing limitation on who could penetrate further, to the innermost sanctuary where only the high priest, in solitude, acted as the intermediary to atone for the sins of the nation.

The tabernacle was also known as the Tent of Meeting, a name adopted after the tent Moses used to pitch outside the camp to meet with God (Ex. 33:7). Joshua spent long periods of time there (Ex. 33:11). While God met with Moses, the pillar of cloud came down and stayed at the tent entrance. With the development of the tabernacle, this idea of intimate communication with God was incorporated into Israelite worship.

Overall, the structure consisted of a series of same-sized fabric panels with acacia wood frames. The tabernacle's walls and panels that ringed the outer court were set vertically. The side frame boards were extended into sockets fixed in the ground to keep them from falling over. The frames had a crossbar to keep the rectangles rigid.

The tabernacle's rectangular enclosure (the Holy Place) was set just west of center in the court. Attached to its west end wall was the Holy of Holies, the most sacred of all places in the court enclosure. It was accessed only by the high priest on the Day of Atonement. It was separated from the tabernacle proper by a specially constructed veil or canopy. Exodus 40:3 explains its purpose as a cover, opening up the possibility that it was a type of roof and veil combination. This possibility has caused much scholarly debate with no consensus. Either the Holy of Holies was open to the sky, or it had a flat covering (after the typical Eastern nomadic tent design accommodating a fifteen-foot span). To give you a sense of the debate, several late nineteenth- and early twentieth-century scholars suggested the "middle bar" acted as a ridge pole to slope the roof. Proposals over the years regarding the panel connection methods and arrangement of curtains with post supports are too many and technical for us to be concerned about here.

As is common with the Bible, the more you penetrate its wording, the more gold is revealed. The Hebrew word for tabernacle is rooted in the verb "to dwell," another root word that we use for *landscape* (discussed in chapter 1). If we look again at Exodus 25:8–9 in the context of this word definition, we have Yahweh desiring to dwell in his dwelling, which is to say, he R-E-A-L-L-Y wanted to situate himself. Worship was not to be conducted in a religiously sterile environment; Yahweh wanted it to occur in his home, an intimate setting not unlike a place where one would conduct family life and lay one's head at night. This is not to say worship was a casual affair. The strict tenets of ritual would be scrupulously followed; there was no doubt as to the seriousness of the setting. Yet this built environment possessed certain intimate associations that extended worship to more personal terms. Sacrifice was a matter of a people leaving one home to worship in another.

This emphasizes the intent (excuse the meaningful pun) behind the tabernacle's construction. Though there were many hands at work on it from day one, this was entirely God's project. He conceived it in Moses' mind by projecting its form on his mental canvas. He gave explicit and precise measurements of its dimensions and specified the decoration, colors, fabrics, the design of its objects, and the garments the priests wore.

As a woodworker I find it interesting that God preferred acacia wood for its sturdy and lightweight nature. Most likely it was also locally available. Amazingly, he infused within certain persons the technical skill to carry out his designs and the ability to teach others specific tasks (we might place them in the hierarchical order of master craftsman, journeyman, and apprentice). Just before making critical (expensive) and very complicated saw cuts (for instance, the compound miter which friends of mine have humorously called the "confounded miter"), I have prayed for God to bless me with this type of wisdom. . . .

From Exodus 25:8–9 it is clear that God's intent was to "dwell" in a very simple structure. With the exception of the wood frames, it mostly consisted of hanging fabric, rope, and anchoring stakes. The symbolic religious accoutrements of the ark, sacrificial altar, laver, showbread table, lampstand, and incense altar were exclusive to Israel. However, architecturally, the tabernacle did not physically dominate.

God's instructions were not to have it situated on an elevated plane or built to monumental proportions as typical of many pagan temples in ancient times. In an architectural sense, elevation and size express social self-image and the human desire to create a lasting remembrance (see chapter 12). God was working in a different paradigm of religious architecture. Though this was the highest expression of Israelite tent construction, the place exuded immense humility in the context of who it was built to house. To me it is the epitome of self-restraint on the part of the Creator of the universe. Let's reflect on this more deeply.

God and My Wall Calendar: A Reality Check to His Immensity

At the beginning of this year I went through the difficult task of choosing what calendar to purchase to hang on the wall in front of my writing table. I was extremely disappointed to find that Gary Larsen did not produce a Far Side calendar, and in my despondence I searched the Web for an alternative. I became attracted to calendars with photographs taken by the Hubble space telescope. The one that is facing me now is of Supernova 1987A, which was a massive star that exploded on February 23, 1987, in what astronomers define as a large Magellanic cloud. Apparently, it is 150,000 light years away, which, if we do the math, I think is a smaller number than our national debt. It is the closest supernova to have exploded in modern times. The specifics of this dwarfs my intelligence (flips my mental breakers), but all I know is that its image above the calendar day-grid of May 2009 is staggering. And this is one tiny micro event happening in a universe of these things. Choosing which Hubble or NASA calendar was really tough, as they were featured alongside all the earthly nature ones put out by the National Geographic, the national parks, environmental societies, and professional photographers. It was like choosing which mind-boggling images fabricated by the hand of God I would like to post on my wall.

Of all the incredible possibilities, God, in dark cloud form, chose to dwell behind colorful goat-hair curtains fabricated by a people he inspired and, above all, loved. He could have housed himself in a supernova or prematurely landed the city of heaven and resided in that. I find the tabernacle an astonishing revelation.

The movement of going further into interior spaces, where each progression signifies a deepening of sacred space (from outer court to the Holy Place to the Holy of Holies) is a common attribute in religious architecture going back to earliest time. Early church architecture from the fourth century AD uses nave, chancel, and apse to reflect this same attribute with a division between the layperson standing in the nave and the priest presiding over the Eucharist at the rear of the chancel and apse. It seems to be within our human nature to deepen our spiritual experience, and our architectural representations oftentimes reflect this. Somehow our bodies react to the way we move further into interior places. I think Jesus had this in mind when he said,

> But when you pray, go into your room[39]
> close the door and pray to your Father, who is unseen.

MATT. 6:6

His complete humanity understood this principle when he made his solitary journeys to pray somewhere out in the countryside away from the crush of people. Enclosure can be found in nature as well as within a building. In regard to the tabernacle, this deepening interiority was processed by a lineage of priests—a class of exclusive folk. No one could go anywhere they liked. Thus I am not sure what the common Israelite felt about the tabernacle: whether he considered it a machine for forgiving national sin, an intimate zone where God lived, or a beloved material representation of the hope of his people becoming a great nation.

Perhaps I should not consider this context, but I imagine most modern-day evangelical Christians would become frustrated by not being allowed to enter the Holy of Holies. But perhaps (implied by Jesus' statement above) God's people had been going off to pray and commune with God long before the temple curtain was torn and Christ became our high priest. I do not think ancient Israelite prayer warriors were limited to the select few we read of in the Bible. I believe the righteous in the Lord have always prayed in their hidden, quiet spaces, whether they happened to be in their domestic tents or out in the vastness of the wilderness landscapes. Tabernacle worship could have been a manifestation of their spiritual walks, a coming together of a nation of tribes to obediently follow the tenets of the God with whom they loved to commune.

Tent-related Names and the Apostle Paul's Fleshly Tent

Further tent-word studies connect personal names with

spiritual meanings. Aaron's Hebrew name is directly linked to the word for sacred altar or shrine. A close Egyptian linguistic and phonetic connection to the words *Ahr-on* has his name mean "tent man." The combination of terms "altar" and "tent man" for the name Aaron is noteworthy since they piece together his identity as the first high priest to operate within the tabernacle.

> *"Have Aaron your brother brought to you from among the Israelites, along with his sons Nadab and Abihu, Eleazar and Ithamar, so they may serve me as priests. . . . Tell all the skilled workers to whom I have given wisdom in such matters that they are to make garments for Aaron, for his consecration, so he may serve me as priest.*
>
> Ex. 28:1, 3

It is also noteworthy that the name of the master craftsman, Oholiab (Ex. 35.34), means "the divine Father is my tent." In Oholiab's name we capture the perception of God as protector from life's harsh elements, whether they are natural or human generated.

A Symbolic Meaning for the Tent of Meeting

For us, in a symbolic way, the Tent of Meeting is then a tent of refuge from the storms life throws at us, the place where we may meet with God and find a balm that soothes the painful things that always seem to plague us (like dysfunctional family members). Or perhaps it is a refuge in a more severe sense, as when one learns a terminal illness is attacking their fleshly tent that has been so dependable at resisting foul weather. It is vital that we can claim entrance to the "tent"—a tent that does not perish—to meet with a God who is always faithful to show up and dwell with, comfort, and deliver us. His cloud saturates relational space, no matter the pain, disappointment, and impossibility of a good outcome. He is there protecting us with his abiding love.

The tent is a symbol that this is not all there is to the story of existence. Fabric deteriorates, rope unravels, and wood decays.

Sunlight bleaches color; sand and grit cut fiber as winds and foot traffic grind them deep into the fabric, shortening its lifespan. The mobile nature of the tent is a metaphor for our transience here on earth. Paul fully relates this concept nine hundred years after Solomon:

> *For we know that if the earthly tent we live in is destroyed, we have a building from God, an eternal house in heaven, not built by human hands. Meanwhile we groan, longing to be clothed instead with our heavenly dwelling, because when we are clothed, we will not be found naked. For while we are in this tent, we groan and are burdened, because we do not wish to be unclothed but to be clothed instead with our heavenly dwelling, so that what is mortal may be swallowed up by life. Now the one who has fashioned us for this very purpose is God, who has given us the Spirit as a deposit, guaranteeing what is to come.*
>
> 2 Cor. 5:1–5

We may find protection under the covering of our physical bodies, but it is only for a while. The fact that we can acknowledge this is testimony to the indwelling of the Spirit within our present temporary natures. The Christian narrative expounds that one day we all will exchange our temporary, earthly tents for ones that do not decay, ones of eternal permanence. For us in the here and now, our tents are temporary, disposable instruments.

This brings us to the final question of this chapter: whatever happened to the tabernacle?

What Ever Happened to the Tabernacle?

We are not sure. After Solomon completed the temple in Jerusalem, we have faint references as to the fate of the tabernacle, though we do know its sacred furnishings were transferred into its precincts. The Scriptures do not definitively say whether the tabernacle's frames were disassembled and stored within the temple treasury or whether sections of it were incorporated into the temple's Holy of Holies.

First Kings 8:4 records that the Tent of Meeting accompanied the ark and the sacred vessels from the City of David into the temple. The tabernacle is never mentioned again in the book of Kings, but two passages in the book of Chronicles indicate that until the end of Hezekiah's reign, the tabernacle resided within the temple. Desiring to renovate the temple, King Joash asked the head Levite why the priests had not collected funds "for the tent of the testimony." And in 2 Chronicles 29:6, Hezekiah initiated his religious reforms by acknowledging that the current generation's fathers "were unfaithful; they did evil in the eyes of the LORD our God and forsook him. They turned their faces away from the LORD's dwelling place [literally, "tabernacle"] and turned their backs on him." Passages such as these suggest that either for over two centuries following the temple's completion the tabernacle continued to exist, or its terminology lived on in the temple precincts while it lay somewhere (as our fleshly bodies will one day) obsolete.

Devotional Questions

1. Have you ever spent a night in a tent? How did that feel? What was it like to have a thin piece of fabric between you and nature?

2. What connections can you make between your tent experience(s) and the Israelites living in tents?

3. What insights can we learn about God from the fact that he chose a tent structure for his first constructed place of worship rather than a temple of stone like other nations?

4. How does the tabernacle develop a progression of sacred spaces that work from the outside into the innermost space? Name these spaces. Why did God instruct it to be designed this way?

5. How does the apostle Paul relate our bodies with tents (2 Cor. 5:1–5)? What do they have in common?

6. How are our bodies like tabernacles? By what means does God dwell in our Holy of Holies? How do our bodies symbolize God's eternal promise?

7. Knowing these things, how should we take care of our bodies?

CHAPTER 8

PATTERNS IN THE MIND
The Hand of God

*After the king was settled in his palace and the LORD had given him rest
from all his enemies around him, he said to Nathan the prophet, "Here
I am, living in a house of cedar, while the ark of God remains in a tent."
. . . But that night the word of the LORD came to Nathan, saying:*
*"Go and tell my servant David, 'This is what the LORD says: Are you the
one to build me a house to dwell in? I have not dwelt in a house from
the day I brought the Israelites up out of Egypt to this day. I have been
moving from place to place with a tent as my dwelling. Wherever I have
moved with all the Israelites, did I ever say to any of their rulers whom I
commanded to shepherd my people Israel, "Why have you not built me
a house of cedar?"'*
*"Now then, tell my servant David, 'This is what the LORD Almighty says:
I took you from the pasture, from tending the flock, and appointed you
ruler over my people Israel. I have been with you wherever you have
gone, and I have cut off all your enemies from before you. Now I will
make your name great, like the names of the greatest men on earth. And
I will provide a place for my people Israel and will plant them so that they
can have a home of their own and no longer be disturbed. Wicked people
will not oppress them anymore, as they did at the beginning and have
done ever since the time I appointed leaders over my people Israel. I will
also give you rest from all your enemies.*
*"'The LORD declares to you that the LORD himself will establish a house
for you: When your days are over and you rest with your ancestors, I will
raise up your offspring to succeed you, your own flesh and blood, and I
will establish his kingdom. He is the one who will build a house for my
Name, and I will establish the throne of his kingdom forever.*
2 SAMUEL 7:1–2, 4–13

THIS INTERCHANGE between David and the Lord portrays a significant time of transition in the perceptions of the home and the place of worship in the nation of Israel. Israel had, for the most part, left their tent culture behind and had now settled in Jerusalem and in many of the towns and villages of the previous tenants. The Lord, however, continued to reside within the fabric environment of the tabernacle.

David finally had a little peace in his life, the same type of peace that later allowed his eyes to wander to Bathsheba—but that is another story about rooftops and baths. It dawned on David that he resided within four solid walls and the house of the Lord did not. Apparently, David had the opinion that living within walls lined with cedar constituted a more sophisticated lifestyle than living within enclosures of animal skins and fabric. Clearly, there was a discrepancy between his and the Lord's houses, and he felt it was time (he had the time) to upgrade an outmoded thing of the past to his level of elite status.

At first I was ready to point the finger of guilt at David pertaining to a sin he would later pay dearly for or of which he would write another agonizing psalm. But having sat in very comfortable worship settings with compelling digital environments, I am not so sure I should pull the trigger on this one. There is nothing wrong with investing in technologically enhanced worship if the focus of the investment is to attract the unsaved through musical and artistic performances, make the gospel message clear, and boost the spiritual life of the believers. Regarding David, we have to see what the Lord had to say about this.

Yahweh responded to David with a reality check. First, God did not need human hands to improve his prestige. Did God reside in the realm of status? Did God need a nicer house? It should have taken only an instant to see these questions were pretty ridiculous.

However, God's questions resonated: "Did I ever say . . .?" "Why have you not . . .?" The instruction to build, up to this point in the biblical narrative, had always come from the Lord, and it was clear to David that the Lord would lay down the exact parameters of his earthly dwelling.

At the end of the day, a humanly conceived structure, particularly one genuinely intended for the glory of God, will always be tainted with some degree of pride. Not to keep kicking an old tire, but the Babel job was problematic in this way. It is part of our human condition. When pastors gather, the ones who are building cannot help but become elevated. I try to shield my eyes from the nakedness of their egos as they climb the steps of the ecclesiastical altar—though I wouldn't mind a nicer house.

For the second reality check, the Lord reminded David that he was a product of the pasture. And the only reason he left the sheep was because God chose him; the only reason he did not end up a pin cushion for his enemies' sharp pointy things was because of God's divine protection.

However, we see the summation of this dialogue taking a different tack than what we might expect. God's priority with the business of building a new worship center was not as much about what David wanted to do for the Lord but what the Lord was building *in* David. The revelation in this interchange was the formation of the institution of the house of David centered in Jerusalem. It was to be a continuous succession of generations made secure via the nation of Israel's obedience to Yahweh and, correspondingly, Yahweh's promise to preserve his people. After putting David in his place, the Lord then blessed him with these great words. However, he informed David that David's successor would build the temple:

> *King David rose to his feet and said: "Listen to me, my fellow Israelites, my people. I had it in my heart to build a house as a place of rest for the ark of the covenant of the LORD, for the footstool of our God, and I made plans to build it. But God said to me, 'You are not to build a house for my Name, because you are a warrior and have shed blood.'"*
>
> 1 CHRON. 28:2–3

Among kings and their successors, transition was often uneasy and bloody. Between David and Solomon, the issue of building the temple could have been a flash point of contention, but happily we see a wonderful handing off of responsibility. David grasped the vision, for God had affirmed him completely; he knew his name would, in perpetuity, be installed at the head of Israel's kingly lineage and be associated with the future temple he would never live to see. The Lord would forever sustain him, just as he had since before he was a shepherd boy.

The typical act of kings and successors hacking off parts of the kingdom (and heads) would be pointless. The eternal vision of the house of David was infinitely more than he could imagine; David was overwhelmed with this honor and could only respond with humility.

King Solomon fully appreciated and applied the lesson of his father in respect to his position in building a temple to the Lord. Clearly one of the attributes of his wisdom was a teachable spirit. When he thought about the task, the question, "Who am I?" was critical:

> "The temple I am going to build will be great, because our God is greater than all other gods. But who is able to build a temple for him, since the heavens, even the highest heavens, cannot contain him? Who then am I to build a temple for him, except as a place to burn sacrifices before him?"
>
> 2 Chron. 2:5–6

The Lord revealed his mind behind the creation of his temple. He chose the place, formulated its design, and consecrated it for his eternal glory:

> "I have heard your prayer and have chosen this place for myself as a temple for sacrifices. . . . I have chosen and consecrated this temple so that my Name may be there forever. My eyes and my heart will always be there."
>
> 2 Chron. 7:12, 16

Moses and David: The Neurology of Built Form

As I read through the following passages, I cannot help but think of Moses and David and the plans God instilled in their minds for the tabernacle and the temple:

> *"Then have them make a sanctuary for me, and I will dwell among them. Make this tabernacle and all its furnishings exactly like the pattern I will show you."*
>
> Ex. 25:8–9

> *"Consider now, for the LORD has chosen you to build a house as the sanctuary."*
> *. . . Then David gave his son Solomon the plans for the portico of the temple, its buildings, its storerooms, its upper parts, its inner rooms and the place of atonement. He gave him the plans of all that the Spirit had put in his mind for the courts of the temple of the LORD and all the surrounding rooms, for the treasuries of the temple of God and for the treasuries for the dedicated things.*
>
> 1 CHRON. 28:10–12

> *"All this," David said, "I have in writing as a result of the LORD's hand on me, and he enabled me to understand all the details of the plan."*
>
> 1 CHRON. 28:19

Over the many years I have spent in construction, I have known fellow carpenters who simply were inspired builders. They were gifted with the ability to visualize a project and without hesitation make the cuts and assemble the wood pieces from what was formulated in their minds. Unfortunately, I was not gifted with this ability; my processing is more mechanical and time consuming. The names of these guys over twenty years are Bard Sherman, Mark Twistleman, Brett Fowler, Doug Starr, Rob Law, Rubin Lopez, Matt Lindsay and Gerard Power. They were all great and I could only try to imitate them. When I read how the Lord infused the images of the tabernacle and temple in the minds of David and Solomon (I think Noah had the same vision for the ark), I cannot help but think of these guys. They simply had "it."

God, through the work of the Spirit, engraved in the minds of Moses and David perfect prototypes of the tabernacle and the temple. The Hebrew root words for *pattern* (*tabniyth*) in the Exodus passage are structural terms: "model," "figure," and "form." This indicates that the pattern was likely three-dimensional, not flat imagery. This same word is used again in 1 Chronicles 28:19.

The word *mind* in the NIV translation of 1 Chronicles 28:12 is not there in the word-for-word Hebrew translations. The key phrase is more accurately translated from the Hebrew as "of all that *he had* by the Spirit" (*Tanakh*, HPS).[40] In the Hebrew, *had* is *hayah*, meaning "to exist, with the emphasis on becoming." It is rooted in the term *ayeh ah-yay*, simply meaning "where." These words seem identical to the concepts the German philosopher Heidegger (see chapter 1) used to define the meaning of landscape in the early twentieth century.

Also, in 1 Chronicles 28:19 David uses the word *understanding* to describe how the "hand of the LORD" wrote "upon him" the details of the plan. The word for "understanding"—*sakal*— is "to wisely understand" or "to look at with comprehension in reference to the figure and likeness of something."[41] This understanding involved "all the details of this plan" or "all the works of this pattern." The term for *works* is the same word used in Genesis 2:2 to describe God resting on the seventh day from his creative work.

What we may glean from this is that there were precise visual transfers from the mind of God to Moses and David of the detailed plans for the tabernacle and the temple. I can imagine Philo of Alexandria reading over these verses and correlating them to how the mind of God works upon the cognition of the architects and city designers he knew during the first century AD. I recall several sections of his writings from chapter 1:

> God, understood in advance that a beautiful copy would not come into existence apart from a beautiful model, and that none of the objects of sense-perception would be without fault, unless it was modeled on the

archetypal and intelligible idea. Therefore, when he had decided to construct this visible cosmos, he first marked out the intelligible cosmos, so that he could use it as a incorporeal and most god-like paradigm and so produce the corporeal cosmos, a younger likeness of an older model.

Then taking up the imprints of each object in his own soul like wax, he carries around the intelligible city as an image in his head. Summoning up the representations by means of his innate power of memory and engraving their features even more distinctly (on his mind), he begins, as a good builder, to construct the city out of stones and timber, looking at the model and ensuring that the corporeal objects correspond to each of the incorporeal ideas.

Just as the city that was marked out beforehand in the architect had no location outside, but had been engraved in the soul of the craftsman, in the same way the cosmos composed of the ideas would have no other place than the divine Logos who gives the (ideas) their ordered disposition.[42]

Philo's description of memory—engraved images in the mind via the correspondence with the *logos*—resonates clearly with Yahweh placing his building patterns in the minds of Moses and David. This mental aspect pushes me to look into how our minds work in relation to architecture and how we receive shapes through our vision and attach ideas and impressions to them.

How Our Neuro-systems Allow Us to Build

Much neurological study has been made toward understanding how the mind responds to and processes mental images of geometric forms. In my very limited knowledge, I increasingly realize that the mind is a vast universe. Though I believe my brain resides somewhere between my ears, my understanding of its workings is equivalent to the distance between me and Supernova 1987A on the May page of my Hubble Telescope calendar. What I have come to learn is that the mind is geared to receive, process, and file information in an unfathomable number of rational and abstract ways. I am not a neurologist. It was not long ago when I struggled to spell the word. Yet I am compelled to make a few associations with this material. I do not know for sure exactly how the Lord put patterns in his servants' minds, but neurological research into how the mind receives sight images, processes three-dimensional forms, and associates ideas with them offers certain insights. Thus, I sense the following to be possible context for our understanding of Scripture.

Neuroscientist Semir Zeki says,

> "To discern a form is to verify a pre-existing idea, an act that no one, save the man we call an artist, can accomplish without external assistance." But what is this pre-existing idea, save the same stored visual record of a brain that has been exposed to many forms? . . . Gleizes and Metzinger state that under certain conditions, "it incorporates quality, the incommensurable sum of the affinities perceived between that which we discern and that which pre-exists within us." . . . the many cells in the visual cortex are selective for lines of particular orientation, and that they "pre-exist" within us, in the sense that they are genetically determined and need only to be visually nourished to become permanent fixtures of the visual brain.[43]

Though this is heavily debated, neurological evidence suggests that there is a matrix "prewired" into the brain that applies prepared images of form to visual stimuli involving our models of spatial perception.[44] In other words, there is evidence to suggest that we are born with image prototypes preset in our minds and open files ready to recognize and receive visual images that will be automatically broken down and disseminated to innumerable other files. These images are applied to our thoughts and ideas by some type of spontaneous file search-and-retrieval system. For my simple mind, it is like buying a computer with preinstalled operating software . . . times a billion—but at this, neuroscientists would scoff.

The structure of the brain allows individuals to orient themselves in relation to physical forms and certain perceptions that may accompany the images and patterns within the brain's stored visual memory system. It is a place where certain forms and shapes are invariably selected as privileged over other forms as we attach feelings to them.

Neurologists understand that the experience of having a mental image is an indication the brain is processing information in a particular way. When we use imagery to recall information, we generate images of previously seen patterns that are tucked away in our mental filing system. This process hinges on activating previously stored representations of spatial relationships. From this aspect, it is fascinating to consider how the psalmists, prophets, and apostles applied their neurological facilities to articulate their perceptions of God's truth while under the influence of the Holy Spirit. In order to express the impact God was making on their lives, through their myriad of circumstances, they had to cull their mental filing systems for appropriate means of expressing what oftentimes words could not express.

According to Steve Kosslyn, a neurologist at Stanford University, imagery is received through the eyes, producing a pattern of activity in a set of areas in the occipital lobe he calls the "visual buffer."[45] The areas in the visual buffer are organized such that when images from the eyes are scanned by the brain they are arrayed so that their geometric properties may be recognized. Moreover, the visual buffer physically preserves the spatial structure of the same images that strike the backs of our eyes. The visual buffer stores the properties of images that indicate edges and regions of color and texture, allowing us to recognize the same objects or like objects in different locations and contexts.[46]

Scientists Daniel Reisberg and Fridericke Heuer[47] might call this perception an internal stimulus from which a perceptual representation is constructed. The perception ("percept") of an image is remembered in the associative memory differently from the processing of the actual shapes of images. The percept is more of a "depiction" or the idea of shape than the simple remembrance of its lines and form.

The neurological mechanics of the perception of certain

shapes and forms is critical to understanding why Yahweh wanted the Israelites to destroy idolatrous altars and build an altar, in a very similar form, dedicated to him. This holds true with the constant Christian dilemma in relating to the secular world regarding certain places that are determined sacred, secular, and profane. In chapter 5 on altars and standing stones, we saw how the mechanics of perception made a single stone propped to the standing position, or a heap of stones, more significant than thousands of others lying across a field. Though the shape of one's church may be similar to a local Costco, the buildings hold much different values and perspectives. Somehow our minds can sort out this very complicated business.

The spatial structure of the buffer organizes the shapes into separate contexts that preserve the spatial relationships of objects without mixing or confusing them. We not only remember individual objects, but we also abstract properties of objects and remember their prototypes (base forms).

The image of the cross of Christ comes to mind here. The cross signifies physical suffering, infinite grace, and eternal life, and innumerable related perceptions shoot off from these ideas to create a complex web of philosophical, theological, and emotional thoughts and life experiences. From the symbol of two lines intersecting at ninety degrees, I determine the basis of my life.

The natural tendency is to associate things in categories and not as much with individual objects. These objects are organized into parts that some call "geons"[48] (short for geometrical icons), which are stored in the visual memory system. Because of our ability to separate images into parts we have a system that can ignore irrelevant shapes when they are processed in the brain's ventral system,[49] and because of this deep processing into categories, an object can still be thought of long after it has been seen.[50]

In a recent episode of *60 Minutes*, Lesley Stahl interviewed neuroscientists Marcel Just and Tom Mitchell from Carnegie Mellon University.[51] Their research involved the ability to identify thoughts (crudely referred to as "reading the mind") based on brain activity seen while scanned by a MRI. Test subjects were given pictures of ten objects to look at, five of which were buildings. From the image seen on the MRI monitor, Just and Mitchell observed brain activity patterns consisting of neurons firing under different intensities in different places across the surface of the brain. Everything that Kosslyn, Reisberg, Heuer, Zeki, and others have theorized was present in the multiple sparks and flashes of light across the brain's surfaces and its canyonlike depths. The MRIs looked very much like the video images of lightning storms taken by satellites and space shuttles, which show sporadic and simultaneous muted and bright flashes of light when the cameras pass over the seas and the continental land masses.

So when I consider that Yahweh put the tabernacle and temple images in his servants' minds, I think of infinite complexity and sparking synapses. The patterns of the tabernacle and temple were lightning storms flashing across the brain. He did not simply place an image in there, like downloading a program with a single file. Moses and David received an assimilation of images, perceptions, and geometries of functional and abstract natures, sown by Yahweh, as searing light across the furrows of living receptive brain matter.

Yahweh and Deep Processing in the Mind

The idea of deep processing invariably leads me to the books of Psalms and Isaiah. If there was ever deep imagery, it is here. Whenever the things of earth errantly loom larger than my perspective of God, I meditate on these passages:

The LORD wraps himself in light as with a garment;
he stretches out the heavens like a tent
and lays the beams of his upper chambers on their waters.
He makes the clouds his chariot
and rides on the wings of the wind.
He makes winds his messengers,

flames of fire his servants.
He set the earth on its foundations;
it can never be moved.

Ps. 104:2–5

Who has measured the waters in the hollow of his hand,
or with the breadth of his hand marked off the heavens?
Who has held the dust of the earth in a basket,
or weighed the mountains on the scales
and the hills in a balance?
Who can fathom the Spirit of the LORD,
or instruct the LORD as his counselor?
Whom did the LORD consult to enlighten him,
and who taught him the right way?
Who was it that taught him knowledge,
or showed him the path of understanding?
Surely the nations are like a drop in a bucket;
they are regarded as dust on the scales;
he weighs the islands as though they were fine dust.

ISA. 40:12–15

The deep processing of the psalmist (David) and Isaiah in these passages is a master class in applying preexisting imagery while under the influence of the Holy Spirit. The king and the prophet culled their memories for particular objects with which to create abstract concepts of Yahweh. David morphed the effects of God with natural phenomena: light, clouds, and wind. For the heavens he used tent, building, and chariot imagery—all things he was intimately familiar with. He had transitioned from a shepherd's tent to a king's palace, and as a military man he likely fought against the chariots of the Philistines. He could look up in his house and see beams laid over standing walls that established the floor for the upper chamber. The upper chamber, for David and in the contemporary Middle East, was the most pleasant space, as it caught the cool morning and afternoon breezes. It was likely here that David did most of his writing and meditation while in Jerusalem.

For Isaiah, I see him in the marketplace watching someone using their hand to take a drink out of a bucket while vendors used scales to measure produce for sale. To take everyday imagery and apply it to the omniscience of God is to refine him to base forms to express his highest, most complex, divinity. David's and Isaiah's profound knowledge of God came not from what could be seen; how can anyone possibly see these things? Somehow patterns of insight were put in their minds, and their visual buffers went to work, popping all the right percept files open where images with their corresponding ideas were assembled within the matrix of God's wisdom. Only with the Holy Spirit can this be possible. I suppose, in writing this, I am doing the same thing, though in comparison with David and Isaiah, in minuscule.

Devotional Questions

1. What was involved in the transition from worship in the tabernacle to the temple in Jerusalem? Who instigated the idea of temple worship?

2. How did God respond to David's request that God be worshipped in a temple? Why did God respond the way he did?

3. Why did God choose Solomon to build the temple?

4. How did God communicate the temple plans to David and Solomon? How was this similar to his communication with Noah and Moses about building the ark and tabernacle?

5. How do you think God put images and dimensions into his servant's minds? Do we receive inspiration for our creations in similar ways? How do our projects come to us? How do we first envision them?

6. How did the Jewish philosopher Philo describe the mental process?

7. Think of the people you've known who are inspired and gifted builders. What is in them that make them that way? Is it their attention to detail? Is it their ability to envision a project before it begins and to make it in a constant stream of effort? Or are they able to create as they go as their inspiration happens in the midst of the process?

8. Now that you have read how our minds process information, how intricate and immensely complex do our minds seem? How does this knowledge help us better understand Romans 12:2: "Do not conform any longer to the pattern of this world, but be transformed by the renewing of your mind"? What changes do we need to make in what we put into our minds each day?

CHAPTER 9

PRIDE AND EVIL IN BUILT FORM
Lessons from Sodom and Lachish

WHEN I WAS GROWING UP in a Christian family, there were places I could not go. They were bars, brothels, adult bookstores, any place where minors were not allowed (something to do with one's age, not one's occupation), radical leftist bookstores (which often had posters of Raquel Welch in that caveperson bikini that looks pretty conservative today), and certain movie theaters that did not show Disney movies. Churches and religious buildings, to a young kid growing up, were also somewhat of a conundrum (a funny-looking and funny-sounding word which means mystery, puzzle, or riddle).

Growing up Presbyterian, I found a strong desire to go to the nearby Mormon church because this particular one had an incredible gym with a basketball court. I mean, how could one better unite heaven and earth than with glass backboards? A Buddhist temple had a giant gong suspended from a neat wood beam structure in front of it. To my young eyes, this was really cool too. The Presbyterians didn't have a gong nor, at the time, a basketball court. I stayed with the Presbyterian church because I could not leave it (by parental mandate), and they had a youth group that went on wonderful adventures like the bicycling trip we took across the Golden Gate Bridge, up Mt. Tamalpais, down to Stinson Beach, then up the coast to the town of Inverness.

They also arranged the inner-tube (tubing) rafting trip down some California river where I lost my tube in the rapids and almost drowned. I remember a particular backpacking trip when I almost died by sliding, out of control, down a High Sierra glacier in the Desolation Wilderness. It was great! I found the near-death experiences in the high school church youth group to be the best for getting close to Jesus because I came very close to actually seeing him. I was knocking on the door, so to speak. In retrospect, I do not think these life-and-death experiences were an intentional part of the evangelistic strategy of the youth group leadership. But I could not wait until I could go on their next adventure!

Christians and Bad Places

In any case, I discovered that "place" and "Christianity" were connected in positive and negative ways. It was not so much the buildings as it was the behavior that went on within them that mattered. Different religions had their buildings; they were not bad, just different. And in those years difference of belief closed off certain places. I did not have the mentality to ask why; I just accepted it, because I knew that if I did, I would continue to be fed and be allowed to watch *Batman*, *The Wild, Wild West*, and *Mannix* on TV.

While researching my PhD thesis, I discovered the early Church Fathers struggled with their congregations over the same issues. The Christian theologian, Tertullian (AD 150–222) wrote this about 140 years after the apostle Paul's death:

Thus if sacrificer or worshipper, I enter the Capitol or the temple of Serapis, I shall fall from God—just as I should if a spectator in circus or theatre. Places do not of themselves defile us, but the things done in the places, by which even the places themselves (as they have argued) are defiled. We are defiled by the defiled.

There is no law laid down for us as to places. For not merely those places where men gather for the shows, but even temples, the servant of God may approach without risk to his Christian loyalty, if there be cause sufficient and simple, to be sure, unconnected with the business or character of the place. But the streets, the market, the baths, the taverns, even out houses, are none of them altogether clear of idols. The whole world is

filled with Satan and his angels. . . . Places do not of themselves defile us,
but the things done in the places, by which even the places themselves (as
we have argued) are defiled. We are defiled by the defiled. It is on that
account that we remind you who they are to whom places of this sort are
dedicated, that we may prove that they to whom the places are dedicated,
are lords of what is done in the places.[52]

What he is saying is similar to what I understood growing up:
it is the bad stuff going on in places that makes them bad. But
somehow, buildings get labeled, linking the reputation with the
activities for which they are used. A house used for prostitution
is called a "house of ill repute." A rescue mission is a building
used as a blessing and therefore becomes one. Likewise, when
we enter them we become infected by sensations we receive from
their atmospheres. How humans are affected by certain spaces
and buildings have been the study of architectural theorists for
years. Tertullian later describes certain buildings as *inflicted* from
sinful behavior.

A later textual source depicts the debate between two sixth-
century people: the Christian Octavius and the pagan Caecilius,
in the writings of the ancient Latin author Minucius Felix. Three
hundred years after Tertullian we see similar issues:

But in the meantime, in your anxious state of expectation, you refrain
from honest pleasures: you do not go to our shows, you take no part in
our processions, you are not present at our public banquets, you shrink
in horror from our sacred games, from food ritually dedicated by our
priests, from drink hallowed by libation poured upon our altars. Such
is you dread of the very gods you deny. . . . You do not bind your head
with flowers, you do not honour your body with perfumes; ointments you
reserve for funerals, but even to your tombs you deny garlands.[53]

And therefore, we who are ranked by our morals and modesty, we
have good cause for abstaining from your wicked pleasures, from your
processions and your spectacles; we are well aware that they originated in
religious rites and we condemn their pernicious attractions. Who would
fail to be horrified to see at the chariot races the frenzied brawling of the

mob, to see at the gladiatorial contests a school in murder? At the theatre
too, this raving madness is undiminished, and the display of indecencies
is greater.[54]

Octavius laid down a key point: obedient Christians simply did not go to certain places. The church would rather not have their congregations go to an amphitheater or circus to watch combatants hack at each other, sacrifice at pagan altars, and get perfumed and flowered-up for the civic festivals where one would likely eat meat from sacrificial altars. As Caecilius reveals, pagan city officials were noticing those who did not attend and were taking names and numbers. Societies were unified and deeply superstitious things then. Allegiance to the gods was performed in public. Doing the correct worship rituals meant protection and a prosperous year for families and the city. Continuance depended on sacrifice. To consistently not participate in pagan civic festivals and worship rituals was taken as an act of ill will toward a community. Out of this came Christian persecution.

Speaking of Bad Places, How About Sodom and Lachish?

I have selected two cities in the Old Testament that epitomize how sin affects place and how the Lord judges these places. The first is from the well-known Sodom and Gomorrah episode, and the second is a city called Lachish in southern Judea. About Sodom and Gomorrah, Genesis tells us:

Then the LORD said, "The outcry against Sodom and Gomorrah is so
great and their sin so grievous that I will go down and see if what they have
done is as bad as the outcry that has reached me. If not, I will know."
GEN. 18:20–21

"No," [the two men] answered, "we will spend the night in the square."
But he [Lot] insisted so strongly that they did go with him and entered his
house. He prepared a meal for them, baking bread without yeast, and

they ate. Before they had gone to bed, all the men from every part of the city of Sodom—both young and old—surrounded the house. They called to Lot, "Where are the men who came to you tonight? Bring them out to us so that we can have sex with them."

GEN. 19:2–5

The two men said to Lot, "Do you have anyone else here—sons-in-law, sons or daughters, or anyone else in the city who belongs to you? Get them out of here, because we are going to destroy this place. The outcry to the LORD against its people is so great that he has sent us to destroy it."

GEN. 19:12–13

By the time Lot reached Zoar, the sun had risen over the land. Then the LORD rained down burning sulfur on Sodom and Gomorrah—from the LORD out of the heavens. Thus he overthrew those cities and the entire plain, destroying all those living in the cities—and also the vegetation in the land.

GEN. 19:23–25

Though the remains of Sodom and Gomorrah have not been found, it is thought they were twin cities, closely situated along the southern Dead Sea region. For the sake of brevity, I will use "Sodom" in the singular to describe them both. From what we take from these verses, it was a pretty vile place. This was manifest in how Lot did not want his angelic friends sleeping in the plaza because he knew they would be sexually assaulted and likely killed. The idea that Lot would offer his two virgin daughters (19:6–8) to the mob really bothers me; I have a daughter and the thought of this is unspeakable. Maybe he knew their sexual preferences and that they would not take them, but the fact remains: if you hang out in evil places, you will likely have to make nasty compromises and messy decisions.

Sodom was situated on what is called the Plain of Sodom near Mount Sedom, which likely took its name from the city. Mount Sedom, in part, consists of layers of rock salt; the purity of its salinity has been tested to be much higher than what is gleaned from the Dead Sea. The salt trade from earliest antiquity into the medieval period was extremely lucrative. For Sodom to be a city sitting at an important east-west crossroads and be in possession of a mountain of pure salt was to have an easily accessible, unlimited gold supply. Sodom's affluence emanated from the earth.

Geologists tell us Sodom was founded on uncompacted or loose sandy sediments, while the town of Zoar, where Lot and his family fled from during the cataclysm, was situated on bedrock, on the flanks of the southern end of the Dead Sea basin. The theological concept of building on sand and rock should not be lost on us here. I am pretty sure people of that time and place were neither aware of the sediment lying beneath their city nor had knowledge of increasing pressure within the tectonic plates and fault lines throughout the Dead Sea region. But the truth behind the wisdom of building on either rock or sand is constant. The natural forces at work reveal the strength of one over the other. It is no wonder that the Lord occasionally refers to himself in Scripture as the Rock.

Environmental archaeologists tell us that, up to the time of the destruction, the Plain of Sodom was an extremely beautiful, well-watered land with prosperous agricultural/trade cities. It was also at the end of a three-hundred-year wet cycle, which explains why Lot, when given the opportunity, chose this fertile valley to settle. Archaeologists likewise encounter an abundance of fossil flora (plant remains in stone) in their excavations and determine this to be a sign of a well-irrigated, high-yield farming zone. The maturing prosperity of the land accounts for the transition from individual villages to city-states with satellite villages. We see these city-states in the biblical record when the five kings of Sodom, Gomorrah, Admah, Zeboiim, and Bela fought against and were defeated by the four kings from the cities of Elam, Goiim, Shinar, and Ellasar. Lot and his family were caught up in this conflict and were rescued by Abraham north of Damascus (Gen. 14:13–16).

Geologists have determined that, until Sodom's destruction, the valley region from the Galilee to the southern end of Dead Sea had not experienced notable earthquake activity for 3,500 years, until the Early Bronze Age III period. The language of Genesis 19:23–25 illustrates what can be seen only as the unleashing of intense seismic activity. The Dead Sea region possesses a number of fault lines, similar to the tectonic plates and fault zones in the San Francisco Bay Area where my wife and I currently live. Geological study of the region estimates that the severity of destruction increased as the sedimentary layer under the cities slipped toward the center of the valley basin along the down side of what is presently known as the Amazyahu Growth Fault.

The presence of petroleum-like materials in the Dead Sea region is historically well known. The first-century Jewish historian Flavius Josephus described the sea as Lake Asphaltites. Earlier historians, Poseidonius of Aphamia (Apamea) in Syria (second century BC) and Diodorus of Sicily (first century BC) observed many pieces of asphalt (bitumens) along the shores of the sea. Genesis 14:10 says the fleeing kings of Sodom and Gomorrah were trapped in pits of tar (*hemar*) that were not heated but had the consistency of pliable, sticky tree sap. The La Brea Tar Pits in Los Angeles are an example of that kind of pit.

Geological evidence indicates that deposits of cool, pliable, "slimy tar" were more abundant in ancient times than now. During this time, tar was a standard, multipurpose building material. As previously discussed, it was the bonding agent for the bricks in the construction of the Tower of Babel, and was likely the caulking for Noah's ark and baby Moses' basket set upon the Nile.

The Greek historian Herodotus described Babylon as being built of bricks set in tar mortar (hence the name "mortar").[55] Ancient Greek historians Strabo[56] and Diodorus Siculus[57] described the waterproofing agent for the terraces and projecting galleries of the legendary hanging gardens of Babylon, a manmade forest setting attached to the king's palace. A layer of waterproofing consisting of reeds set in thick bitumen or tar was laid over massive stone slabs supported by the garden's towering vaults. The reeds acted as a bonding agent to keep the tar from cracking. It was a waterproof mat that kept the irrigation water from falling through to the lower stories.

Here we have the waterproofing technique of the Moses basket (thin reeds set in pitch or tar) and ancient ship-building principles applied to monumental architecture. The Egyptians also used tar in their mummification processes. In its molten state tar does horrible damage to human flesh and is extremely combustible. Just ask a roofing contractor.

The billowing of smoke and rain of sulfurous fire, as described in the biblical record, are products of hydrocarbons (fossil fuel stuff) escaping from underground reservoirs and igniting upon reaching the surface. Al Gore would have been appalled. The surface and shores of the Dead Sea had for centuries been known to possess heavier hydrocarbons or what we would associate with chunks of tar, asphalt, and oil. As the earth fractured, the source rocks of hydrocarbons were superheated and released under pressure from deep in the ground. It was like an underground oil refinery gone berserk.

As temperatures increased, heavier asphalts exploded into flame. "Rejuvenated faulting" (smaller dormant faults) were likely activated, opening a number of channels for the sudden escape of larger, more explosive, events. Then the percolation of salty water from the sea, mixed with sulfur and hydrogen sulfide, created large plumes of black smoke that emitted sulfur dioxide in the form of acidic rain. When this fell to the ground, it likely caused great loss of life. The sky was filled with a terrible mixture of flaming pieces of tar and noxious acid, all of which came down as rain upon the cities as their brick walls fractured and collapsed from the massive earth tremors. It is no wonder the angels told Lot to hurry. The rush of saltwater into superheated chambers would have also created steam. The ancient Hebrew word that we interpret as *smoke* (*kittor*) has a modern Hebrew equivalent of "steam." Thus one theory has the two words—smoke and steam— as dual elements within the Sodom story.

As a geological event, this was a perfect storm. Everything came together at just the right, or wrong, time. Increasing pressure along fault lines, the abundance of petroleum materials, increasing population density, a rising water table, and a severe earthquake ended an epoch of habitation. This is thought to have initiated a change in climate to a more temperate, dry environment. The consequence changed the region's topography and began a cycle of drought. This drought is reflected in the wanderings of the patriarchs for the remainder of the Genesis narrative and in Israel's four-hundred-year stay in the land of Goshen in Egypt. If you go to this area in the summer, the place is like a heat furnace (yes, I know, it's a dry heat) as bleak and inhospitable as driving through the San Joaquin Valley in July in a '59 Chevy station wagon before air conditioning. It is the kind of heat that could melt your crayons into a globulous mass—not that I am bitter after forty-seven years.

Beauty and Evil

I find it odd that prosperity and beauty could be the breeding ground for abject sin. Beautiful buildings, creative minds, advanced technologies, and aesthetic environments that house and grow evil do not connect with me. It should be the opposite. Beautiful environments should encourage a higher spiritual plane, cleaner thinking, and elevated behavior. These things should naturally draw us to the Lord; their wonder should reflect our wonder of him. But, even today this seems not to be the case. Hitler had Albert Speer and the architect Paul Ludwig Troost design a fabulous world for his Third Reich. The Aztecs who created a staggeringly beautiful civilization centered in what is now Mexico City cut the hearts out of their sacrificial victims and stacked their skulls on framework displays in the city plazas. The Greeks, who produced the foundation of Western civilization and the brilliant philosophical insights I quoted in chapter 2, left their unwanted babies against particular street walls with the intent that they would be "adopted" as slaves, and in the case of girls, as prostitutes or temple servants. Spartan families exposed deformed or sickly infants to the elements on hilltops or threw them into the Apothetae, a chasm under Mount Taygetus. It is estimated that there was a 20 percent infanticide rate among female babies in Athens. The Romans left their unwanted (typically female) babies on city dung heaps where the heat from the decaying matter kept the child alive until someone came along and claimed it as a slave. These children often bore the full or fragment of the name *Koprias,* meaning "from the dung heap."[58] Today you can find partial-birth abortions, child pornography, and other tremendous evil existing within our finest cities. Beautiful aesthetics are not a sign of a moral culture.

I mention this to say that the biblical places where sin brought on the Lord's destruction were not gloomy, slimy, filthy, and grimy (all the "-oomy," "-imy," and "-ilthy" words) places like the castle of the Wicked Witch of the East depicted in *The Wizard of Oz.* Like Sodom, they were fabulous cities of wealth, beauty, and sophistication. It must have been extremely difficult for a child of God not to be sucked into their affluently cool lifestyle. Comparisons must be made to what Christians face today in the environment of digital sin. Their spiritual survival depends on keeping a safe distance from its strong pull, while simultaneously operating within its realm. The apostle Paul's sound bite—"be not conformed to this world" (Rom. 12:2)—is a simple command that understates the spiritual battle one faces daily.

We now come to a battle Israel faced that was indeed as much spiritual as it was physical.

The Temperament of Israel and the Destruction of Lachish

Like the punishment meted upon Sodom, the Lord's destruction always seems to be pretty thorough. Isaiah drew upon the example of Sodom and Gomorrah in his prophecy of the Assyrian invasion of Israel in the eighth century BC. Thus the two—Sodom and latter-day Israel—were linked. In both instances, if it were not for the Lord, there would have been no survivors. Isaiah compared Israel to the once-great city, described as a now-defenseless, rundown shack in a field:

Your country is desolate,
your cities burned with fire;
your fields are being stripped by foreigners
right before you,
laid waste as when overthrown by strangers.
Daughter Zion is left
like a shelter in a vineyard,
like a hut in a cucumber field,
like a city under siege.
Unless the LORD Almighty
had left us some survivors,
we would have become like Sodom,
we would have been like Gomorrah.

ISA. 1:7–9

Before I discuss the city of Lachish, we must look at how Israel treated the temple in Jerusalem. Israel's demise was a gradual process of deliberate, premeditated destructive disobedience.

Turn your steps toward these everlasting ruins,
all this destruction the enemy has brought on the sanctuary.
Your foes roared in the place where you met with us;
they set up their standards as signs.
They behaved like men wielding axes
to cut through a thicket of trees.
They smashed all the carved paneling
with their axes and hatchets.
They burned your sanctuary to the ground;
they defiled the dwelling place of your Name.
They said in their hearts, "We will crush them completely!"
They burned every place where God was worshiped in the land.
We are given no signs from God;
no prophets are left,
and none of us knows how long this will be.

PS. 74:3–9

Now the sons of that wicked woman Athaliah had broken into the temple of God and had used even its sacred objects for the Baals.

2 CHRON. 24:7

Manasseh was twelve years old when he became king, and he reigned in Jerusalem fifty-five years. He did evil in the eyes of the LORD, following the detestable practices of the nations the LORD had driven out before the Israelites. He rebuilt the high places his father Hezekiah had demolished; he also erected altars to the Baals and made Asherah poles. He bowed down to all the starry hosts and worshiped them. He built altars in the temple of the LORD, of which the LORD had said, "My Name will remain in Jerusalem forever." In both courts of the temple of the LORD, he built altars to all the starry hosts. He sacrificed his children in the fire in the Valley of Ben Hinnom, practiced divination and witchcraft, sought omens, and consulted mediums and spiritists. He did much evil in the eyes of the LORD, arousing his anger.

2 CHRON. 33:1–6

It is astonishing to me to read how, over and over, the sacred space of the temple was desecrated and converted into a pagan sanctuary. The meticulous instruction from the Lord as to its design and the wonderful craftsmanship that went into every inch of it was abused. The hours spent on its intricacies became one of the many fragments of Israel's spiritual amnesia. I wonder if the Lord feels the same anger when we destroy our bodies, the temple of the Spirit. We become bloated with inactivity and destructive dietary habits, and we wonder why there is a corresponding drop in our spiritual walk. I had better chuck my sack of Cheetos.

Israel's leadership could only look back to the promises of Yahweh and the prophecy of Isaiah to know what the result would be of their behavior.

"But if you turn away and forsake the decrees and commands I have given you and go off to serve other gods and worship them, then I will uproot Israel from my land, which I have given them, and will reject this temple I have consecrated for my Name. I will make it a byword and an object of ridicule among all peoples. This temple will become a heap of

rubble. All who pass by will be appalled and say, 'Why has the LORD done such a thing to this land and to this temple?'"

2 CHRON. 7:19–21

"Have you not heard?
Long ago I ordained it.
In days of old I planned it;
now I have brought it to pass,
that you have turned fortified cities
into piles of stone.
Their people, drained of power,
are dismayed and put to shame.
They are like plants in the field,
like tender green shoots,
like grass sprouting on the roof,
scorched before it grows up."

ISA. 37:26–27

The threat was palpable. If Israel worshipped other gods, she should get ready for the fallout. But who is ultimately responsible for the temple's ruin and the country's fall: Yahweh or the actions of Israel? The book of 2 Chronicles has a hypothetical passerby attributing it to the Lord, but was it entirely his doing?

Two Kings Go Head-to-Head Over Israel: Hezekiah vs. Sennacherib

Fourteen years before the Assyrian invasion, a righteous man named Hezekiah rose to the throne and worked to repair what generations of evil kings had done:

Hezekiah was twenty-five years old when he became king, and he reigned in Jerusalem twenty-nine years. His mother's name was Abijah daughter of Zechariah. He did what was right in the eyes of the LORD, just as his father David had done.
In the first month of the first year of his reign, he opened the doors of the

temple of the LORD and repaired them.

2 CHRON. 29:1–3

Soon after Hezekiah repaired and cleaned out the temple of pagan refuse, crises occurred. While the Assyrians were completing the destruction of the great city Lachish, only twenty-five miles to the south, Hezekiah made a transaction with the Assyrian king to keep Jerusalem from suffering the same fate:

> *In the fourteenth year of King Hezekiah's reign, Sennacherib king of Assyria attacked all the fortified cities of Judah and captured them. So Hezekiah king of Judah sent this message to the king of Assyria at Lachish: "I have done wrong. Withdraw from me, and I will pay whatever you demand of me." The king of Assyria exacted from Hezekiah king of Judah three hundred talents of silver and thirty talents of gold. So Hezekiah gave him all the silver that was found in the temple of the LORD and in the treasuries of the royal palace.*
>
> *At this time Hezekiah king of Judah stripped off the gold with which he had covered the doors and doorposts of the temple of the LORD, and gave it to the king of Assyria.*

2 KINGS 18:13–16

It is here that Sennacherib, the king of Assyria, is paired with the Judean city of Lachish and enters the frame of biblical history. Sometime around 1000 BC, Assyria began its ascent as a supreme military power in the Middle East. By the time King Sennacherib ascended to the throne in 705 BC, Assyria had reached the pinnacle of its cultural affluence and geographical expansion through conquest. Its army was technologically more advanced than any at the time, including its closest rival, Egypt.

The Assyrians had developed the composite bow that would not be rivaled for a millennium, as well as chariots that enhanced their maneuvering speed, freedom of movement, and intelligence gathering—critical strengths for a great army far from home. The Assyrians' technology was primarily directed toward laying siege to cities rather than open field combat. They developed advanced systems for penetrating and collapsing city walls, which the city of Lachish was to experience at its demise. The Assyrian infantrymen were renowned for all the things that make a fearsome killing force. They were uncompromisingly tough, courageous, tenacious, and did not have a conscience when it came to ruthless brutality. I remember the great archaeologist Dr. Ussishkin calling them the Nazis of ancient time.

In 701 BC Sennacherib was compelled to invade Palestine. Judah and the southern coastal plain cities of Philistia and the northern coastal plain cities of Phoenicia decided to become independent from Assyrian rule. They were likely backed by Egypt and Babylon (which was beginning its ascent as a world power). We know from ancient sources that the real reason for the invasion involved a power struggle between Assyria and Egypt and the control of the critical trade routes linking the Eastern and Western worlds. Like a tiny mouse that decided to burrow into a gasoline refinery and chew through an electrical wire that created a spark, one tiny city (Ashdod) decided not to give its tribute (taxes) to the city of Sargon, which was closely allied with and a clearing house for taxes paid to Assyria. This was not a good idea. The king of Ashdod attempted to gain allies in his little tax evasion revolt. This also was not a good idea. The growing cancer of revolt is how kingdoms fall, and this prompted Sennacherib to invade.

Hezekiah got himself into trouble by imprisoning the overthrown king of Ekron, a guy named Padi, who lost his position in the revolt. Thus Hezekiah took sides with Ashdod, aligning Israel against Assyria. This really was not a good idea. Israel, up to this point, had played a delicate game of neutrality between Egypt and the empires of Assyria and Babylon. Israel was like the Swiss of the Bronze Age Middle East, but not anymore.

Upon arriving in Palestine, Sennacherib quickly intimidated the coastal states back into control. A large Egyptian military force headed by Tirhakah, king of Ethiopia, clashed with the Assyrian army near Eltekeh on the Philistine coast, and the Egyptians were destroyed.[59] Sennacherib's forces swept up to the gates of Egypt but did not invade the country. Instead, Sennacherib turned back and took vengeance on the split kingdoms of Judah and Israel.

The confrontation between Hezekiah and Sennacherib's envoy (2 Kings 18:13–37) is the apex of the story. But first we need to discuss the city of Lachish, the last and most heavily fortified city to fall in the south.[60] The modern archaeological title for the site is Tel Lachish. A "tel" is a conglomerate of rocks, soil, and stratified remnants of civilizations that form higher elevation levels on a hill or promontory overlooking the countryside.

At the time of the Assyrian invasion, Lachish possessed a massive city wall at the edge of its summit. It also had a lower wall (called a revetment wall) built halfway down the hill. The purpose of the revetment wall is thought to have been a first, though minor, line of defense and a retaining support for the steep upper slope and base for the great upper walls. The remains of the main gateway at Lachish are measured to be the largest known all of ancient Israel's cities. The gate entry was designed in what is called the Solomonic style in that it had thick-walled E-shaped chambers that supported its massive superstructure and compartmentalized spaces for administrative/military purposes. Its architecture created an elaborate system of blind corners, multiple-segmented spaces that would have isolated groups of attackers to enfilade from all sides and above. The idea was to create multiple killing fields in the likely event the enemy infantry pushed to breach the gate defenses. Close to the gate, archaeologists uncovered bronze gate hinges, the size of which would qualify to operate the great double-entry doors. This was an unprecedented find. Bonded to the hinge plates were wood fragments that have survived from the original doors; the species was acacia wood.

In the summer of 1977, I worked as a field worker on the Lachish Archaeological Project directed by Dr. David Ussishkin of the University of Tel Aviv. I was twenty-one years old and a student at the University of Oregon. I had attached myself to a group from Northwest Christian College in Eugene, Oregon. We lived in twelve-man army tents in the archaeological camp outside the walls of a kibbutz at Beit Guvrin. The stories about our group could fill a book, so I had better not get started. I will say that the trip made such an impact on our lives that most of the guys' girlfriends became violently nauseous whenever we hauled out the Lachish slides and projector for the thousandth time.

In the middle of the nineteenth century, British archaeologists led by Sir Austen Henry Layard were excavating ancient Nineveh in present-day Iraq, and there they found clear pictorial representations cut in stone-relief panels of Sennacherib's destruction of Lachish. Nineveh sat on the east bank of the Tigris River, opposite of the modern city of Mosul, and was one of the greatest metropolitan cities of the ancient world. The stone panels were discovered in the hallways of Sennacherib's immense royal palace. They show a chronological progression of the siege and demise of Lachish and its inhabitants, with relief cut in extreme detail. They now hang in the British Museum, and to stand before them is worth the flight fare to London.

The reliefs portray an intense struggle as Syrian siege engines—wheeled, tank-like cars with battering rams—are pushed forward on paved ramps lined with timber planks. The ramps were built by slaves who were forced to endure and die under the fire and missiles from their own people on the city walls. This is one of the horrible ironies of siege warfare. During the summer I worked there, an exploratory excavation of the massive siege ramp on the southwest side of the city bore traces of plaster that formed a smooth track for the siege carts. The carts were supported by ranks of Assyrian archers, while lit torches, stones, and debris from the city filled the air and cascaded down from above.

If you look closely at the projectiles carved on the stone panels, you can make out lit torches intended to ignite lamp oil thrown on the cars, and round grinding stones used for processing food. The latter are evidence that the end was very near and time desperate. If you throw a food processor out the window, it is a sure sign there is no more food to process. There are also pieces of chariots (wheels and frame materials) thrown down as projectiles from the ramparts. This may indicate what has long been surmised, that Lachish was one of Judah's "chariot cities," an important administrative center and critical to the defense of southern Judah. Chariot pieces flying through the air

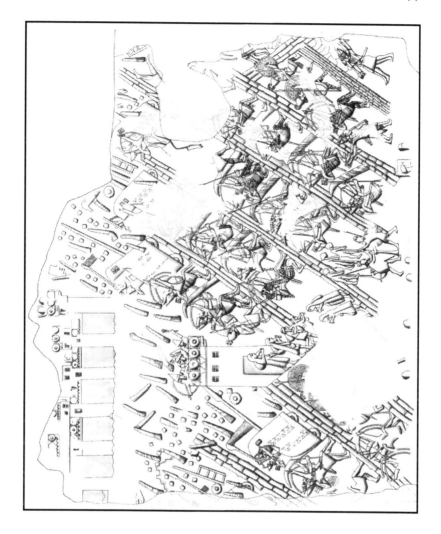

(Above) Drawing of the storming of Lachish and aftermath taken from the Lachish reliefs by Judith Dekel.

(Right) Drawing of the Assyrians attacking the walls of Lachish taken from the Lachish reliefs by artist Judith Dekel.

Images courtesy of the Institute of Archaeology, Tel Aviv University.

also likely meant there were no longer horses waiting around to pull them.

In the bottom left corner of a panel depicting the main siege ramps, captives are shown impaled under their sternums by lances, and then planted vertically in the ground. Suspended in this way, the spear point would slowly travel upward in the victim, just behind the sternum and up the rib cage; the pain and suffering must have been unbelievably excruciating. This was the Assyrian version of "hang em high"; there was no merciful throwing of a rope over a tree limb. Several other captives are shown lying flat on the ground while being, according to the common Assyrian practice, flayed alive. The Assyrians were not the bad guys you wanted attacking your city. For the defenders, the sight of a field of fellow citizens impaled or having their skin pulled from their bodies must have been a visual and audible psychological horror show as screams of agony resonated up the slopes into the city.

These terrible scenes are close to those depicting the events after the fall of Lachish. The carvings portray a line of captives approaching King Sennacherib with their hands raised upward in a plea for mercy. The king is seated on his ivory throne (transported from Nineveh) where captives are kneeling or crouching in subjection and likely pleading for their lives. Dr. Ussishkin believes the tortured victims were the result of Sennacherib's judgment, and the severity of their fate was likely due to their responsibility in Lachish's resistance. Off to the side of the judgment scene, one of the captives is being stabbed to death by an Assyrian soldier, and next to this a similar act exists in a small fragment where the rest has broken away. We see that after every victory, Sennacherib sat in the seat of judgment dispatching life and death as he saw fit. The longest cuneiform inscription engraved in the background near the king says, "Sennacherib, king of all, king of Assyria, sitting on his *nimedu*-throne while the spoil from the city of Lachish passed before him."

Early one morning, several of us in our tent—Gary, Allen, Mark, and I—decided to get up and run from our camp to the site, a distance of around five miles. We were the first of the entire group to arrive at the tel. A freshening breeze off the distant Mediterranean could be felt as the sun broke over the horizon. I stood on the massive wall foundations that once supported its defensive towers, the stone witnesses to sheer terror. If the panels were accurate as to distance, Director David Ussishkin estimated the images, later carved on the stone panels, were recorded approximately two hundred meters from the city's southwest corner, on a hilltop amidst the trees and farms of Moshav Lachish. Thus, it is likely King Sennacherib set up his ivory throne at this point to observe the siege in what is presently a grove of fruit trees safely out of arrow and slingshot range. I could imagine him there casually orchestrating this symphony of death, his massive ego on display, teaching these delusional upstarts the ultimate lesson for their disobedience.

Prophetic Warnings Unheeded

Despite the horrors of an Assyrian siege, it seems Israel was doubly disobedient: first to Yahweh and second to Sennacherib. The first brought on the second. A startling revelation was that Sennacherib knew it was Israel's God who instructed him to invade.

> "Furthermore, have I come to attack and destroy this place without word from the LORD? The LORD himself told me to march against this country and destroy it."
>
> 2 KINGS 18:25

When an idolatrous invading king tells you that he was told by your God to come and destroy your stuff, you've got to be asking yourself, "Who changed the teams? Why didn't I receive the text that this was coming?" Well, ancient text messages came in the form of prophets. They were like audio-textual messages cc'd from Yahweh. The following paragraphs mention a few of these outspoken voices that should have clued Israel in long before the walls started to burn and cave in.

The prophet Micah spoke to the immorality existing in Lachish and the surrounding countryside. Micah pointed to deep religious sin, not some small deviation away from the Lord's commands. His warnings against sin should have been engraved in Israel's spiritual conscience. I like the phrase in the first sentence of Micah 1:13: "harness fast horses to the chariot," which in contemporary language is like saying, "We're leaving right now. Load up the SUV; we're getting out of Dodge!"

> *You who live in Lachish,*
> *harness fast horses to the chariot.*
> *You are where the sin of Daughter Zion began,*
> *for the transgressions of Israel were found in you.*
>   MIC. 1:13

> *"In that day," declares the LORD,*
> *"I will destroy your horses from among you*
> *and demolish your chariots.*
> *I will destroy the cities of your land*
> *and tear down all your strongholds.*
> *I will destroy your witchcraft*
> *and you will no longer cast spells.*
> *I will destroy your idols*
> *and your sacred stones from among you;*
> *you will no longer bow down*
> *to the work of your hands.*
> *I will uproot from among you your Asherah poles*
> *when I demolish your cities."*
>   MIC. 5:10–14

The prophet Isaiah revealed many times the reason for the national trauma. In their audacity, the people had become like Sodom, and when they abandoned the Rock, they lost their fortress.

> *Jerusalem staggers,*
> *Judah is falling;*
> *their words and deeds are against the LORD,*

defying his glorious presence.
The look on their faces testifies against them;
they parade their sin like Sodom;
they do not hide it.
Woe to them!
They have brought disaster upon themselves.

Isa. 3:8–9

In that day their strong cities, which they left because of the Israelites, will
be like places abandoned to thickets and undergrowth. And all will be
desolation.

Isa. 17:9

You have forgotten God your Savior;
you have not remembered the Rock, your fortress.

Isa. 17:10

"Have you not heard?
Long ago I ordained it.
In days of old I planned it;
now I have brought it to pass,
that you have turned fortified cities
into piles of stone.
Their people, drained of power,
are dismayed and put to shame.
They are like plants in the field,
like tender green shoots,
like grass sprouting on the roof,
scorched before it grows up."

Isa. 37:26–27

"Listen to this, you descendants of Jacob,
you who are called by the name of Israel
and come from the line of Judah,
you who take oaths in the name of the LORD
and invoke the God of Israel—
but not in truth or righteousness. . . .
For I knew how stubborn you were;

your neck muscles were iron,
your forehead was bronze. . . .
You have neither heard nor understood;
from of old your ears have not been open.
Well do I know how treacherous you are;
you were called a rebel from birth."

ISA. 48:1, 4, 8

Similarly, Jeremiah spoke nearly one hundred years later of the Babylonians, who repeated the destruction of Judah and sacked Lachish and Jerusalem. His words transcend the centuries:

"And when the people ask, 'Why has the LORD our God done all this to us?' you will tell them, 'As you have forsaken me and served foreign gods in your own land, so now you will serve foreigners in a land not your own.'"

JER. 5:19

"This is what the LORD Almighty, the God of Israel, says: You saw the great disaster I brought on Jerusalem and on all the towns of Judah. Today they lie deserted and in ruins because of the evil they have done. They aroused my anger by burning incense to and worshiping other gods that neither they nor you nor your ancestors ever knew. Again and again I sent my servants the prophets, who said, 'Do not do this detestable thing that I hate!' But they did not listen or pay attention; they did not turn from their wickedness or stop burning incense to other gods. Therefore, my fierce anger was poured out; it raged against the towns of Judah and the streets of Jerusalem and made them the desolate ruins they are today."

JER. 44:2–6

The prophets' warnings and judgments during the Assyrian and Babylonian invasions went unheeded because Israel had rejected their Yahweh-istic heritage and adopted idolatry. Worshipping in the manner of the old Canaanites (I use *Canaanite* as a cover term for all idolatrous tribes and nations in Palestine) was forever their Achilles' heel. I mean . . . turning from temple worship to witchcraft? How does a nation reject their God who blessed and forgave them despite their repetitive lapses? This betrayal was so "in your face."

As the Assyrian storm clouds were gathering, we have a story of a king who worked to turn his nation around from sin. Hezekiah had a good heart, and though his country was infected with idolatry, he began the spiritual cleanup by taking a squeegee and leaf blower to the temple. He restored the temple to proper worship and reinstalled the Levitical priesthood. But, as with every person working to do the right thing, Hezekiah had to face his days of trial.

After all that Hezekiah had so faithfully done, Sennacherib king of Assyria came and invaded Judah. He laid siege to the fortified cities, thinking to conquer them for himself. When Hezekiah saw that Sennacherib had come and that he intended to wage war against Jerusalem, he consulted with his officials and military staff about blocking off the water from the springs outside the city, and they helped him. They gathered a large group of people who blocked all the springs and the stream that flowed through the land. "Why should the kings of Assyria come and find plenty of water?" they said. . . .

Later, when Sennacherib king of Assyria and all his forces were laying siege to Lachish, he sent his officers to Jerusalem with this message for Hezekiah king of Judah and for all the people of Judah who were there:

"This is what Sennacherib king of Assyria says: On what are you basing your confidence, that you remain in Jerusalem under siege? When Hezekiah says, 'The LORD our God will save us from the hand of the king of Assyria,' he is misleading you, to let you die of hunger and thirst. Did not Hezekiah himself remove this god's high places and altars, saying to Judah and Jerusalem, 'You must worship before one altar and burn sacrifices on it'?

"Do you not know what I and my predecessors have done to all the peoples of the other lands? Were the gods of those nations ever able to deliver their land from my hand? Who of all the gods of these nations that my predecessors destroyed has been able to save his people from me? How then can your god deliver you from my hand? Now do not let Hezekiah deceive you and mislead you like this. Do not believe him, for no god of any nation or kingdom has been able to deliver his people from my hand

or the hand of my predecessors. How much less will your god deliver you
from my hand!"

2 CHRON. 32:1–4, 9–15

Even though Hezekiah ransomed Jerusalem by stripping the temple and the city of its wealth, Sennacherib's true plan was revealed. He wanted Jerusalem to fall; the money bit was a ruse. As Sennacherib's chief officer stated, this was as much a war of religions as it was a territorial tiff. The strength of kings was directly related to the strength of their gods. Quite often kings became megalomaniacs (huge headed) and deified themselves, and I think Sennacherib followed this pattern common among Eastern kings.

The passage above includes a small portion of the Assyrian chief officer's narrative. His condescending tone was similar to that of a man named Sanballat who derided Nehemiah when he was restoring the fallen walls of Jerusalem some 250 years later:

When Sanballat heard that we were rebuilding the wall, he became angry
and was greatly incensed. He ridiculed the Jews, and in the presence of his
associates and the army of Samaria, he said, "What are those feeble Jews
doing? Will they restore their wall? Will they offer sacrifices? Will they
finish in a day? Can they bring the stones back to life from those heaps of
rubble—burned as they are?"
Tobiah the Ammonite, who was at his side, said, "What they are
building—even a fox climbing up on it would break down their wall of
stones!"

NEH. 4:1–3

Sennacherib's chief official and Sanballat used similar tactics of deriding truth and castigating a faithful one's obedience to God. The Assyrian was talking Tower of Babel and Eden snake talk; he spoke the language of deified man. Sanballat's goal was to discourage through cynical condescension. Both degraded God and those who were doing his will.

Hezekiah's response in the face of an overwhelming and relentless enemy was to pray. The last words of his prayer revealed his mind. This was a battle exposing the core issue in the conflict between the worship of idols and the worship of Yahweh. Stripped down to the essentials, this was a confrontation between the created and the Creator. It was quite silly, really. One party was delusional; the other created the universe. One side mattered, the other didn't really.

Hezekiah's prayer of deliverance was from a righteous man to an almighty God. Now that his city was surrounded with the water turned off, it was "go time."

> *"It is true, LORD, that the Assyrian kings have laid waste these nations and their lands. They have thrown their gods into the fire and destroyed them, for they were not gods but only wood and stone, fashioned by human hands. Now, LORD our God, deliver us from his hand, so that all the kingdoms of the earth may know that you alone, LORD, are God."*
>
> 2 KINGS 19:17–19

And Now for Paul Harvey's "The Rest of the Story"

> *Then the angel of the LORD went out and put to death a hundred and eighty-five thousand in the Assyrian camp. When the people got up the next morning—there were all the dead bodies! So Sennacherib king of Assyria broke camp and withdrew. He returned to Nineveh and stayed there.*
>
> *One day, while he was worshiping in the temple of his god Nisrok, his sons Adrammelek and Sharezer killed him with the sword, and they escaped to the land of Ararat. And Esarhaddon his son succeeded him as king.*
>
> ISA. 37:36–38

After taking massive losses, Sennacherib wisely gathered up the fortune he amassed from the invasion and headed home. Sennacherib's annals count the deportees sent to Assyria at 200,150. This was a veritable population shift and an immense transfer of wealth from the west to the eastern part of the Middle East. In 681 BC, exactly twenty years after the fall of Lachish,

Sennacherib was murdered by his protégé while praying in front of his gods. Following his death, a revolt broke out in Assyria and his palace was sacked and burnt. The relief depicting Sennacherib sitting on his throne before Lachish was deliberately mutilated, his face completely eliminated. After the tirade against Yahweh, he ended up nothing more than patricide fodder—his life wrapped up in a single verse.

Despite Hezekiah's reforms and the miraculous defeat of Assyria, Israel went back to their idolatrous ways. Yahweh, forever consistent in his discipline, brought the Babylonians under King Nebuchadnezzar to inflict a heavy penalty for their disobedience. This time Israel did not have a righteous king to pray for Jerusalem's deliverance.

> He brought up against them the king of the Babylonians, who killed their young men with the sword in the sanctuary, and did not spare young men or young women, the elderly or the infirm. God gave them all into the hands of Nebuchadnezzar. He carried to Babylon all the articles from the temple of God, both large and small, and the treasures of the LORD's temple and the treasures of the king and his officials. They set fire to God's temple and broke down the wall of Jerusalem; they burned all the palaces and destroyed everything of value there.
> He carried into exile to Babylon the remnant, who escaped from the sword, and they became servants to him and his successors until the kingdom of Persia came to power. The land enjoyed its sabbath rests; all the time of its desolation it rested, until the seventy years were completed in fulfillment of the word of the LORD spoken by Jeremiah.
>
> 2 CHRON. 36:17–21

The destruction was complete. The story of the nation of Israel shifted to Babylon as if Yahweh, his people, and the land needed to take a break from the unending cycle of sin-affliction-repentance-deliverance. It was like taking a national cleansing breath to rid the place of impurity. Years later, a new generation with righteous and sensitive hearts would be directed to return and rebuild. Chapter 10 will present the story of Nehemiah's return to rebuild the walls of Jerusalem.

Conclusion

After the dust of this chapter settles, we are left with two smoking cities. As the stories of Sodom and Lachish portray, there is more to these places than an assembly of buildings standing behind concentric walls. Their architectures are a battleground of morality and immorality where behavior determines outcomes. The Scriptures open an invisible drama. Buildings stand or fall based on obedient worship to Yahweh.

The most poignant images from the Lachish panels are those showing families of survivors (men, women, and children) being led off into captivity carrying sacks of belongings over their shoulders, and on carts driven by oxen. Women are depicted carrying babies, and it is impressed on me that these children will grow up never seeing the land of their birth. There is another equally disturbing panel where the deported captives, now back in Nineveh, work to build Sennacherib's royal palace. Men are shown carrying huge stones and piling them up to form a foundation for the great building. Another relief shows a great bull stone colossus being dragged to the building site by long ropes pulled by scores of captives. If we look closely, the exact detail in the carvings allow us to make some connections. We see that each row of captives manning their ropes is dressed in a particular style. Amazingly, we can match exactly the dress style of the men pulling on one of the ropes to those captives depicted in earlier panels leaving Lachish. The comparison is unmistakable. They are being cruelly driven by Assyrian taskmasters. This was Egypt all over again. It must have been humiliating to know you were building in captivity what you could have been building at home. To see the panels glorifying the destruction of your city be mounted on the walls you sweated and were beaten to build must have been agony.

In our world where it's difficult to apply meaning to anything, here we have cities and their peoples on the edge of the abyss. Irony lurks here like the invisible elephant standing in the room. The heaps and standing stones are mute. The key to abundant blessing, the blessing that always came when Yahweh was worshipped and his statutes followed, was discarded for the one thing that had always proved to be self-destructive.

This reminds me of the wonderful education my children and their generation in the public school system received from the DARE Program and the many sexual-prevention classes that taught them, explicitly, not to use drugs and that if you have sex, be sure to wear a condom. The "just say no" and "wear a layer of latex" admonishments were given in the hope that they would counter the downward spiral of STDs and unwanted pregnancies. Police dutifully visited classrooms, and nurses from Planned Parenthood came to inform and prepare the students for what was coming their way and hand out condoms like Chiclets gum.

Hormonally, it later became something like the running with the bulls in Pamplona. It did not take long to see the result of the years of education played out on too many of these young lives. Tragically, the end result was a nightmare of drug addiction, STDs, and unwanted pregnancies for some we knew by name. This happened in an affluent area with scholastically competitive kids.

I cannot help but make an association between Israel and raising children. You teach, discipline, and warn. You try to model, and you try to be real. You patiently instruct and point out examples of success and failure. You send youth pastors to be surrogate prophets and holy men to present a vibrant environment, a new perspective on biblical truth. But at the end of the day you are dealing with the irrepressible force of human nature and its indomitable will. We decide for ourselves what to accept and what to discard. The psychology behind this is, like many things, beyond me and the bounds of this book.

But I came close to doing the same thing when I was young. Then, after a number of near misses, I closed the doors on the dangerous things and opened the temple doors to those who I remembered would be a blessing to me. I remembered because the blessing had been demonstrated and proven in the past, and I yearned to go back to those days. I could visualize the beautiful faces of the kids I knew in our amazing youth group and the youth pastors who taught undeniable truth—and likewise lived that truth. How could I have rejected that for the superficial joy the world offered, only to be cast, as an infant, on the *kopra* heap and be adopted by an abuser as a slave? Perhaps the remnants of Israel, residing in Assyria and Babylon, had felt the same way.

Devotional Questions

1. When you were growing up, were there places your parents would not let you go? Where were they?

2. Are there some places you have banned yourself from as an adult? Where are they and why?

3. There is a stream of thought that accepts that beautiful places (cities, towns, landscapes) inspire higher levels of culture and human behavior. In your experience, is this true? Is this biblically correct?

4. How did God destroy Sodom? What prompted him to act? We are back to Noah; what is similar and/or different this time in God's destruction?

5. How was the destruction of the city of Lachish similar to and/or different than what occurred at Sodom?

6. The events surrounding the demise of Lachish did not involve a natural cataclysm as at Sodom, but why does God use other nations to inflict punishment on his children?

7. Does God punish nations for their immorality today? Or do you think he's in a holding pattern biding his time before he kicks off the Apocalypse? If he does punish nations today, what are his methods?

CHAPTER 10

NEHEMIAH
Building Amidst Ridicule

But when Sanballat the Horonite, Tobiah the Ammonite official and Geshem the Arab heard about it, they mocked and ridiculed us. "What is this you are doing?" they asked. "Are you rebelling against the king?" I answered them by saying, "The God of heaven will give us success. We his servants will start rebuilding, but as for you, you have no share in Jerusalem or any claim or historic right to it."

NEHEMIAH 2:19–20

When Sanballat heard that we were rebuilding the wall, he became angry and was greatly incensed. He ridiculed the Jews, and in the presence of his associates and the army of Samaria, he said, "What are those feeble Jews doing? Will they restore their wall? Will they offer sacrifices? Will they finish in a day? Can they bring the stones back to life from those heaps of rubble—burned as they are?"

Tobiah the Ammonite, who was at his side, said, "What they are building—even a fox climbing up on it would break down their wall of stones!"

NEHEMIAH 4:1–3

"Why is this taking so long?"

"Why did you build it this way?"

"Why is this costing so much?"

"This looks: out of level, out of plumb, not straight, too big, too small, too thin, too tall, too weak, too beefy, too wimpy, too out of proportion, too wood grainy, too rough, to smooth, too knotty."

"The colors in the wood grains are too varied in their spacing and color; can't we *do* something about that?"

"Can we *do* something about this knot?"

"I wouldn't let him build my dog house."

"Good thing you don't do this for a living...What, you do?"

"You missed this." "You missed that."

"What were you thinking?" "You need to start thinking."

"Don't you know how to do that?"

"You've never done this before?"

"Stop desecrating nature; put the board and saw down and step away from the job site."

"Be a good lad, kindly pick up your tools and kit and be off with you; you're sacked. Anyway, thank you for coming." (The British version of, "You're fired," related to me by a New Zealand carpenter who overheard this while working on a high-rise project in London, England).

WHAT YOU HAVE JUST READ is a power-spray of verbal ridicule I've heard, received, and (with some latent guilt) said over the years. It is somewhat amusing to read the words of Nehemiah's enemies, Sanballat, Tobiah, and Geshem, and see them carry a similar tune to my litany. Sarcastic criticism spans 2,500 years.

For Nehemiah and his crew, the stress in rebuilding Jerusalem's walls was as much a physical beating as it was the daily mental harassment and psychological fear caused by their oppressors. Mentally each had to carry a stress-packed suitcase in addition to the courses of stones they had to lift and set each day.

In this chapter we encounter a work-place truth: our jobs are as much battling psychological demons as they are accomplishing tasks. Many of us painfully know that *oppression* and *work* are two words often paired together in our daily experience. Coping with malicious criticism and abusive supervisors is often the most difficult part of our lives, and since much of the book of Nehemiah is taken up with confronting it, we must dedicate this chapter to it. This time archaeology will not be at the forefront of our discussion.

In construction I have come to realize criticism is a two-edged sword. In a positive sense, it keeps quality control in check, people from getting killed or dismembered, and (to use a highly technical word) "wonky" things from being built. It upholds the integrity of the trades. Criticism, properly given and accepted, is a good thing. Yet there are times it is better if a person finds something else to do for a living. "Be a good lad; just step away from the jobsite."

In the biblical narrative we see a critical precedent where Jesus, Stephen, and Paul expressed their opinions without much delicacy. Rather than being emotional tirades, their disciplining had to do with correcting the practice of profaning the worship of God, the sacred space of the temple, treatment of Israel's prophets, and immorality among the saints who should have known better.

Confidence is critical to a builder. When I make a good cut, when my joinery fits tight and the job flows, my spirit is high, my vision of the job is clear; I can't wait to tackle the next task. When I receive criticism (just or unjust) a mental battle commences and all the happy thoughts dissipate. In their place arise anger, frustration, and bitterness that reduce the quality and raise the frustration of my work. While I am in this state, my vision is distorted. I miss my cuts (not to mention my fingers). I doubt my plan and want to do something else for a living—like be a travel writer on the Discovery Channel. A friend of mine likens criticism to race cars flying round and round a dirt track, spewing dust and rock every-which-way. To the builder, criticism is as much a mental as it is a physical battlefield.

The most unexpected problem I find in construction is not the technical work. Most of us working in the trades know how to do, very well, the specific tasks required of us. What is most surprising to me is how strong the subcurrent of emotion, the bad-mouthing, gossip, and anger issues, can run during the course of a project. This emotional freight weighs heavily on the mind, often cripples the quality of craftsmanship, and extends the schedule of completion.

The homeowners on a particular project became aware of this dramatic undercurrent when a workman foolishly told them that so-and-so subcontractor was doing a bad job on their granite countertops, just as they had on a previous job. The owner-contractor confrontation that immediately followed was equivalent to laying a thick bed of habanera chilies in a breakfast omelet.

Destructive criticism and ridicule are pervasive throughout life. They are an invasive psychological cancer that operates well beyond the workplace to feed on our minds when we are alone with our thoughts. It takes many rounds of spiritual chemotherapy to kill these destructive voices. It is in this difficult realm that we connect with Nehemiah and his builders. Fortunately, Nehemiah's book is packed with practical insights to cope with adversity in the workplace. Following the very different perspective of this book, we will find our answers through a deeper architectural knowledge of walls.

The Problem and the Solution

Then I said to them, "You see the trouble we are in: Jerusalem lies in ruins, and its gates have been burned with fire. Come, let us rebuild the wall of Jerusalem, and we will no longer be in disgrace."

NEH 2:17

Nehemiah's national rallying cry for Jerusalem's reconstruction boils down to the condition of its walls. This might seem strange, but walls affect human emotion; they may induce passionate responses. Much earlier in the biblical record, the spies reporting to Moses from their reconnaissance mission into Canaan were filled with fear after seeing cities with insurmountable walls, and massive gates (Deut. 3:5). We've seen Jericho's tumbling walls provoke joy and victory songs for centuries, and in our postmodern era, sarcasm. In the first verses of Nehemiah we have the Jews in deep mourning over Jerusalem's broken walls (1:3–4). All of this emotional venting seems Oprah-esque for something so seemingly simple. What's going on?

Fundamentally, a wall is . . . well . . . a wall. A wall is a vertical slab that blocks off, separates, divides, hems in, and protects. Yet walls may impose varying degrees of sensations. In chapter 6 we saw how deepening interiority within walls led to more intimate spaces. Probing deeper, we saw the symbolism of the collapsed walls of Jericho depict the brokenness of Rahab's heart (her most internal space), her coming to God, and her infusion into the genetic line of the coming Christ-child.

So walls can have deep connections with our beliefs and psyches. Perhaps walls are more complex than we think. Nehemiah said Israel was humiliated because of them. Jerusalem's walls mirrored the guilt of the nation's overall spiritual condition, as a vertical reflecting pool casting a true image of the one gazing into its still waters. And this image was not pretty. Jerusalem's missing gates, a fragmented-jagged wall profile, and blackened stones looked like the broken teeth and black eyes of a bare-fisted fighter. The walls stood as an architectural metaphor for a nation's covenant with their Lord. Once strong and proud, they now stood broken, stripped of their power and the spiritual vision that once energized their construction.

Here we have biblical evidence of a national identity embedded in standing architecture. The nation stood in the same broken disgrace as Jerusalem's walls. On a happier note, restacking stone in a concentric pattern around Jerusalem was a physical sign of spiritual restoration, a renewed commitment between a people and their God. But as we know, restoration of any type is not an easy task.

Nehemiah leading the charge to rebuild of Jerusalem's walls must place high on the list of Scripture's most inspiring construction projects. After the depressing examples of the Tower of Babel, the walls of Jericho, Sodom and Lachish, and prophecy of civic and national destruction (walls breached and crashing down, and people deported), it is quite a relief to hear something positive (walls going up and people moving in).

From a secular point of view, Nehemiah's account is the classic story of how a small group out of a displaced nation, an underdog team, won the day by overcoming tremendous odds through their faith in their God and extremely competent leadership. This brilliant example of spiritual leadership, logistics, and organization has been applied, in many creative ways, by pastors guiding their flocks through church building projects and business consultants in group leadership and teambuilding seminars.

Before we go further, we must acknowledge that the Jerusalem Wall Restoration Project (JWRP) could only have been accomplished through the power of Almighty God working through a righteous, repentant, and humble leader. The book of Nehemiah screams this fact. Nehemiah's earthly support came through hard-working individuals, self-sacrificing families, and trades-people of the same character. It was a synergy of the physical and the spiritual.

As the work progressed, Jerusalem's walls made Nehemiah's enemies feel excluded, jealous, and vulnerable. They vented their violence not through sword thrusts or arrow shots but in verbal ridicule. Their goal was to discourage the building effort by reducing the self-image and confidence of the builders. Yet power shifted as the wall heights rose and gates were repaired. The haters raged as they became more "vertically challenged," and the builders were raised up in spiritual and social confidence in their Lord and in their efforts.

Walls might be as much a key player in this narrative as is the character of Nehemiah. It is important that we further our architectural knowledge of them; this will lead to deeper applications at the conclusion of this chapter.

Walls: Capturing Space

Walls divide. They have two sides: physically and metaphorically. They compress and make tangible distances between things by making a solid barrier that provides security and separation. They extend the territory of what they contain to a precise boundary, and set limits to what is inside and what is outside. With walls space can be used more economically than without. The compact city is made possible by walls.[61]

The built wall is an instrument of the mind, and a powerful one. A wall manifests its architect's purposes. It is born of intention and infused with attitude.[62]

The architectural theory behind the meaning and necessity of walls goes back many centuries. Four hundred years before Christ, Aristotle said the area around us (what he called "space") is captured in invisible containers from largest to smallest, like thousands of envelopes of successive sizes stuffed within each other, or like Russian dolls that fit within one another. This imagery helped to explain his theory that everything has its place, its location. By "everything" he means air, sky, people, nature, things—everything. Because everything is where it should be, there is no earthly void, a place where nothing exists.

We can relate Aristotle's idea to the Bible. When God approved his creation in Genesis I, it was a planetary environment of bounded and filled places. Excuse the double negative, but there were no places of nothingness. God left nothing blank as if he would get back to it and fill an earthly void with some random stuff, like expanding foam insulation, on the following Monday (the eighth day). Every space, from a pin prick to the limitless horizon, is packed full ("chock-a-block," as the British say) with life and matter. Everything is in its proper place.

Aristotle went further to say the space around us, no matter if we are standing in a Sierra meadow or a library reading room, is like a hollow with external boundaries and internally filled. Everything is contained in something else. For instance, a gnat is consumed and is in the digestive tract of a rainbow trout; the trout swims in a lake immersed in its waters; a shoreline rings the lake contained in a valley, surrounded by mountains, within a coastal range, under the sky's hemisphere, and so on.

To borrow Aristotle's concept, architecture has been said to be the art of "filling the hollow." We erect buildings of all sorts and their effect bounds or partitions open space with walls. We fill their insides (hollows) with our families, professions, and the other limitless number of things we use them for.

Walls are humanity's means of establishing boundaries to make the natural world a human world. It is in *our* nature to contain things (as we imitate this divine principle in nature), whether out of necessity or psychological desire. Walls fulfil this need.

As a side-note: Spatially speaking, we are never truly "free." No matter if we quit our jobs and move out into the forest to live in a hollow Redwood tree or open sky, we are always bounded or limited by something. In his song, "Gotta Serve Somebody," Bob Dylan lyrically exposes the lie that we hold complete sovereignty over our lives.[63]

Beyond their obvious functions of protecting, containing, dividing, and making an alien territory indigenous ground, walls take on many types of significance. Their meaning may be moral, social, personal, political, military, philosophical, symbolic, religious, psychological, and aesthetic. In Nehemiah a number of these symbolic types can be identified with Jerusalem's walls. To complete the wall's circuit enabled Jerusalem to define itself as a viable place. All other conceptions of the city rested upon this piece of territory being bounded by vertical stone. The temple and Jerusalem's commercial, administrative, and residential zones lay within this captured space.

Walls are two-sided things, and their exterior faces are as architecturally important as their interior ones. They are equally potent from their interior and exterior perspectives. As their interior faces rose upward, Jerusalem's walls brought joy and security to the inhabitants. Their exterior elevation brought out a radically opposite response from the Jews' outside adversaries. Joy and confidence, anger and fear—it's amusing how much of an emotional contrast they were.

The walls became a key player in the Nehemiah narrative. They were a statement of resistance representing the Jew's determination to be permanently placed on this particular point on the landscape. The Jews built like mad to present their stark, elevated faces to the enemy. The higher the walls rose, the more desperate the enemies' resistance grew, and the more the builders' vision of success was affirmed. This people would not be moved (4:7). In a similar way, a common trait of those who oppose God is hatred toward fixed and immovable things: a secure, confident faith; rigid standards of morality; and a planted, righteous people.

A Biblical Discussion of Nehemiah

*"Lord, let your ear be attentive to the prayer of this your servant and to the prayer of your servants who delight in revering your name. Give your servant success today by granting him favor in the presence of this man."
I was cupbearer to the king.*

NEH. 1:11

*The words of Nehemiah son of Hakaliah:
In the month of Kislev in the twentieth year, while I was in the citadel of Susa, Hanani, one of my brothers, came from Judah with some other men, and I questioned them about the Jewish remnant that had survived the exile, and also about Jerusalem.
They said to me, "Those who survived the exile and are back in the province are in great trouble and disgrace. The wall of Jerusalem is broken down, and its gates have been burned with fire."
When I heard these things, I sat down and wept. For some days I mourned and fasted and prayed before the God of heaven.*

NEH. 1:1–4

*The king said to me, "What is it you want?"
Then I prayed to the God of heaven, and I answered the king, "If it pleases the king and if your servant has found favor in his sight, let him send me to*

the city in Judah where my ancestors are buried so that I can rebuild it."
Then the king, with the queen sitting beside him, asked me, "How long
will your journey take, and when will you get back?" It pleased the king
to send me; so I set a time.
I also said to him, "If it pleases the king, may I have letters to the governors
of Trans-Euphrates, so that they will provide me safe-conduct until I
arrive in Judah? And may I have a letter to Asaph, keeper of the royal
park, so he will give me timber to make beams for the gates of the citadel
by the temple and for the city wall and for the residence I will occupy?"
And because the gracious hand of my God was on me, the king granted
my requests. So I went to the governors of Trans-Euphrates and gave
them the king's letters. The king had also sent army officers and cavalry
with me.
When Sanballat the Horonite and Tobiah the Ammonite official heard
about this, they were very much disturbed that someone had come to
promote the welfare of the Israelites.

NEH. 2:4–10

The date was 444 BC. It had been 257 years since Lachish
fell to King Sennacherib of Assyria (chapter 9), 142 years after
the Babylonian destruction of Jerusalem (586 BC), 70 years
after Esther married King Darius (see the book of Esther),
and fourteen years after Ezra received permission from King
Artaxerxes of Persia to go back to Israel and restore the temple
and priesthood in Jerusalem. Now Nehemiah entered the
biblical timeline.

We quickly discover a number of factoids about Nehemiah.
He lived in Susa, one of the capitals of the Persian Empire used by
its emperors.[64] He worked as the cupbearer to King Artaxerxes.
A cupbearer was a provocative profession. He was responsible
for pouring wine for the king. He was in charge of the cup and
often tasted the king's food before giving it to him. We might
think this was a pretty cool job, like being a *sommelier*[65] at a Five
Star restaurant, but this was not the case. Though he existed in a
culinary world, a cupbearer lived on the ragged edge of political
intrigue and empire-wide power plays. Simple tasks were life
and death events. Don't even think of spilling the wine or

fumbling the cup. A little later in the historical record, a Roman aristocrat would have thrown his wine servant into his pool of huge lampreys for breaking a wine glass had Augustus Caesar not intervened.[66] His impulse to cast his servant to the lampreys to be eaten alive meant he had done so previously and considered it good entertainment. Yuck!

From ancient to modern times, an assassin's favorite method of doing away with royalty was to place poisons in their food and drink. To be a cupbearer was to perpetually wonder if you only needed a few Tums for indigestion or a quick sword blow to the noggin to forego the gagging and last bit of thrashing around before dying. If any bad dates got through Nehemiah's taste test (see the movie *Raiders of the Lost Ark*, where that monkey died after wolfing down a bowlful of bad dates), he would have immediately paid with his life. There was no antidote to inject, no white bread to stuff down his gullet to counteract the poison. Nehemiah had to show up every day for work bringing his "A" game. It was imperative that Nehemiah be infinitely trustworthy and wise in the realm of human nature. He needed the gift of anticipation, to see what was coming and prepare for it.

The king was dependent on Nehemiah. Artaxerxes was anxious to know exactly when Nehemiah would be back from his Jerusalem expedition (2:6). His anxiousness to know the date of Nehemiah's return ticket seems a subtle statement that Nehemiah was not allowed permanent residency in Palestine. His service was critical to Artaxerxes' existence as king.

We wouldn't think someone with his resume qualified to be a restoration kind of guy, someone who could mobilize a force to complete a tactical mission. However, we see in the opening verses that Nehemiah was politically and spiritually savvy.

On the spiritual side, he carried a repentant heart (1:4–11). He knew his place before a holy God. He accepted the just effects of his people's spiritual disobedience and possessed the means to repair this broken relationship. It is not surprising then that Nehemiah was prone to pray. It was a knee-jerk reaction before answering a question and before a significant event requiring special insight and protection from evil (4:4–5; 6:9, 14; 13:14, 22).

After he prayed, he acted. His behavior reflected a deep spiritual life. In moving on what he received through prayer, his life became one of substance. This was how he came to the king each day with the complete package. And people like this are easy for others to follow. We sense that when crunch time comes, when the sky is about to fall on everybody's head, this guy won't panic and bail. He'll always have a plan and tell each person what is required so they, together as a team, may carry the day. However, the spiritual person of substance is not self-absorbed; they will never hesitate to give God full credit for the victory (4:14–15).

Politically, Nehemiah knew he earned the king's empathy through faithful service that extended way beyond his job description and pay grade. They had a history, which was astonishing because anyone of the millions Artaxerxes ruled was required, on pain of death, to approach his throne by crawling face-down on their stomach across a very long carpet. They must have had an extraordinary friendship for the king to notice Nehemiah's troubled heart and ask the timeless, wonderful question, "What is it you want?"

Nehemiah answered the king by presenting a specific task within a specific timeframe. He requested a building permit and complete access to the king's forests, the equivalent to a vast lumberyard. Again, preparation and anticipation were hallmarks of Nehemiah's character. I wonder if, in his mind, he had already worked out the entire reconstruction process and could envision Jerusalem's walls and gates in their finished state.

First Things First

I went to Jerusalem, and after staying there three days I set out during the night with a few others. I had not told anyone what my God had put in my heart to do for Jerusalem. There were no mounts with me except the one I was riding on.

By night I went out through the Valley Gate toward the Jackal Well and the Dung Gate, examining the walls of Jerusalem, which had been broken down, and its gates, which had been destroyed by fire. Then I moved on toward the Fountain Gate and the King's Pool, but there was not enough room for my mount to get through; so I went up the valley by night, examining the wall. Finally, I turned back and reentered through the Valley Gate. The officials did not know where I had gone or what I was doing, because as yet I had said nothing to the Jews or the priests or nobles or officials or any others who would be doing the work.

NEH. 2:11–16

I also told them about the gracious hand of my God on me and what the king had said to me.
They replied, "Let us start rebuilding." So they began this good work.

NEH. 2:18

The first activity on Nehemiah's to-do list after arriving in Jerusalem was to take an inspection tour of the wall perimeter. Typically, one who bore the king's mantle would have paraded around Jerusalem with a retinue of sycophants and a musical troupe of cymbal and tambourine bashers. However Nehemiah chose to run a nocturnal special ops mission with only a few trusted men.

Working his way around the walls, Nehemiah could take in the lay of the land (from the strategic height of a donkey's back) and formulate the order of work, a materials list, a means of supply, and distribution of labor. Though we are never told their names, the men accompanying him were very likely knowledgeable builders whom he could depend on to sort out the logistical specifics and discuss alternate ideas. Though Nehemiah's reconnaissance is barely mentioned, it was perhaps the most crucial event that enabled a successful outcome. Preparation in prayer and exhaustive planning are keys not only to completing a difficult task but also to overcoming personal ridicule.

Nehemiah was also aware that danger was afoot, and enemy eyes were watching. Stealth was necessary so his adversaries could not anticipate his next move. Nehemiah surveyed the landscape, formulated a plan, and presented it to Jerusalem's Jewish leadership for approval. Amazingly, everyone climbed on board. The plan must have been prayerfully considered, well thought out, intelligently and rationally supported, optimistically presented, and physically doable. These things breed confidence, and confidence is a ridicule killer. Anyone out there planning a church building project, I advise taking notes.

The Workers

In ancient literature it is very rare, if not completely unknown, to know the names of the common workers credited for building a civic project. We know of only a few great sculptors and architects in the ancient Greek and Roman periods, and we will never know their assistants and apprentices who solved the limitless design issues, made the difficult cuts in timber and stone, and did the heavy, very dangerous lifting. The names of the thousands of skilled craftsmen and laborers who built the great temples and magnificent civic centers of antiquity are forever lost to us. So do not merely skim over Nehemiah 3. It is a wonderful blessing to have the individuals and family names of those who risked their lives to rebuild Jerusalem's walls. Let's go over some of them.

Eliashib the high priest and his fellow priests went to work and rebuilt the Sheep Gate. They dedicated it and set its doors in place, building as far as the Tower of the Hundred, which they dedicated, and as far as the Tower of Hananel.

NEH. 3:1

The repairs next to him were made by the priests from the surrounding region.

NEH. 3:22

The men of Jericho built the adjoining section, and Zaccur son of Imri built next to them.

NEH. 3:2

The next section was repaired by the men of Tekoa, but their nobles would not put their shoulders to the work under their supervisors.

NEH. 3:5

Uzziel son of Harhaiah, one of the goldsmiths, repaired the next section; and Hananiah, one of the perfume-makers, made repairs next to that. They restored Jerusalem as far as the Broad Wall.

NEH. 3:8

Next to him, Malkijah, one of the goldsmiths, made repairs as far as the house of the temple servants and the merchants, opposite the Inspection Gate, and as far as the room above the corner; and between the room above the corner and the Sheep Gate the goldsmiths and merchants made repairs.

NEH. 3:31–32

Rephaiah son of Hur, ruler of a half-district of Jerusalem, repaired the next section.

NEH. 3:9

Adjoining this, Jedaiah son of Harumaph made repairs opposite his house, and Hattush son of Hashabneiah made repairs next to him.

NEH. 3:10

Beyond them, Benjamin and Hasshub made repairs in front of their house; and next to them, Azariah son of Maaseiah, the son of Ananiah, made repairs beside his house.

NEH. 3:23

Above the Horse Gate, the priests made repairs, each in front of his own house.

NEH. 3:28

Shallum son of Hallohesh, ruler of a half-district of Jerusalem, repaired the next section with the help of his daughters....

NEH. 3:12

Nehemiah grouped the workers by their natural distinctions of family, business, and priestly classes. Each group came to the work site already bound by natural ties. Wisely they were given a wall section to build next to each other so one could look over and monitor the other's progress. It encouraged a self-perpetuating competitive work atmosphere.

Speaking of competitive atmospheres, have a look at 3:12! Shallum son of Hallohesh had his daughters up there building the wall with him. I'll bet that got the testosterone flowing among the men! No wonder the wall was finished in 52 days (6:15)!

We must pause to consider Shallum's daughters. I think it is wonderful that we have proof of women up there laying stone with the guys. If I were Shallum, I would be so proud to have my girls up there with me. This was pretty dangerous stuff, loading and mortaring stone at height, not to mention the possibility of attack by Sanballat and Tobiah's men (4:11–23). It is likely they alternated bearing arms while the others worked and were on call to sortie to the weak spots on the wall when the horns blew in case of attack. Here we have Shallum's daughters up there during the worst of it. It is a treasure to have this single verse to contemplate.

The high priest Eliashib and other temple priests are mentioned, as well as the other priests living in the surrounding area (3:22). It is encouraging to see they were not a privileged class above doing physical work, but got stuck in along with the rest of them. The priests' participation in the heavy lifting was a foretaste of the priests rebuilding the temple during King Herod's reconstruction project hundreds of years later.

In Nehemiah the priests are listed first in a long list of participants comprising a variety of occupations, backgrounds, and towns. Men from the cities of Jericho and Tekoa came to work, though the nobles from Tekoa weren't interested in getting their hands dirty. It's amusing that this appropriate criticism of Tekoa's nobles has survived over 2,400 years of history.

I am reminded of when an affluent mother asked me to use her young sons to carry up from the garage a giant stuffed swordfish her husband caught off Barbados. After they helped me set it before the wall on which I was to hang it, one of them exclaimed, "I can't believe we actually had to work during the summer!"

Many others at Jerusalem did not mind working outside their more delicate social class. Goldsmiths, perfume makers, and others from the merchant district participated in rebuilding sections of walls. I can imagine some of these had sore muscles after days of carrying stone.

Another important strategy Nehemiah used was to have a number of Jerusalem residents work on wall sections adjacent to, in front of, and beside their family's homes. Their interest was now personal. It reduced the anonymity of working on a national or civic work project to the more intimate level of the individual. For those working in sight of their homes, each stone they lifted and set in place held serious personal implications, like sandbagging your home as a local rain-swollen river reaches its flood limit. Building the walls and building them well was vital for family survival. It's in our natures to want a strong fortification where we lay our heads at night.

The more I ponder this, the more I think this was a brilliant strategy. For lunchtime, the workers only had to drop down to get a bite to eat, while their wives could keep an eye on their men and made sure they didn't dilly-dally around.

The Enemies

But when Sanballat the Horonite, Tobiah the Ammonite official and Geshem the Arab heard about it, they mocked and ridiculed us. "What is this you are doing?" they asked. "Are you rebelling against the king?" I answered them by saying, "The God of heaven will give us success. We his servants will start rebuilding, but as for you, you have no share in Jerusalem or any claim or historic right to it."

NEH. 2:19–20

When Sanballat heard that we were rebuilding the wall, he became angry and was greatly incensed. He ridiculed the Jews, and in the presence of his associates and the army of Samaria, he said, "What are those feeble Jews doing? Will they restore their wall? Will they offer sacrifices? Will they

*finish in a day? Can they bring the stones back to life from those heaps of
rubble—burned as they are?"*
*Tobiah the Ammonite, who was at his side, said, "What they are
building—even a fox climbing up on it would break down their wall of
stones!"*

Neh. 4:1–3

I've come to realize that whenever someone attempts to do
something constructive in life, there will be opposition. You
would think people would applaud their bravery in stepping out
of their comfort zone to better themselves. Most of us must work
immeasurably hard to achieve a vision that's been in our minds
for years, or something we desperately need to do because our
lives depend on it. We deserve a squad of cheerleaders standing
on the sidelines encouraging us on to victory. But alas, unless
you have friends who happen to be cheerleaders, it's doubtful
you'll see pom-poms when the going gets tough. There will be
plenty of Sanballats and Tobiahs to cast refuse on our efforts.

A nasty part of the human condition reacts in opposition to
someone moving in a positive direction, whether out of jealousy,
an emotional expression of their crummy lives, sense of personal
failure—the sources for resentment are endless. The upwardly
progressing person may be a carpenter who becomes a general
contractor, an addict leaving rehab, an overweight person
reducing calorie intake and upping exercise, an earnest Sunday
school attendee who becomes a Bible teacher, or a pastor who
wants to expand a ministry or campus. Ridicule is reminiscent
of that arcade game Gopher Bop, in which one smacks the little
critter's head with a foam bat when it pops its head above the
ground. You try to rise above your current state, and there
waiting for you is the guy with the big stick to smack you back in
your hole where he thinks you belong.

The building project in the book of Nehemiah gives practical
insights to overcome life's gopher bashers. Chapters 4 and 6 of
Nehemiah describe these threats in detail. For the sake of brevity
I will keep the focus to the verbal ridicule.

Nehemiah's situation was similar to the ones in which we

find ourselves at any time of the day. We are not literally building walls, but we do so in a metaphorical sense when we build to reinforce the structures of our spiritual, personal, family, and professional lives. We may not have bad people with sharp pointy things outside our homes wishing to kill us (well, most of us anyway), but we do have adversaries. Somehow people enter our lives to make our days difficult. And in the spiritual dimension there is that "roaring lion looking for someone to devour" (1 Peter 5:8). The book of Nehemiah is a timeless treatise in overcoming those who desire to kill our spirits.

Coping by Having a Good Laugh

For you created my inmost being;
you knit me together in my mother's womb.
I praise you because I am fearfully and wonderfully made;
your works are wonderful,
I know that full well.

Ps. 139:13–14

Many books are available to help us protect our emotional boundaries, but there is no better affirmation than what the psalmist wrote above concerning our personal value.[67] We must remember we are "fearfully and wonderfully made." What can ridicule do against such knowledge? Our self-worth is bestowed on us from the Creator of the universe. All our strength for self-esteem and practical methods for battling ridicule come from our being crafted by God.

The insights of both secular and Christian authors on self-esteem directly relate to lessons from Nehemiah. Rather than rehashing their many fine points, I will relate what I believe is an important spiritual gift in dealing with ridicule.

The most effective tool I have for battling verbal abuse is a sense of humor. I know this doesn't sound overly spiritual. I pray for those who persecute me. But my immediate response in hearing destructive language is to find the irony in comparing what they say with who they are and how they behave. Take, for instance, a friend I once had who told me I had loyalty issues and was deceitful (I wouldn't do something he wanted me to do). This came from a guy who, some years before, ran off to Paris to have an adulterous three-year affair. When he said this to me, I just bent over in hysterics. It seems our most critical people are merely projecting their sins on us. They want to make us more like the worst of themselves. Then they can condemn us in the way their guilt condemns them. Every act of ridicule is a confession of unhappiness, and unhappy people love company. It's like creating an anti-support group. Meanness is a profession of self-loathing.

Imagining our abusers in this way should prompt empathy from us. We should be motivated to pray and do small physical things to make them feel cared for. And we should let them know from what spiritual source we are doing these things.

"Laughter is the best medicine." This truth has kept me sane over the years. The great benefit of humor is that there is much less energy available for anger and stored bitterness. The times in my life when I lapsed into deep depression were when I lost the ability to find humor in the dark times. I am uncertain whether the self-help books focus on humor for dulling the pain from our abusers, but I have found it to be the best medication for emotional wounding.

Humor, finding the comedic take in the most difficult times, allows me to turn away from being hurt to looking at the funny hair coming out of the mole on my abuser's face or noticing how short they are and the funny quirks they use to appear taller and more dominant (loud voice, intense facial features, arching the back while rearing up on the toes). Their voice becomes loud; their head projects forward and sometimes shakes. (We see these same gestures in critters in the animal kingdom.) Conversely, gangly tall people lean over you like a redwood tree whose root ball has been weakened by erosion from heavy rains. In this posture they typically speak in firm, punctuated language as if to jam the sound waves through the solid bone of your skull. From this vantage point the abuser becomes a comedic prop.

At work, hilarity helps take the edge off the sting of a bosses' anger. Here are some examples.

Years ago a close friend and coworker and I were up on scaffolding to nail siding boards on the downhill side of a garage. Our boss had just vented a tirade of anger and then roared off down the driveway in his truck. Somehow I was inspired to imitate the harsh, shrill scream of Reichsführer of the SS, Heinrich Himmler. (I had been watching World War II Nazi documentaries on TV at the time.) It didn't take long for my friend to join in.

"Panzer Gruppen Carpenters, ju vil nail der entire ziding to dis garrage by za end of zis day or ju two vil spend 30 days untz der cooler! Zat iz unt oder! Unt zen aftervards zu vil proceed unt to da hoff unt begin siding it. All ziss must be completed before der vinter or you vil be ziding der Eastern Front!!!"

Unfortunately, we weren't aware that our boss had forgotten something and returned to the job. He didn't say anything to us, but we had the feeling he had heard our Germanglish ranting. When we heard his truck drive off for the remainder of the day, we bent over in gut wrenching hysterics to the point where I had to descend the scaffolding to get my asthma inhaler.

In the early 1990s I worked with a guy named Jim Donovan who had an amazing ability to deflect a boss's anger. Jim would admit that he looked like a giant blonde walrus. I had a toy stuffed walrus as a child, so I instinctively wanted to hug the guy and rest my head on his shoulders (but I didn't for all the obvious and correct reasons). Jim was endowed with the typical walrus-like big body, eyes, snout, long front incisors, big face cheeks, and bristly mustache. Jim was the complete walrus package.

Unfortunately for Jim, our boss was the kind of guy who wanted to see people flying around the jobsite, banging things, lifting framed walls, sliding rafters in bunches up to the ridge beams—lots of frantic action, no music, no dogs, no talking. But Jim was not naturally attuned to those things. (Nor were the rest of us, for that matter). He was more of a plodding, happy, social creature with another unfortunate habit of alcoholism. During very hot days, he would literally sweat Jim Beam from his pores. But that is another sad story for another day.[68] Jim simply wanted a mellow working home where he could hang out and work with the guys for eight hours. That's all he wanted from a job.

Eventually our angst-ridden boss noticed Jim's placid nature. I was in the jobsite trailer that sat in the court in front of the house. The boss, several other workers, and I were going over the plans. From the trailer we saw Jim walking down a long hallway of windows to complete a carpentry task in one of the bedrooms. This hallway was about forty feet long, and Jim, as I have said, was not a fast mover. The moment the boss's eyes lifted from the plans to the windows, the temperature in the trailer became noticeably warmer as his blood pressure skyrocketed and his face muscles twitched in rage.

The tall bank of windows was spaced evenly in one-foot intervals, and they made it look as though Jim was set in a filmstrip as he happily sloughed along the hallway, chatting with whomever he passed. The funny part was, with the windows spaced one foot apart, we could see his stomach's curvature enter a window frame first, before any other part of his body. Then with his next stride the rest of him showed up, then with the next step his belly disappeared, and then it showed up first again in the next window frame. To see this repeatedly was mesmerizing. Then, just as he was mercifully about to reach his goal and enter the end bedroom, he slowed to a halt, slumped his shoulders in a giant sigh, turned around, and proceeded back the way he had come to get the piece of material he was supposed to do his job with. Poor Jim had forgotten the piece of wood, the very material with which he was to do his job.

For those of us witnessing this off-Broadway play from the job trailer, it couldn't have been scripted any better—or worse, depending on perspective. We all knew Jim's forgetfulness was due to years of heavy drinking, and being a good sort, the crew happily accommodated this. It was our little secret. But now the secret was out.

Later, the boss's confrontation with Jim was not pretty—lots of intense verbiage in increasing decibels. Hearing a coworker being yelled at is not a happy occasion. We felt really bad for Jim, the kind of really bad that makes you happy it was not you who were the object of wrath. And we knew there would be fallout from this: lots of bitterness from Jim, more scrutiny for all of us from the boss. As the boss's truck (angry diesel) roared off in a cloud of dust, it placed a final exclamation point on the event. I believed the truck and our boss mutated into a single demonic being in a Steven King, *Carrie* (1983), kind of way.

What happened next is the reason for this long recital from a jobsite long ago. It was now lunchtime, and we had gathered in a small group, waiting to bring Jim back into the fold and heal his wounds. We could tell he was hurt, maybe carrying a bit of anger from the abuse, yet when he lifted his big walrus head we could see a glimmer in his eyes and knew there was life there. Jim came to a stop in front of us, and before any of us could say a word, Jim said in his best Yosemite Sam impersonation, "Oooh, I hate that wabbit!" He then immediately went to the classic Tweety Bird, "Ooh, he's a mean ole putty cat," I'm telling you, it was pure bedlam. The hilarity was infectious, and many of us reached further for more Looney Tunes cartoon references (Foghorn Leghorn, Daffy Duck) that became a cacophony of hysterics.

I remember it being one of our more enjoyable breaks as we, in humorous metaphor, had our boss for lunch. I must add that our conversation was not malicious; it was necessary emotional therapy. We understood that our boss carried tremendous stress and pushed himself beyond our capabilities to find the next job to keep us working and, equally, fulfill his ambitions. Venting was his way of coping, a pressure release. I think he sometimes regretted it, though for Jim a bit of discipline was necessary. However, we coped that day by forming an empathetic small group.

Conclusion to Working under Ridicule

Humor aside, Nehemiah offers many practical lessons in counteracting malicious criticism. We defeat those who attempt to damage our self-image by possessing an impregnable sense of ourselves as children of God, designed and formed in his image. We will always have the high ground in any confrontation, and from our vantage point we are able to pray for those who persecute us.

Prayer is a hallmark of Nehemiah's character. Reinforced through constant honest prayer, Nehemiah keeps a thoughtful, aware mind. He doesn't react in emotional immaturity to the next assault. Threats are things to be discerned and countered with an immediate controlled response.

I believe Nehemiah's time in prayer gave him the quiet mental space to prepare. Through time meditating in prayer he was able to give King Artaxerxes a detailed plan and timeframe before he even left Persia. Extensive preparation gave Nehemiah flexibility in countering his adversaries' strategies and managing the work and his people.

Nehemiah knew cohesive, productive groups are made from individuals bonded together by common skills, interests, and adversities. The precious metals merchants and perfume makers likely had the same muscle strains in the same places from lifting stones all day, and families came preset with hierarchies and divisions of labor. The groups rebuilding Jerusalem's walls may have been the first documented example of what we know as support groups. They were not only productive but self-medicating as they coped with physically injuries and emotional stress from prolonged effort under constant threat from forces outside the walls. Giving them the responsibility for completing a wall section, often close to their residences, was brilliant planning that drove fast, quality work.

A prayerful, self-confident person encourages others in their work and personal lives. They pray for other's success rather than judging and criticizing. I can't tell you how important this is to our Christian witness. Nehemiah was an encourager and people's advocate before God. He was a passionate leader who likewise instilled passion in his people. Can you see the contrast here with the Babel job in chapter 4?

Humor is my bold addition to this list, but I'm uncertain how biblically appropriate it is. I don't see Nehemiah and some of the workers cracking jokes on the wall, mocking Sanballat and Tobiah—though I think it could have happened. I get the impression everyone involved was in a constant state of exhaustion. However, I imagine some of Nehemiah's correspondence with Sanballat was laced with sarcasm with a few facial expressions I would have loved to see.

There is nothing ground shaking in what I'm saying. We defeat those who attempt to damage us by not reacting in kind. We must transcend the verbal garbage and ascend the heights of our identity as redeemed children of the Most High God. We are crafted in his image, perhaps in more dimensions than we are capable of knowing. Our responses to difficult encounters should mirror our identities.

After taking abuse from supervisors for years, I believe we should respond by confronting a habitual abuser head-on (publically or privately) with firm, calm condemnation to nip it in the bud. If a solution is not possible or productive, we, like Nehemiah, may use our forces (support groups, etc.) to alter our situations. We can try to move to a new department, look for another company, or become self-employed. Certainly we can rid ourselves of friends with degrading habits.

I realize this is extremely difficult, and there are occasions when we cannot escape abusive people. For some reason, we are lashed to them for a period of time. A friend of mine told me that the worse his supervisor's behavior became, the more he worked to love him or her into the kingdom. I think this is righteously cool. Rather than fleeing, he worked to love such people through prayer and daily gifts of kindness.

However, there are some abusers who can't be loved into the kingdom. They must be dealt with in a harsher manner. The last section of this chapter deals with physical threats. Ridicule can be a short step away from physical confrontation. Nehemiah again provides an example for us to follow.

Coping with Physical Threats

But we prayed to our God and posted a guard day and night to meet this threat.

NEH. 4:9

"Don't be afraid of them. Remember the Lord, who is great and awesome, and fight for your families, your sons and your daughters, your wives and your homes."

NEH. 4:14

Nehemiah and his people were threatened daily by those who wished to do them physical harm. We too, when there are no other options, must know how to physically defend ourselves. Nehemiah certainly had no qualms about it. His words, "We prayed to our God and posted a guard" and "Remember the Lord . . . and fight for your brothers, sons, daughters, wives, and homes" are not those of a pacifist.

While attending seminary, I took an ethics class taught by a professor whose personal moral code would not allow him to resort to physical self-defense, even when life was at stake. His interpretation of "Blessed are the peacemakers" (Matt. 5:9) was literal and all-encompassing. Though I know his view is popular, I found it astonishingly naïve and a comfortable identity for a man who lived in academia and an upper class neighborhood. A good friend and fellow classmate from Compton, California, thought he was insane. As a youth pastor working "in the hood," his greatest challenge came, not in handing out condoms to his kids, but keeping them from shooting each other. The following section will expand on this important topic.

Why Build Walls When God Protects Us?

Also our enemies said, "Before they know it or see us, we will be right there among them and will kill them and put an end to the work."

NEH. 4:11

Therefore I stationed some of the people behind the lowest points of the wall at the exposed places, posting them by families, with their swords, spears and bows. After I looked things over, I stood up and said to the nobles, the officials and the rest of the people, "Don't be afraid of them. Remember the Lord, who is great and awesome, and fight for your families, your sons and your daughters, your wives and your homes."
When our enemies heard that we were aware of their plot and that God had frustrated it, we all returned to the wall, each to our own work.
From that day on, half of my men did the work, while the other half were equipped with spears, shields, bows and armor. The officers posted themselves behind all the people of Judah who were building the wall. Those who carried materials did their work with one hand and held a weapon in the other, 18 and each of the builders wore his sword at his side as he worked. But the man who sounded the trumpet stayed with me.

NEH. 4:13–18

This business of defending one's space brings up an important side-topic. We, like Nehemiah, interact with the spiritual world when we pray and trust the Lord for protection. Yet we must *do* things to ensure our safety just as we must *do* things to prove the effectiveness of our prayer and spiritual lives. We don't drive like maniacs, don't roam dangerous neighborhoods at night. We might learn self-defense, carry pepper spray, lock our doors, leave a safety light on, and maybe activate a home alarm system before we hit the sheets. (Make sure the dog or cat doesn't have access to rooms that have motion sensors—just saying.)

Years ago, a close friend of mine in the trades (I'll call him Al) read a book about Richard Ramirez, "The Night Stalker." That led him to read several other biographies about serial killers and rapists (see Ted Bundy, yikes). His immediate response to his nightmares and leaping out of bed when raccoons traversed his roof was to arm the bed he shared with his wife with enough firearms and sharp-edged weaponry to hold off Seal Team VI. The semi-auto 12-gauge shot gun I noticed leaning by the nightstand was not a shock, but I had never seen a holstered 44 mag. pistol strapped to the side of a mattress before. He told me it took every tool he owned to fabricate intricate systems of removable sharp-pointy things and barriers to seal off his interior and exterior doors each night.

A brief comment about his wife; she was absolutely understanding throughout this entire ordeal. She gently worked through his neurosis and subtly, gently (little by little) chucked most of his work in the bin.

I was mesmerized by the devastating, simplistic beauty of his defenses. I told him he had created the most ingenious and dangerous thing I had ever seen. It reminded me of the progressive entrapment and enfilade defensive systems I wrote of earlier at the ancient cities of Jericho and Lachish. If some idiot was stupid enough to attack them at night, the flying lead would turn his house into Swiss cheese; that is, if he got through the reinforced doors, electrified copper wire strung along his deck, and carefully placed trip wires. A short time of uneventful safe living (see his wife) has caused much of his work to be cut up and used for other purposes (swords into ploughshares kind of thing), but every night his doors are locked tight and the shot gun remains by the nightstand.

I tell this story because Al is a rational Christian who maybe went a bit over-the-top for a while. (I suggest not reading many terrifying true biographies of mass murderers.) But he illustrates the point that we still live in dangerous times. Killers roam the streets, and we have to be wary as foxes.

Unless the LORD builds the house,
the builders labor in vain.
Unless the LORD watches over the city,
the guards stand watch in vain.

                                                            Ps. 127:1

The Lord does indeed protect us. We should not be paranoid, but we live in a fallen world, so we have to keep our minds about us, just as Nehemiah kept his. The spears, bows, and swords the Jews carried on the walls were not a fashion statement. They were ready to kill if necessary. As it turned out, this show of force was enough to intimidate the aggressors, just as we know today the best way to deal with a bully is to confront him at first with overwhelming nonviolent force (a crowd of serious family members within his personal space should do it). However you choose to do that is up to you.

Christian pastor, political columnist, and author Doug Giles is a strong advocate for teaching women, from early age to adulthood, martial arts and marksmanship.[69] With his young daughters in mind, he is tired of seeing bodies of raped and murdered young girls and women splashed across our news media. He believes that it's time for women of all ages to stand up and care for themselves, since their protection has been largely abdicated by men. The philosophy he's teaching his daughters and promoting in his books is, "if you're between a rock and a hard place, be the rock (or know how to rock in a hard place)." "When the septic matter hits the fan, be the fan." His advice is brutal, but when we see images of torn, ruined little girls lying dead in a field or floating in a river and the law is too convoluted to administer justice, are we left to only shake our heads in impotence?

The fact that we have to build walls is the reality check of the dichotomy between our spiritual and worldly realities. I know this is not a popular stance, but we must learn how to bear and wield arms when our lives demand it. We are not helpless lambs. Like Nehemiah, we should be simultaneously heavenly minded and earthly savvy.

Devotional Questions

1. What was Nehemiah's occupation under King Artexerxes? What job responsibilities did it involve?

2. What important role did those job responsibilities play in rebuilding Jerusalem's walls?

3. Looking at Nehemiah's relationship with King Artexerxes from an employer/employee perspective, how would you describe their relationship?

4. What spiritual qualities did Nehemiah have? How was his spiritual life an asset? What role did it play in accomplishing his task?

5. What strategy did Nehemiah use to organize and conduct the reconstruction of Jerusalem's walls?

6. Who were Nehemiah's enemies? What strategies did they attempt to stop construction?

7. In what ways did Nehemiah defeat his enemies' strategies?

8. Thinking about your experiences at work and at church, have you experienced people who ridiculed your participation on projects? These destructive people seem to rise out of the ground. Why do you think they work to tear down rather than build up others?

9. What strategies did Nehemiah use to defeat the negative, condescending threats of his enemies? (For example, humor.) How can we use them in our daily lives?

10. What is your position on self-defense? Do you "turn the cheek" with the first blow, then come out swinging on the second? What should be our strategy against physically intimidating people? When should we ever go on the attack? What did Nehemiah demonstrate?

CHAPTER 11

A CARPENTER'S VIEW OF JESUS

Jesus has been found worthy of greater honor than Moses, just as the builder of a house has greater honor than the house itself. For every house is built by someone, but God is the builder of everything.

HEB. 3:3–4

A NUMBER OF TIMES while driving I have come upon vehicles, generally pickup trucks, with bumper stickers that say, "My Boss is a Jewish Carpenter." Intrigued, I searched online and found sites that sell stickers with similar messages: "The Love of my Life is a Jewish Carpenter," "My Father is a Jewish Carpenter," or "I Work for a Jewish Carpenter." These bumper stickers come in a variety of fonts with Christ symbols that clue in even the most biblically illiterate as to the carpenter's identity.

I've never been a fan of Christian bumper stickers. I know many ardent evangelicals spend a lot of time praying over these things before peeling off the back and rubbing them onto their chrome parts and back windows. I cannot justify this. I have a conviction that to relegate the deep things of God to short, cheesy ditties on our car bumpers is an abomination. Would Jesus have engraved a plaque and hung it on the back bumper of his work cart with the words, "I and the Father are One" or "I am a Jewish Carpenter" or "I Don't Build on Sand; Call the Rock, Jesus of Nazareth"?

Perhaps a better witness would be for Christian drivers with *ichthus* fish stickers to not drive like bats out of hell and to try to not run over church parking attendants on Sunday mornings. Let's start with that and work our way up.

I found another bumper sticker to contrast with the Jesus-carpenter ones. When driving on the South San Francisco peninsula roads, I occasionally see a bumper sticker that proclaims, "I Am a Rocket Scientist." There must be a good number of rocket scientists living here. I happened to meet one the other day while hiking in the Rancho San Antonio Open Space Reserve. His name was Fred, and he was one of those responsible for creating the software used for rocket guidance systems—something having to do with telemetry. Fred thinks the "I am a Rocket Scientist" stickers are very funny, but he does not have one on his car. Fred said he knows who he is and does not feel the need to inform the world of what he did for a time in his life. I think it is important for many of us to proclaim things: who we are, what we do, what we believe or don't believe. Jesus proclaimed himself the Good Shepherd, one with God the Father, the Way, the Truth, and the Life. The rocket scientist bumper sticker is pretty straightforward; the "My Father is a Jewish Carpenter" sticker is cryptic. It raises a few questions.

We must ask ourselves: "Are the Jesus-carpenter bumper stickers theologically correct?" Is it biblically accurate to say Jesus was a carpenter?

Jesus as Carpenter

Our knowledge of Jesus of Nazareth as a carpenter comes from the following two gospel passages:

> *Coming to his hometown, he began teaching the people in their synagogue, and they were amazed. "Where did this man get this wisdom and these miraculous powers?" they asked. "Isn't this the carpenter's son? Isn't his mother's name Mary, and aren't his brothers James, Joseph, Simon and Judas? Aren't all his sisters with us? Where then did this man get all these things?" And they took offense at him.*
> *But Jesus said to them, "A prophet is not without honor except in his own town and in his own home."*
>
> MATT. 13:54–57

When the Sabbath came, he began to teach in the synagogue, and many who heard him were amazed.

"Where did this man get these things?" they asked. "What's this wisdom that has been given him? What are these remarkable miracles he is performing? Isn't this the carpenter? Isn't this Mary's son and the brother of James, Joseph, Judas and Simon? Aren't his sisters here with us?" And they took offense at him.

MARK 6:2–3

That's it. There's nothing more—enjoy. Authors writing centuries after Jesus' death wrote fanciful stories about his woodcraft that never made it into the canon of Scripture, so I will not delve into them here. Theologians and Bible expositors have come at the above passages from different contexts, as they do with the entire body of Scripture. There is a general consensus that Matthew and Mark are describing the same event with different perspectives, the common situation police find when taking witness statements after a car accident.

By the way, what would happen if a "My Boss is a Jewish Carpenter" driver ran into an "I am a Rocket Scientist" one? Would we finally have an answer to the intelligent design issue? And would their insurance companies ever be able to settle? Sorry.

There is no doubt about the amazement the Jews felt when they heard Jesus' teaching that day in the synagogue. It must have been like listening to an eight-year-old playing a difficult violin or piano concerto. Those listening to Jesus in the synagogue were genuinely amazed at how a guy they knew as a tradesman could teach from the Torah like a veritable prophet. It was like witnessing a living *non sequitur*: a genius, a master out of context with what they knew him to be. I suppose this was a little scary for them. And some byproducts of fear are not pretty: anger, jealousy, and derision—the type of things we face from others whenever we excel at something and receive acclaim.

Jesus thought the comparisons, especially involving family, were the stuff of public discourse: "How can you be like this if you come from them?" The "Isn't this the carpenter" line could be changed to whatever object fits the circumstance. And don't forget the ridicule. In addition to amazement, the listeners were displeased. They took offense. But Jesus, never the one to back down, reminded them of their historical tendency to reject their prophets, particularly those who were considered to be relationally closest to them.

A few peculiarities remain unknown. Matthew speaks of Jesus as "the carpenter's son," while in Mark the crowd says he is "the carpenter." In a trade family it would be assumed that the son would follow the father in the craft, so Matthew's rendition makes sense. Mark links "carpenter" with Mary's son, which makes us ask, "Where is Joseph?" Some have interpreted this mix of identity questions tempered with a nasty attitude as an attempt to demean Jesus' character, which in this case was to allude to Jesus as a fatherless son (bastard). Now, if this was truly their intent, I *do not* want to be standing in line with the guys who uttered that line when we hand in our numbered tickets to the archangel at go time in front of the Seat of Judgment. However we interpret this, Jesus' response was a harsh rebuke.

We now focus on the term "carpenter."[70] The Greek word *tekton* defined one who worked with almost any hard material: stone, wood, or metal. Thus we have the profile of a well-rounded builder who could build just about anything. It is interesting that the ancient Church Fathers in the Greek-speaking Eastern Roman Empire thought of Jesus as a woodworker, and the Church Fathers in the Latin West thought of him as an ironworker. I cannot find out why, but with the broad definition of this word, either or both could be true. *Tekton* is translated for us as "carpenter" to give us the sense of a local, residential craftsman.

I am sure of one thing: Jesus of Nazareth was a builder whose job required the skills of many disciplines of building and artisan handwork. Yet perhaps as the word *tekton* hints, his specialty was in woodworking, more specifically milling rough timber with hand saws, adzes, and planes to be used for housing, agriculture, and furniture. As is primarily the case with wood joinery, the board attachments would entail bonding joints with glue (they did have glue then), often without nails, though with heavier materials iron nails had been used by carpenters for many centuries. He could well have used cool, pliable tar as mastic for bonding and waterproofing.

A carpenter has to work somewhere. For Jesus it was obviously in Nazareth and possibly in a wealthy city called Sepphoris, which lay only four miles from his home. We will look at these two places, Nazareth and Sepphoris, as likely work environments for our Savior. Though our evidence for Jesus' workaday life is tenuous at best, we are faced with two very different towns in which he may have worked.

Nazareth

Up until the 1980s, Jesus' pre-ministry work was thought to have been carried out in the tiny backwater town of Nazareth without much contact with the sophisticated Greco-Roman world. The archaeological remains of buildings in Jesus' Nazareth are difficult to unravel, and theories for their type and dating are highly debated. During the early to mid-twentieth century, initial probes leading to exhaustive, systematic excavations were carried out. Archaeologists uncovered only flooring pavements, foundation outlines, water cisterns, and burial caves. From this we may infer a system of buildings typical of a relatively primitive agricultural community, yet the dating of this evidence cannot be narrowed to an exact time period.

Nazareth's long heritage of Christian pilgrimage began in the fourth century. It is from this that we securely fix the town's locale on the Galilean landscape. Unfortunately, much of the first-century residential fabric of the town was obliterated. Its materials were used to build Christian churches, pilgrimage sites, and support buildings for the influx of the early Christian tourist trade beginning after Constantine the Great in the early fourth century. I cannot help but see this as ironic. Presently, Nazareth is home to twenty-three churches and monasteries.

Jesus' very residence may have been dismantled and its pieces inserted into the walls of a church built to venerate him or his mother. This is simultaneously ironic and full of spiritual insight. Jesus never thought of himself as a residential homeowner: "Foxes have holes and birds of the air have nests, but the Son of Man has no place to lay his head" (Matt. 8:20).

So perhaps it is best we do not have a house with Jesus' name scratched on the door lintel. He came to pave the way for the church through his resurrection, not to leave bits of his material presence for us to go crazy over. In chapter 14 we will see the apostles Peter and Paul use architectural imagery to integrate Jesus, his church, and the prophets into a theological temple.

On December 21, 2009 I read a press release from the Israel Antiquities Authority reporting a discovery of a first-century Jewish house under a convent courtyard in Nazareth, adjacent to the Church of the Ascension.[71] This was very exciting news. Broken pottery fragments of clay and chalk vessels found amidst the foundation walls provided the general dating and Jewish identity for the building. The excavation director was quoted saying that Jesus and his childhood friends likely knew of this house and that the excavators found a small hole that was used to hide valuables during the fall of Jerusalem in AD 70. Sell it, baby! A few pottery fragments, a tiny area of foundation remains, and we have Jesus and his pals kicking a soccer ball off its walls. Get ready for the critical fallout within the archaeological community, a new flood of Christian tourists, and CAD experts designing the digital house of Jesus. Sorry about the cynicism—archaeology has always been an uneasy tightrope walk between the empirical approach and an embellished sales promotion to attract funds for further excavation.

Evidence from pocket excavations (like this one) asserts that Nazareth's population likely reached four hundred and was not developed in the Roman civic pattern with a street grid and paved streets or public structures with columns, mosaic floors, and marble décor. Nazareth appears not to have had wealthy patrons injecting money into a miniature Roman prototypical city as was done at Caesarea, Tiberius, Scythopolis (Bet Shean), and other cities of the Decapolis region in present-day Israel and Jordan.

Residences were simple structures of unfinished stone and mud brick walls. The town was devoted to agricultural production. This has led many to assume that Jesus' work involved very simplistic construction and repair of farming implements.

Sepphoris

With the recent excavation of Nazareth's neighbor, the ancient city of Sepphoris, new perceptions of a working-class Jesus are being drawn. Sepphoris lay approximately four miles from Nazareth. It had been a significant city during the Hasmonean period (140 to 63 BC). Later, before the great city of Tiberius was built, Sepphoris was Herod Antipas's first capital in Galilee. He rebuilt it after the Romans destroyed it.

The mistake that led Rome to annihilate the community in 4 BC was made by Judas the Galilean (not to be confused with Judas Iscariot), the son of the outlaw Hezekiah, whom Antipas had put to death years earlier (talk about pruning a family tree!). Judas led the residents of Sepphoris in rebellion after Antipas's father, Herod the Great, died. Judas apparently became very upset with his Roman tax bill, gathered likeminded folks, and whipped them up in to a revolt. (Remember, as we discussed in chapter 9, refusal to pay taxes prompted the Assyrians to invade Israel.) Very soon they realized they should have written their checks to the Roman Palestine Tax Board. The city of Sepphoris died along with Judas the Galilean. That was the way Rome handled business: rebellion = destruction. If you are going to revolt against Rome, you really have to have a good bailout plan. If not, don't do it.

With the excavation of Sepphoris, new hypotheses are being made about Jesus' early years. Excavation has determined that after Antipas rebuilt Sepphoris, it became a wealthy community with a strong Jewish population of between eight and twelve thousand inhabitants. What is coming out of the ground is a small city in the Greco-Roman prototype with paved streets laid out in an orthographic pattern (a grid pattern of squares and rectangles) consisting of a main street (*cardo maximus*) and cross streets (*decumanai*). Large cut limestone pavers were set in a herringbone pattern to create a central avenue approximately forty feet wide. The immense street had sidewalks lined with shops and was covered by a roof system supported by continuous rows of pillars. Uncovered in the lower market area was a great first-century basilica, probably used for administration and commerce. The basilica was designed with the typical central nave and two aisles separated by columns. Its roof covered over fifteen thousand square feet (not including its covered porches).

The city had a theater (late first century) that was carved into a hillside, a synagogue with beautiful mosaic flooring, and a neighborhood of houses described as upper-class mansions with internal (ritual) baths common in wealthy Jewish homes. In order to operate a city of this size, Sepphoris must have possessed a centralized governing infrastructure that produced and, more importantly, maintained these places.

Despite its impressive features, Sepphoris does not show signs of Roman extravagance. The city has a conservative nature expressed in the commonness of the archaeological remains of household and personal items. The city itself was not covered in marble, and the theater (which could seat four thousand or nearly half the city's population) was built with frugality in mind compared to theaters throughout the East.

This then was a city that, in its architecture and population, had invested itself in the Greco-Roman image (at the direction of Herod Antipas) but had not sold out to its indulgences. It did not fully devote itself to the Roman prototype like other cities that wished to impress Roman governmental aristocracy in order to attract funds for further growth. There are no remains of pagan statues; shrines or temples; images of pagan deities on coins; or their names mentioned on stone, pottery, and mosaic inscriptions. Importantly, there are no inscriptions honoring deified Roman emperors. This is unusual in comparison to all other Greco-Roman city remains of this size covering this broad reach of time.

Perhaps the community's lower level of wealth could not

push it into the Roman luxury-edition lifestyle. However, it is more likely that being a primarily Jewish community, political and religious convictions compel it to remain separate and not convert to a Roman identity. It is telling that there is no sign of a monumental public bath in Sepphoris. A bath complex was one of the defining elements of Roman culture, and it is likely Jewish laws against baring the flesh in public negated its construction. Rather than a violent revolt, a subtle architectural statement against Rome was perhaps a wiser course. Apparently, the Jewish population met Rome halfway.

The dating of the theater and a number of other monuments runs past the time of Jesus. The time frame of the excavated synagogue is roughly between AD 400 and 650. Remnants of structures under the synagogue floor are dated, by pottery and coin deposits, to no earlier than the second century, about one hundred years after Christ. So, somewhat regretfully (for those scholars who are desperately searching for a dissertation topic), we cannot place Jesus carving seats in the theater or accompanying his family there on a Saturday night (after Sabbath) for a little light entertainment. We also should not pose an imaginary theatrical confrontation between Christ and the pagan gods, hurling thunderbolts at each other and enacting life-and-death narratives, as if in Greek tragedies.

Sepphoris is not mentioned in the Bible. Though Jesus lived four miles from this place, there is no evidence to indicate that he ever went there. Yet a city of this size, with its initial civic form and the first of its monumental construction happening during the years of Jesus' working career, cannot be ignored. In the unlikely event that Jesus did not enter its gates, he must have at least met builders working there or seen the carts loaded with materials moving along roads to its construction sites.

Theologians have speculated why Sepphoris is absent from the Jesus narrative. Some theories relate it to Jesus' teachings on the morality of wealth and economic justice between the poor (Nazareth) and the rich (Sepphoris). The two cities become metaphors for one of the key social issues Jesus often confronted. Jesus could not, simultaneously, be seen to have professional associations with the wealthy and be a spokesperson for the poor. Thus, Jesus would have avoided Sepphoris. Jesus could not be labeled "cosmopolitan."

Another reasonable theory is that Jesus avoided Sepphoris because of his uneasy history with the family of Herod. Antipas is heavily associated with the city, and Jesus' family (after arriving in Nazareth from Egypt) was likely wary of his movements. During Jesus' later ministry years, John the Baptist was imprisoned and beheaded, and Luke 13:31–33 tells us that Jesus evaded "that fox" Herod, who was intent on killing him. We also do not see Jesus entering Tiberius, which was another seat of Herodian power. Instead we see Jesus, in the gospel of Mark, centering his ministry in the fishing (working-class) community of Capernaum (Mark 2:1; 9:33). Matthew records it as Jesus' "own city" (Matt. 9:1).

However, going back to Jesus' construction years, I feel compelled to say that Jesus and his father Joseph could very well have worked in Sepphoris at the outset of Herod's building program. Nazareth was seemingly a stagnant place for a builder to operate. Theological theories aside, simple logic presents the overwhelming opportunities at Sepphoris as too good to pass up.

I know we would like to impose our impressions of Jesus and say that if Sepphoris is not in the Bible, Jesus did not go there. But, the Scriptures are not the first-century version of the Biography Channel—a program that shows, in chronological order, every event in Jesus' life (with commentary). We can make tentative conclusions outside the canon of Scripture and call them tentative.

Others might desire to impose on Jesus a life of poverty by restricting him to the confines of Nazareth. Forbid that Jesus made a decent living. Here we see the ugly face of working-class bias and the twisted view that a pious Jesus should epitomize a life of penury.

Perhaps, if Paul were there, he would comment, "Anyone who does not provide for their relatives, and especially for their own household, has denied the faith and is worse than an unbeliever" (1 Tim. 5:8).

So, from a builder's standpoint, I see a young Jesus and his foster father Joseph load their cart with tools, hitch their donkey, drop down the two-hundred-meter gradual descent from the Nazareth ridge, head north-northwest across the Nahal Zippori valley, and climb the Sepphoris acropolis to work their day.

Jesus Dies by What Defines His Craft

I have thought many times over the years of the irony of Christ dying by the materials and tools of a carpenter. There is nothing of this in Scripture other than the verse below, so I will be brief.

> *"Unless I see the nail marks in his hands and put my finger where the nails were, and put my hand into his side, I will not believe."*
>
> John 20:25

From these words of the apostle Thomas, we know that Christ was attached to a cross structure by hammer and nails. More accurately, it was likely a heavy iron-headed mallet and spikes long enough to penetrate two crossed feet. The wood cross material was hewn from timber with saws and adzes, and maybe cleaned up somewhat with hand planes. Crucifixions outside Jerusalem were common, and permanent scaffolding probably existed to facilitate the process, for the wood supply was depleted and the Romans were efficient. Death by wood and iron—again I go back to the ancient Eastern and Western churches' belief that Jesus was a woodworker and ironworker, respectively.

Jesus the Redemptor

Just as the resurrection came after the crucifixion, Jesus' carpenter terminology should follow with a similar progression in meaning. The Latin term for an independent building contractor was—wait for it—a *redemptor*. I am not making this up. I have searched for the genesis of the word, but it seems that contractors were always called that (along with *conductor*). A *redemptor* was someone who built and repaired public works and private houses—really anything involving construction (buildings in a poor state that needed to be redeemed for common use). Normally, he would have a crew of men working under him. He signed legal agreements with his clients, typical of the contractor profession today.

The redemption process in construction agrees with what Isaiah says: "The bricks have fallen down, but we will rebuild with dressed stone" (Isa. 9:10).

Redemption is the process of reparation—a restoration of something from its base or ruined form. It is a state of brokenness in need of repair. Isaiah gives the sense that the repair is not with like materials, making it again as it once was. True redemption and restoration occurs when what is broken is improved upon with new materials of a higher grade.

There is also redemption in the use of our natural resources. I am not ignoring the issue of ecology; if any society should have a mandate in caring for nature, it should be the church. Yet there is a redeeming factor in raw materials when trees, stones, sand, and bitumen are converted into elements for human habitation.

In chapter I we saw how we take what is exhibited in the natural world and apply its materials and design prototypes to enhance human life. Resources lying dormant find value and purpose in new applications. The elements are changed when we cut off the weak and diseased, and intense heat bleeds away impurities. This is equally true for our spiritual natures and our corresponding behavior. As Paul says,

If anyone builds on this foundation using gold, silver, costly stones, wood, hay or straw, their work will be shown for what it is, because the Day will bring it to light. It will be revealed with fire, and the fire will test the quality of each person's work. If what has been built survives, the builder will receive a reward.

1 COR. 3:12–14

I picture Paul coming up with this example as he stitched

the fabric of a tent. The qualities of architectural structures, including those made of fabric, are under continuous testing by their resistance to wind and air pressure, stability during ground movement, temperature variation, and shear and load stresses. This testing begins as soon as the structure takes shape and becomes elevated. In the same way, as soon as we become redeemed by the blood of the Lamb and stand as his child, we face resistance from a number of directions. Whether that resistance is the desires of the flesh or conformity to the world, we are constantly tempted to incorporate destructive behaviors into our bodily temples. Sometimes we have to put ourselves to the test, to undergo a little fire to see what remains, which habits are worth chucking and which are worth keeping.

Paul goes on to write,

Do you not know that your bodies are temples of the Holy Spirit, who is in you, whom you have received from God?

1 COR. 6:19

We see that the principle of redemption is not only an event of salvation but an ongoing lifestyle program. Paul extends the construction metaphor to the architecture of a temple to express how we are to consider the formation of our Christian communities as well as our physical bodies. Christ redeems us, and we are to maintain the quality of our lives knowing that one day all the extraneous, unnecessary stuff that we have added to ourselves will be burned away. The burning will leave us standing naked in the truth of who we are and what we've done.

I would like to securely connect the profession of *redemptor* to the person of Jesus of Nazareth, but it is only speculation. Yet Jesus would likely have operated as an independent builder in a family business in the Roman world. Like the IRS in the United States, the Roman tax collectors were extremely interested in how a family claimed itself as a taxable identity (note the previous life of the apostle Matthew). It follows that Jesus would not have avoided paying tax on his services, and he would have likely done so as a professional tradesman. It is not known whether he employed anyone; yet, it is possible, maybe probable, that he entered into contractual agreements with someone in Sepphoris to perform certain work. This was required under Roman law just as it is today with the general contractor law here in the state of California. Thus, Jesus likely worked as a *redemptor* in the professional world, just as he was to become the Redeemer for our sins.

Devotional Questions

1. In Mark 6:2–3 the people of Nazareth are astonished at Jesus' healings and his teachings in the synagogue. They understand him to be a tradesman, not a holy man. Why does this confrontation happen now and not earlier in Jesus' life? What does this say about Jesus' early working years?

2. Have you ever heard of Jesus as the carpenter? Why is this profession an important aspect of his life? How does it help us identify with God in knowing that he actually worked for a living?

3. What does it say about Christ that for a time in his earthly life, he chose to work with hand tools? What aspect of God do we see in the fact that, for the few years he had before the advent of his ministry, he chose to be a builder?

4. When someone is learning an art form, trade profession, or craft hobby, how important is the roll of the instructor? Who was Jesus' carpentry teacher? What practical things should fathers be teaching their sons today?

5. We can visualize Jesus and his father Joseph working together on projects. What priority should parents today place on taking time to work on projects with their children?

6. The Roman term for a building contractor was *Redemptor.* How does this fit with Jesus' earthly work?

7. The means for Jesus' crucifixion were the elements of his early profession: wood, nails, and a hammer. What, if any, symbolism can we see here? Perhaps the passing of the old into new life?

CHAPTER 12

HEROD'S TEMPLE
A Description of Transcendent Architecture

THE LAND OF ISRAEL *is situated in the center of the world,
and Jerusalem in the center of the Land of Israel, and the Holy Temple in
the center of Jerusalem.*

Midrash Tanhuma, KEDOSHIM 10

*There is a river whose streams make glad the city of God,
the holy place where the Most High dwells.*

Ps. 46:4

*The man brought me back to the entrance to the temple, and I saw water
coming out from under the threshold of the temple toward the east (for
the temple faced east). The water was coming down from under the south
side of the temple, south of the altar.*

EZEK. 47:1

WE HAVE COME to the temple at the time of Christ, and here
we reach the summit of earthly biblical architecture. Only John's
description of the heavenly City of God can eclipse its brilliance.
The Bible refers to the temple in dynamic imagery. Though a
real place and fixed in real time, it is transcendent.

The temple seems otherworldly in end-of-time
(eschatological) passages. Rivers of water gush forth from its
foundations to nourish the earth. This is incredibly surreal, like
a Maxfield Parrish painting (1870–1966) with its iridescent skies,
landscapes, and neoclassical motifs. We might think of the temple
in only functional terms, but it appears in the Bible's prophetic

books as the stuff of Tolkien. It is very real and strangely the stuff of legend.

In medieval rabbinical commentaries on the Bible, the temple exists during the Creation of the earth and the flood of Noah. One narrative has the rock that protruded up through the floor of the Holy of Holies (now in the Dome of the Rock) as the touchstone where the world was created and as the entry into the abyss, the chaos of the deep first mentioned in Genesis 1 and discussed earlier in this book.[72] Another passage portrays King David digging the Temple's foundations and discovering a slab of stone whose purpose was to restrain, like a chock-stone, the turbulent primordial waters from flooding the earth a second time.[73] Yes, these temple stories are a bit fantastic but have continued through the centuries to enhance the hidden mythic power behind the place.

Most Jews continue to accept the Temple Mount as the spiritual center of the world (literally, the earth's naval[74]). Like the effect a drop of water has when landing in a still pond, concentric rings of lessening sacrality spread out across Israel from this spiritual axis-point. The majority of synagogues built after the temple's destruction in 70 AD were oriented toward Jerusalem. The most sacred space of the synagogue, the specially made niches (at the opposite end from their main entrances) where the Torah and sacred writings were kept, faced the Temple Mount. Synagogues pointed like compass needles toward a spiritual magnetic-north just as the apse, the most sacred space of ancient churches, faced not Jerusalem but eastward, symbolizing the resurrection and the direction of Christ's return.

God intended to make the temple his permanent earthly residence and have his people come with obedient hearts to worship him there. Through this symbiotic relationship between God and his people, rushing, tumbling streams of blessing would pump out from beneath the temple not only to enliven Israel but also to cascade over the landscape and nourish the world.

Unfortunately, for many reasons, this sacred relationship was not always present throughout the Old Testament period. And you get a strong sense from reading the gospels that temple life was not as it should have been during Jesus' lifetime. As a whole, the waters of blessing seem at best frustrated imagery.

Though the temple was functioning as intended, Jesus seemed to be in constant conflict with the administrative practices and the legalistic lifestyle with those in religious leadership. Scripture paints the Pharisees, chief priests, and temple leaders as pretty vicious folks.

AND NOW AN IMPORTANT STATEMENT: The following is not a bashing of Judaism and a moral judgment on every Pharisee, scribe, and temple priest who ever lived. My comments are directed only at those Jesus confronted, those who plotted to kill him, and more importantly, the religious system and mindset that produced these people. Lest we point fingers, Christianity has produced and continues to produce similar mean folk, and confronting the reasons for this is critical for the future of the Christian church.

I return to ask, "How did the Jewish religious leadership come to hate Jesus to the extent of premeditated murder? What influenced these leaders to become other than what God intended?"

The aim of the next two chapters is to approach these questions from this book's perspective: how the temple's architectural character casts light on the errant mentality behind those who built and controlled its spaces, the first-century religious authorities operating on the Temple Mount. Perhaps we may see how very religious people can hate enough to kill someone.

This chapter will give a brief overview of the temple's architecture, and the following chapter will discuss its meanings from several aspects. I wish to probe deeper into how the temple's architecture relates to the concept of "remembrance," Jesus of Nazareth's experiences there, and its behavioral effects on those who created and administered its spaces.

The discussion will ultimately speak to the paradox of a Christian person who attempts to live in the dual worlds of sin and sanctity. I am referring to the disparity between religiosity and behavior, the dilemma of doing religion vs. living one's faith in God. Much like the Pharisees of old, this particular Christian also lives by a code of legalistic or deed-oriented spirituality. This person takes pride in knowing some mostly irrelevant theological, historical minutia. In this, he considers himself a self-important, religious authority. Yet this contrived holiness is an illusion. It masks deep personal and emotional flaws. This person has great spiritual knowledge but is blind to the principles of application spelled out in Jesus' Sermon on the Mount, and in the New Testament letters of the apostles Peter and Paul. Simply, he lacks love.

In construction terms, this type of blindness reminds me of a story, related to me by an old carpenter from Missouri, about his farmer-friend who set about to reroof his two-story farmhouse. The farmer saw the roof pitch was steep, and he needed to belay himself with a rope to keep him from falling to the ground in case he slipped.

Okay, prepare yourself. His first move was to tie the rope to the rear bumper of his family station wagon parked in his front driveway. With the rope tied off to his car, he threw the remaining coil over the ridge of the roof to the opposite side. The farmer climbed a ladder to the roof and tied the rope around his waist. Up high, deep in his own world, he began nailing shingles. Then his wife had to rush to the market to buy a missing ingredient for dinner. She didn't notice the rope attached to the car, and her husband had forgotten to mention his cunning plan to her.

Let me reset the stage. We have the farmer's wife driving off in a car that her husband decided to umbilical cord himself to while working on the far side of his roof. We are talking about a man about to be jettisoned off his roof's ridge, say thirty feet in the air, at 25 miles an hour. We're talking about an Olympic ski jumper on the ninety-meter hill on his *gluteus maximus* (see buttocks) without skis. (On an unrelated note, I remember a friend of mine stapling his wallet to his buttocks while shooting wood shingles on a roofing job. He had the unfortunate habit of resting his gun on his hip until . . .)

The farmer never said whether he heard the car start up

and frantically tried to cut the rope with his "futility" knife or yelled for his wife to wait. What we do know is that one spouse had two broken legs and many assorted injuries—and substantial bitterness. The other wished she had dragged him a little further along the gravel driveway to ingrain a common-sense lesson within the noncompliant brain of her difficult man. To this day, each blames the other for the incident.

The connection point here is how the Jewish leadership in Jesus' time possessed a mental disconnection from the obvious lessons, instructions, and commands spelled out in their Scriptures. Rather, they attached their lives to a rigorous religious lifestyle that sat like an oppressive one-ton station wagon upon Jewish society. The Jewish ruling elite lost the lessons of humility, empathy in leadership, and compassion for the Lord that were once hallmarks of their religious predecessors. Their adverse reaction to Jesus of Nazareth bears this out. To complete the metaphor, the temple destruction by the Romans in 70 AD jettisoned the Jews off the heights of the Temple Mount into a world dispersion, the effects of which lasted for nearly 1900 years. You can't blame the wife for not noticing the insanity of a rope tied to her car's bumper or the Romans for ruthlessly quelling a revolt. Both were simply going about their business.

Now I will describe the Temple Mount and the temple after its reconstruction by King Herod the Great, when Jesus of Nazareth and his disciples walked through its courts.

Herod's Temple Background

The images I'm using of Herod's Temple Mount come from Leen Ritmeyer Archaeological Design.[75] They are undoubtedly the finest accessible images of biblical Jerusalem and the Temple Mount. They are essential when trying to make sense of the temple site.

For our purposes I must limit myself to a general survey of King Herod's reconstruction of the Temple Mount. Our knowledge of it is imprecise. The Jewish historian Josephus, who saw the temple with his own eyes, is our primary and most quoted source. Archaeological findings confirm much of his writing but raise many questions. It is well beyond the scope of this chapter to delve into the myriad of debates the Temple Mount has raised over the years. The futility of it would be like condensing all the views of the Apocalypse, and for that reason alone I hope it either comes soon or not at all.

The archaeological pedigree of this area is fragmented. The site was not investigated until six hundred years after the Crusaders abandoned Jerusalem in the twelfth century. Fredrick Catherwood (1833), disguising himself in Muslim garb of that day, was the first western European to investigate the mount since the Crusader period. Edward Robinson (1836), Dr. James Barclay (early 1850s), Marquis Charles Jean Melchior de Vogue (1862), and, in particular Charles Wilson (1864–1865) working on behalf of the Palestine Exploration Fund (PEF), and Charles Warren (1867–1870) made significant contributions in advancing our archaeological understanding of the site. Though a number of other archaeologists worked through the turn of the century, Wilson and Warren's contributions stand out above all others and were of great help to Professor Benjamin Mazar, who conducted the most intensive excavations a century later.

In 1911 a rich idiot named Montague Brownslow Parker and his team, under the guise of being a legitimate archaeological expedition, were discovered by a security guard after they illegally entered the Dome of the Rock seeking the lost temple treasures. Unfortunately they escaped the ensuing riots and unrest that swept Jerusalem and Palestine. From that point all exploration was prohibited until the Six Day War, when the Israelis took Jerusalem in 1967. Thank you so much for that.

In 1968 Professor Benjamin Mazar, on behalf of the Hebrew University of Jerusalem and the Israel Exploration Society, systematically excavated the mount. His team recorded and examined every stone and architectural element until they could determine a complete plan of the site that spanned from the Iron Age to the Turkish period.

Published texts on Herod's temple are many, but my main

source is Leen Ritmeyer's wonderful book, *The Quest, Revealing the Temple Mount in Jerusalem* (2006). Ehud Netzer's *The Architecture of Herod the Great Builder* (2006) and Joseph Patrich's "Reconstructing the Magnificent Temple Herod Built" (1988) were also extremely helpful. My quotations from Josephus and the Jewish *Middot* come from Ritmeyer.[76]

Description of the Temple Mount in Jesus' Time

Thus, in the fifteenth year of his reign, he [Herod] restored the temple and, by erecting new foundation-walls, enlarged the surrounding area to double its former extent.[77]

They further broke down the north wall and thus took in an area as large as the whole temple enclosure subsequently occupied. Then, after having enclosed the hill from its base with a wall on three sides, and accomplished a task greater than they could ever have hoped to achieve.[78]

When we look at the remains of Jerusalem's Temple Mount today we might think, "Ooh, that's very big," and if we imagine what it looked like back then we would expand the dimensions somewhat in our minds and be a little more impressed. Yet it is a mistake to think in these terms.

Every phase of Herod's expansion and reconstruction of the Temple Mount was monumental on a scale that staggered Josephus's imagination. This was a man who had seen Rome! I find his descriptions faintly similar to the apostle John's attempt to describe the City of Heaven in the book of Revelation.

If we read Josephus' eye-witness account, we should likewise be amazed at the dimensions he gives when we convert his cubits to feet and stades to yards. We struggle to imagine the temple proper being over 172 feet tall and Herod's Royal Portico (or the Stoa Basileia) completely covering the entire 919 feet of the southern wall and rising to nearly 100 feet over the temple plateau (Hebrew: *rachava*). At the southwestern and southeastern corners of the Stoa, the retaining walls fell another 103 and 136 feet to their foundations, respectively.

From the levels of the valley floors looking upward, the temple roof was 270 to 300 feet high. We can only imagine the visual impact this would have made on the first-century visitor whose only frame of reference was their mud brick and stone mortared house in the countryside. For the agrarian Jewish family traveling to Jerusalem for Passover, the temple must have been spellbinding and a continual topic of discussion back home over the following year.

Temple Mount Walls and Entrances

But wonderful and surpassing al description, and even, one might say, all sight, was the [third] sacred precinct which he made outside of these, for he filled up with earth great valleys, into which because of their immense depth one could not without difficulty look down, and bringing them up to a height of four hundred cubits he made them level with the top of the mountain on which the temple was built; in this way the outer precinct, which was open to the sky, was on a level with the temple.[79]

Herod . . . prepared a thousand wagons to carry the stones, selected ten thousand of the most skilled workmen, purchased priestly robes for a thousand priests, and trained some as masons, others as carpenters, and began the construction only after all these preparations had diligently been made by him.[80]

Herod's Temple Mount project changed Jerusalem's topography. To bring the temple plateau to a level height, the lower part of the Tyropoeon Valley and the entire Bezetha Valley had to be filled with earth. We're talking about a lot of guys with shovels, picks, and wheel barrows. To retain this immense amount of earth, the newly extended walls surrounding the mount were built 14 to 16 feet thick. On the street level along the southern wall, excavators discovered a horizontal course of massive stones they termed the Great Course or the Master Course. They were set horizontally at pedestrian eye level. Four of the largest of these stones are legendary. The greatest of these is 45 feet long, 11 ½ feet high, and (though its thickness is debated) likely five feet thick (as the other stones in the wall). Its estimated weight is 175 tons. The northernmost stone is 16 feet long, weighing 200 tons. Its northern edge forms the southern door jam to Warren's Gate, a door opening discovered by archaeologist Charles Warren that has been deduced to give direct access to the Temple Mount from a street no longer in existence. To the south of the largest stone there are two others measuring seven and 38 feet long weighing 27 and 150 tons, respectively.

Below the Great Course there are 12 courses of much smaller stones (typical of those higher up on the walls) before one reaches bedrock. From an engineering perspective this massive course would normally rest on bedrock, but it is clear the courses were presented at public eye level to convey a message. We might impose our impressions on the ancient passerby and think these great stones foretell the magnificence and power of what is to come after they enter the Temple Mount complex. It's as if they are calling out to us, "Prepare to be astounded!"

By first enclosing his new Temple Mount with retaining walls, Herod doubled the original area of the Temple Mount to 34.5 acres. The area was not perfectly square: the western wall was 1,591 feet; the eastern wall 1,542 feet; the north wall 1,033 feet; and the southern wall 919 feet long. The increase in area came primarily from pushing outward the north-south wall lines, and to a lesser extent, the western wall.

Each wall had several entrances to the Temple Mount. The largest entry on the western wall was a staircase (built on what is called Robinson's Arch) near the southwest corner that led up to the Royal Stoa (Herod's huge covered structure supported by massive columns). The second largest was accessed by a level bridge (supported by Wilson's Arch) over the Tyropoeon Valley. The most significant entry along the east wall is the Golden Gate. There was another much smaller opening to the south, which gave access to underground storage areas. What stands visible today was built during the (early medieval) Muslim Umayyad period, but inside the gate's structure, ancient remains are still visible from the Herodian period and earlier.

The northern wall possesses a triple gate near its center with the Pool of Israel to the northeast. Josephus does not mention this pool, though it obviously served as an open fresh water reservoir and added to the mount's defenses. The great Antonia Fortress on the northwest corner covers nearly a third of the wall and was surrounded by a moat and supplied with water from the Strouthion Pool.

Though access to the Temple Mount was available from the north, south, east, and west, the main pedestrian entrance to the Temple Mount could well have been from the south. The staircase, which ran the entire length of the south wall, was subdivided by two buildings thought to have been a public building and a *mikva'ot* (ritual baths). The top landing faced a street running against the wall. From here a visitor would have entered through either the double or the triple gate openings. Both corridors from these gates ran under the great Royal Stoa, then up staircases to the main temple plateau (or *rachava* in Hebrew).

The reason for the odd paring of the triple and double gates (why not either triple or double?) has been long debated. Though both give access to the *rachava*, the section of stairs that led up to the double gate was much broader and led directly to the temple plateau, then straight to the Hulda Gate, which accessed the Inner Court.

The subterranean chambers inside the double gate possessed ceilings of particular beauty. Four domes made of close fitting stones remain, two of which possess lavishly carved decorations. The beauty of these fabulous domes can only hint at their original glory. Perhaps this was the Beautiful Gate mentioned in Acts 3, where the apostles Peter and John healed the lame man.

The triple gate was likely more for priestly purposes as it was situated close to the administrative building on the great southern staircase and its inner corridor accessed the underground vaulted structures where supplies were kept. (Those structures have been given the misnomer of Solomon's Stables.)

The Porticoes

> *The porticoes, all in double rows, were supported by columns five and twenty cubits high—each single block of the purest white marble—and ceiled with panels of cedar. The natural magnificence of these columns, their excellent polish and fine adjustment presented a striking spectacle, without any adventitious embellishment of painting or sculpture. The porticoes were thirty cubits broad, and the complete circuit of them, embracing the Antonia, measured six furlongs. The open court was from end to end variegated with paving of all manner of stone.*[81]

As the worshipper reached the temple plateau, they would have seen the entire perimeter covered with double rows of roofed colonnades. The porticoes were 49 feet wide and 41 feet high, and if someone were to walk around an entire circuit, they would go nearly three-quarters of a mile (or if the Antonia Fortress intruded into the courts, just under five-eighths of a mile). The covered colonnades were not heavily decorated, but their brilliantly polished white columns and cedar ceiling panels made a spectacular site. Solomon's Portico (Porch) ran along the eastern edge. It was likely built during the Hasmonean period and untouched by Herod.

Here is how Josephus describes Herod's Royal Stoa:

> *The fourth front of this [court], facing south, also had gates in the middle, and had over it the Royal Portico, which had three aisles, extending in length from the eastern to the western ravine. It was not possible for it to extend farther. And it was a structure more noteworthy than any under the sun. For while the depth of the ravine was great, and no one who bent over to look into it from above could bear to look down to the bottom, the height of the portico standing over it was so very great that if anyone looked down from its rooftop, combining the two elevations, he would become dizzy and his vision would be unable to reach the end of so measureless a depth.*
>
> *Now the columns (of the portico) stood in four rows, one opposite the other all along—the fourth row was attached to a wall of stone—and the thickness of each column was such that it would take three men with out-*

stretched arms touching one another to envelop it; its height was twenty-seven feet, and there was a double molding running around its base.

The number of all the columns was a hundred and sixty-two, and their capitals were ornamented in the Corinthian style of carving, which caused amazement by the magnificence of its whole effect. Since there were four rows, they made three aisles among them, under the porticoes. Of these the two side ones corresponded and were made the same way, each being thirty feet in width, a stade in length, and over fifty feet in height. But the middle aisle was one and a half times as wide and twice as high, and thus it greatly towered over those on either side. The ceilings [of the porticoes] were ornamented with deeply cut wood-carvings representing all sorts of different figures. The ceiling of the middle aisle was raised to a greater height, and the front wall was cut at either end into architraves with columns built into it, and all of it was polished, so that these structures seemed incredible to those who had not seen them, and were beheld with amazement by those who set eyes on them. [82]

Again, dimension plays a key part in understanding the immensity of the Temple Mount. Ritmeyer has calculated that in order to get all 40 columns to fit the dimensions Josephus gives in his description, the Royal Stoa covered the entire 914 feet of the southern wall. The support structure of the underground storage rooms had to carry this tremendous load down to bedrock.

The Stoa was made up of four parallel rows of 40 columns (160 columns in all) centered 23 feet apart. The southernmost row was imbedded or engaged with the southern wall, which gave the structure its lateral stability. In this way, Herod could build an airy, open building to a great height without risk of collapse. The columns were four feet, nine inches in diameter and were 47 feet tall. Add the entablature (horizontal support beams) above the columns, and we have a height of 57 feet. Josephus tells us the center aisle was twice the side aisle's height, so we are looking at a structure around 100 feet high.

The Royal Stoa was comparable in size to a medieval cathedral. Josephus struggles to find words to describe its magnificence. It stands apart from the other colonnades that ring the mount.

The embellishments of Corinthian columns and heavily carved accents and sculptures in Herod's Stoa were in direct contrast to the other beautiful but plainly executed colonnades. We will discuss a possible reason for this in the next chapter.

The Temple Plateau

The Temple Mount platform was a series of sacred zones. Its spatial principles faintly resembled those of the tabernacle but were magnified by immense dimension and seemingly endless wealth. In applying Aristotle's theory of space (see chapter 10 on Nehemiah), the Temple Mount contained a series of increasingly sacred areas, in the way successively smaller envelopes are tucked within larger ones. The further one moved inside enclosures, up stairs, through doorways walls, and through veils, the closer one moved (for the Jews, literally and symbolically) toward God. The requirements to pass into each zone limited the number and type of people (Gentiles and Jews, then only Jews, then only Jewish men, then only priests, then only the high priest). Sacrality was a procession through architectural screens that acted as strainers. Its final synthesis ended in one person, the high priest, who accessed the most sacred place only once a year on Yom Kippur, the Day of Atonement.

On the Temple Mount the huge paved square (and the colonnades that surrounded it) was open to men and women, Jews and Gentiles. Within this great platform was a 500-cubit square (430,000 square feet) inner court bounded by a low railing called the *soreg,* which according to Josephus stood five feet, two inches tall. The Mishnah called the *soreg* the "holy enclosure,"[83] and it enclosed the temple, its sacrificial court, and the Court of Women (*ezrat nashim*). Inscribed in Greek at various points along the wall was the warning prohibiting Gentiles from entering this area:

> *No Gentile may enter within the railing around the Sanctuary and within the enclosure. Whosoever should be caught will render himself liable to the death penalty which will inevitably follow.*[84]

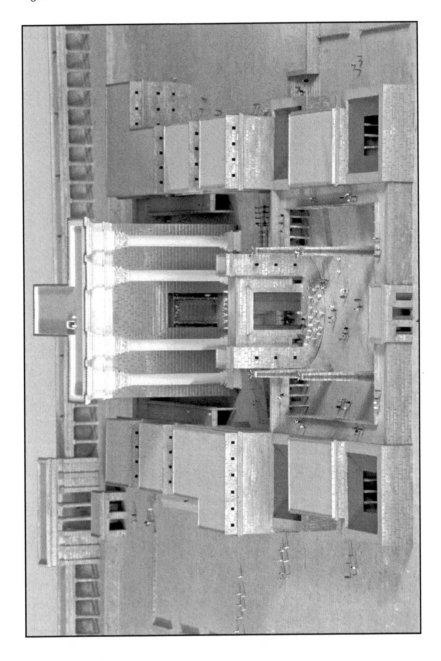

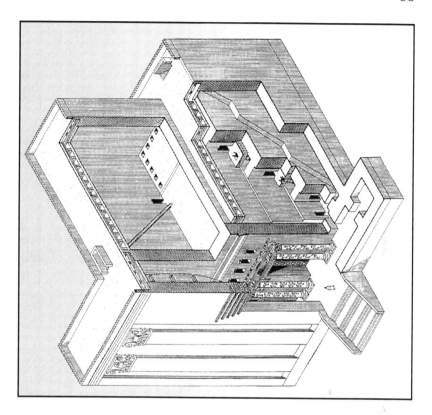

(Above) West elevated view of the Court of the Women, Court of Sacrifice and Temple proper.

(Right) Cut-away section of Temple building proper.

Images courtesy of Ritmeyer Archaeological Design.

The Court of the Women

The Court of Women was not for women only; it was the closest a woman could approach the temple. It was a square court (52,900 square feet), with square buildings at each corner. It was accessed primarily by the Eastern Gate and two smaller Southern and Northern Gate openings. The interior was surrounded by colonnades, with four lampstands, 86 feet tall, spaced evenly in the court. They must have shown like great beacons in the night. The Court of Women was attached to and accessed the inner enclosure at the eastern front of the temple. The four corner buildings at the corners were called the Chamber of the Lepers (where healed lepers were ritually cleansed according to Mosaic code), the Chamber of the Woodshed (where wood for sacrifices was scrutinized for worms), the Chamber of the Nazarites (for those who completed their Nazarite vows, brought their offerings, and fulfilled the requirements of their vow), and the Chamber of the House of Oil (where wine and oil for the courtyard lamps were stored). The buildings were 69 feet square and their inner courts were open to the sky and surrounded with roofed colonnades.

> *Beforetime the Court of the Women was free of buildings, and afterward they surrounded it with a gallery, so that the women should behold from above and the men from below and that they should not mingle together.* [85]

The portico roofs over the Court of Women were accessed by at least one staircase and used by the women as an observation gallery. The roof walkways also provided separation from the men. The New Testament refers to the Court of Women as the Treasury (John 8:20), and here thirteen collection boxes for money were placed. These were called *shopharot,* or shofar chests. *Shofar* is Hebrew for "trumpet," and here refers to the bronze trumpet-like funnels attached to the boxes for the purpose of channeling coins into the chests. The funnels amplified the sound of the coins like the sound slot machines make when they pay out. The richer the offering, the louder the sound; the poorer the offering . . . see Jesus' teaching on the poor widow's mite (Mark 12:41–44; Luke 21:1–4).

At the west end of the Court of Women were fifteen semicircular steps leading up to the Nicanor Gate (Josephus called it the Corinthian Gate),[86] which had great bronze doors (40 cubits or 63 feet high) and two smaller side gates, called wickets. The gates were usually kept open so that the worshippers could observe the priests at their sacrificial work from the lower Court of Women. On the eastern side of the Nicanor Gate was the Court of Israel, where Jewish men went to drop off their sacrificial offerings. Four more steps upward led to the Temple Court where the altar, laver, and Place of Slaughtering were located.

The temple courtyard, the uppermost court where the temple sat, was flanked to the west and east by buildings with gates facilitating priestly worship and sacrifices. I will not take time to describe them other than to say they were accessed from the outer court (inside the *soreg*) by a flight of twelve steps leading up to a narrow continuous landing running along the east, north, and western perimeter of the temple court platform. This landing was called the *hel*.

To describe the temple proper, I will let Josephus speak.

The Temple

But the temple itself was built by the priests in a year and six months.[87]

The sacred edifice itself, the holy temple, in the central position, was approached by a flight of twelve steps. The façade was of equal height and breadth, each being a hundred cubits [172 feet]; but the building behind was narrower. . . . The exterior of the building wanted nothing that could astound either mind or eye. For, being covered on all sides with massive plates of gold, the sun was no sooner up than it radiated so fiery a flash that persons straining to look at it were compelled to avert their eyes, as from the solar rays. To approaching strangers it appeared from a distance like a snow-clad mountain; for all that was not overlaid with gold was of the purest white. From its summit protruded sharp golden spikes to prevent birds from settling upon them and polluting the roof.[88]

First of all, I can't resist commenting on the golden bird-poop-proof spikes lining the edge of the temple's roof. God never specifically ordained these things for the temple's architecture. They seem more of a practical necessity for an ongoing problem. The spikes are referred to in the Jewish Mishnah (*Middot* 4:6) as *kaleh orev*, literally "eliminate the crow." I love it; amidst this shining grandeur we must deal with bird poop. I must rein in the metaphors that flood my mind. But I find it fascinating that an architectural feature significant enough for Josephus to mention, amidst the gold plating and towering stone, is one that keeps birds from soiling not only the roof, but the front face of the temple façade. I mean, for bird-guano to drop into the laver or on an offering on the altar? Yikes! All I'm saying is that it's interesting that birds affected, to a noticeable degree, the temple's ornamental design.

Eliminate the Crow

For me, the temple's roof immediately brings up Satan's temptation of Jesus (Matt. 4:5–6) when Satan took him to its "pinnacle" to see if Jesus could or would jump and then call on his angels to save him from hitting the deck.

Then the devil took him to the holy city and had him stand on the highest point of the temple. "If you are the Son of God," he said, "throw yourself down. For it is written:
"'He will command his angels concerning you,
and they will lift you up in their hands,
so that you will not strike your foot against a stone.'"

MATT. 4:5–6

The Greek word describing exactly where this "highest point" was is vague.[89] It is commonly interpreted as "pinnacle." Off hand, the highest places on the mount were the temple's roof (172 feet) and the south-east corner of the outer wall, standing on Herod's Royal Stoa (estimated at 236 feet). What we do know was that Jesus and Satan were way up there.

Personally, I think Satan led Jesus to the rooftop of the temple. It's a place packed with symbolism. First of all, Satan could have taken Jesus to any building in the world with a sheer drop, maybe the temple of Marduk in Babylon, or the Cheops pyramid in Egypt, or a natural setting somewhere in the mountains like the north face of K2 in the Himalayas, or the northwest face of Half Dome in Yosemite National Park. Yet he chose the temple. I don't think height was the issue here. On the edge of the temple roof, Jesus and Satan would have stood gazing down over the great sacrificial altar and the front *Ulam* doorway that admitted the high priest into a spatial progression that led ultimately into the Holy of Holies. The tension must have been unbelievable with the amount of redemptive freight hanging in the balance as these two stood there.

The second reason I believe the temple rooftop was the location for this temptation was because of the bird-poop-proof spikes that lined the rooftop. As I mentioned earlier, their literal Hebrew meaning was "eliminate the crow," which in the context of Jesus undergoing this temptation is pretty compelling.

Although Satan is never mentioned in the Bible with crow terminology, I think it's theologically cool to attribute the crow image to him anyway. Crows look sinister, a flock of them is known as a "murder of crows," and they make a terrible racket, so why not? In mythology and movies they are known as harbingers of death and doom, and Hollywood has starred them in many demonic movies that I will never see. Here, the poor old crow is a perfect match.

With Satan in crow's clothing, I might take the architecturally packed symbolism hidden within "eliminate the crow" and relate it to the death of Satan in the lake of fire at the great judgment (see Rev. 20:10). It would be hysterically ironic to see Satan standing amidst the spikey things whose hidden meaning forecasts his doom while he tempts Jesus to summon his angels to save him.

But as I read about crows, I'm unsure of this interpretation.

A Word about Crows

No source in the Bible mentions a crow problem on the Temple Mount. But for the following reasons, I'm going to run with it as if there were. The mere presence of the spikes meant the temple property management people must have had a serious crow problem.

First, crows are social birds; they establish strong family bonds. I worked several months with another carpenter named Gordon, who at lunchtime fed a pair of crows that flew in over the hills every day like clockwork. Gordon cawwed like crows, and they dropped out of their aerial circling, landed on a particular telephone pole, and came down to eat the chunks of bagel he scattered on the ground.

Despite a wonderful relationship potential with our micro-raptor friends, this is problematic for the temple, because crows can often roost not by the bagful but in the many thousands. They reproduce like rabbits; the turnover rate from egg to flying bird is only four months, though crows may only have one brood a year.

Ornithologists (bird scientists) believe crows move into heavily populated places because of the heat bubble that forms an invisible dome over towns and cities. Crows enjoy this warmth as well as the night light cities create that offers some security when owls, their primary predator, drop silently upon them. Also, crows habitually drop their kills (anything they can subdue) into water to soak and soften, enhancing their taste as we do when curing beef or cheese.

Crows are extremely intelligent animals. They typically score at the top of Avian IQ tests (I am not making this up). Astonishingly they are capable of human facial recognition. They can remember a person's face and particular articles of clothing. This is particularly the case when someone enters their territory and behaves in an odd or threatening manner. Crows also learn human routines, especially when a series of acts leads to a rewarding end, for instance the clockwork order of Jewish sacrifice on the great altar. The crow then is an intense, highly intelligent, calculating observer. It is the border collie of the avian world.

For these reasons crows would have loved the Temple Mount. The temple roof would have been a perfect pad to congregate in great numbers (lots of level room), and there are plenty of other wonderful buildings to settle on during a family kerfuffle (this is a great word).[90] The heat from the sacrificial altar, the light cast from the four massive beacon towers in the Court of the Women, the plentiful food supply (grain offerings and sacrificial scraps) offered like clockwork by uniquely garbed people, and open water (the laver, the Pool of Israel) in which to store their kills—all of these would tick the proper boxes on a crow's wish list. Also crow poop comes in little pellets, and if you do some quick math, several thousand crows could produce a lot of these in a day. I don't have the numbers nor do I really want to know, but it must be a lot to have underfoot.

Dealing with crows and their habits must have been a huge distraction during worship and a constant threat to ritual purity. When disturbed (which is often) they take off in great numbers with a raucous sound that would have resonated across the temple courts. While sitting on their perches, crows may make a sound like the one the Predator creature made in the Schwarzenegger movie *The Predator* (1987). This is pretty unnerving stuff.

Imagine serious priests offering sacrifices and going about their duties while stepping on bird pellets. Imagine hundreds of "caw-aw-ahs" and weird Predator-like sounds rending the air.

If there is a lesson to be gleaned here, it is how important it is for us to remove the things in our lives that distract us from communing with the Lord. They can be the voices that mock our spiritual lives and self-images, the temptation to leap into unhealthy situations, and people who pollute our minds with endless chatter. In order to live a life of purity, we must "eliminate the crow."

Inside the Temple

The temple proper was two storied and flat roofed. Though Josephus does not describe its columns, a coin discovered during modern archaeological excavations shows, stamped on its face, four massive columns standing across the front entry. The temple's overall dimensions (height, breadth, and depth) were a symmetrical 172 feet. The temple's great interior rooms (the *Ulam* porch, Sanctuary, and Holy of Holies) formed the shape of a T. The other lower, single-story rooms connected to the building's sides and rear made the entire building square shaped.

A flight of twelve steps led from the sacrificial court through a doorway into the temple's porch, called the *Ulam*. The entry opening into the *Ulam* was 70 feet high and 35 feet wide. Its lintel (over the doorway) consisted of five carved oak beams, with the topmost projecting longer and out further than the one below it. This design dropped to the top of the door opening in an inwardly descending pattern. A horizontal row of stones separated each beam from the other. Ritmeyer makes a great point in saying this design is not seen in Greek or Roman architecture of that time. I must consider this a local ethnic Hasmonian or Herodian artistic concept. This focal point to the temple's entry made a significant architectural statement. We might interpret this element as saying, "We might be a friend of Rome, but our God is not a Roman god."

The entire face (of the Ulam) was covered with gold, and through it the first edifice was visible to a spectator without in all its grandeur and the surroundings of the inner gate all gleaming with gold fell beneath his eye.[91]

The *Ulam* was a narrow, long, and very high room (19 feet wide, 120 feet long, 146 feet high). It separated the outer temple wall from the inner Sanctuary wall. One of the chambers at the end of the *Ulam* was called the Chamber of the Slaughter-knives, which was where the knives used for ritual slaughter were kept. If you had entered through the *Ulam* doorway and looked up, it would be the equivalent of gazing at the face of a fourteen-story building. Up high, a number of horizontal cedar support beams spanned between the *Ulam* and Sanctuary walls to prevent their bulging and causing the structure to collapse.

Even though the surfaces inside the *Ulam* were entirely covered with gold, the most dramatic site (according to Josephus) was the grapevine made of solid gold that turned and twisted up a pair of golden pillars. This golden grape arbor was likely set up in front of the entrance to the Sanctuary. The Sanctuary was also called the Holy (I will use both terms interchangeably).

Josephus wrote about the vine above the Sanctuary entrance:

> . . . *it also had golden vines above it, from which clusters of grapes hung as tall as a man's height.*[92]

> *The temple had doors also at the entrance, and lintels over them, of the same height with the temple itself. They were adorned with embroidered veils, with their flowers of purple, and pillars interwoven: and over these, but under the crown-work, was spread out a golden vine with its branches hanging down from a great height, the largeness and fine workmanship of which was a surprising sight to the spectators, to see what vast materials there were, and with what great skill the workmanship was done.*[93]

The entrance to the Sanctuary was 34.3 feet high and 17 feet wide. The golden vine must have reached over that height on both sides and crossed over the sanctuary doorway. Gold chains attached to the *Ulam* ceiling hung down on both sides of the Sanctuary entry, close to the golden vine. The chains were thick enough for priests to climb up to inspect and clean the four crowns (it's uncertain what these were, perhaps window ornaments) above the doorway.

The Holy Sanctuary

Entry into the Sanctuary required passing through a very fine curtain, which hung over two sets of double folding doors. Josephus describes the curtain as a "Babylonian tapestry, with embroidery of blue and fine linen, of scarlet also and purple, wrought with marvelous skill. Nor was this mixture without meaning: it typified the universe."[94] There must have been a cosmic flavor to this place.

Behind the curtain and now completely out of eyesight of any observer, a priest continued the process into the Sanctuary by opening a pair of folding double doors, then entered into a narrow space, closed the doors behind him, and turned to (reminds me of a decompression chamber) open another set of folding double doors that hung on the interior sanctuary wall. He stepped into the Sanctuary room.

The Holy (*heikhal*) was nearly 69 feet long, 34.4 feet wide, with a ceiling 68.5 feet high. Inside this room stood the golden lampstand, the table of shewbread and the altar of incense. On the west end of the room hung the veil (*parokhet*).

The veil was one handbreadth thick [3 inches] and was woven on seventy-two rods, and over each rod were twenty-four threads. Its length was forty cubits [69.5 feet] and its breadth twenty cubits [34.4 feet]; it was made by eighty-two young girls, and they used to make two in every year; and three hundred priests immersed it.[95]

In the gospels, Matthew, Mark, and Luke mention the veil at the climax of the crucifixion when Jesus died and the veil was torn (I love the King James here: "rent in twain," Matt. 27:51) from top to bottom. When I heard about this as a child in Sunday school classes, I was pretty blown away. Not much then could make me stop and think, but this did. A seven-story tall, three-inch thick curtain being ripped in half (from the top) by an invisible hand must have been a major cardiac event to the unfortunate high priest who was very likely at that time operating in the Sanctuary.

The Holy of Holies

The Holy of Holies was a square of 20 cubits (34.4 feet) with the same ceiling height as the Sanctuary. Josephus describes it in startling terminology:

> *In this stood nothing whatever: unapproachable, inviolable, invisible to all, it was called the Holy of Holy.*[96]

Josephus says the room was bare (though its walls were plated with gold) but loaded with serious spiritual freight. To the Jewish mind this was the ultimate sacred space. The biblical book of Leviticus explains that the Holy of Holies was entered only once a year, on Yom Kippur:

> "He [the High Priest] is to take a censer full of burning coals from the altar before the LORD and two handfuls of finely ground fragrant incense and take them behind the curtain. He is to put the incense on the fire before the LORD, and the smoke of the incense will conceal the atonement cover above the tablets of the covenant law, so that he will not die. He is to take some of the bull's blood and with his finger sprinkle it on the front of the atonement cover; then he shall sprinkle some of it with his finger seven times before the atonement cover.
> "He shall then slaughter the goat for the sin offering for the people and take its blood behind the curtain and do with it as he did with the bull's blood: He shall sprinkle it on the atonement cover and in front of it."
>
> LEV 16:12–15

The ark of the covenant, whose lid was called the atonement cover, had been taken as a war trophy by the Babylonians in 586 BC. But the exact place where the ark once stood could be discerned in the etchings in the bedrock stone that protruded approximately nine inches out of the floor. So in Jesus' day, the high priest entered the Holy of Holies during Yom Kippur and placed the censer full of burning coals, taken from the altar sacrifice, on the rock where the ark had once sat. The Mishnah, a record of Jewish oral tradition written down around AD 200, tells us this:

After the Ark was taken away a stone remained there from the time of the early Prophets, and it was called shetiyah. It was higher than the ground by three finger-breadths [about nine inches]. On this he [the High Priest] used to put [the fire-pan].[97]

It hadn't dawned on me until I finished this section what it would have been like for the Lamb of God to enter the Temple Mount, and whether nature and the cosmos hiccupped at the auspiciousness of it. Did the earth tremble a bit or the planets stutter in their rotations for a millisecond? There is no answer to these things, but I wonder.

I am stuck on the biblical phrase: "But the temple he had spoken of was his body."[98] Jesus knew he was to be the final sacrifice. There would be no further purpose for this massive complex. The high priest offering the shovel of burning coals and incense to a nonexistent ark must have hinted that the heart of temple worship was no longer there. Rather, the Holy of Holies was flesh and blood, standing just outside, conversing with people in the courts.

We must now turn to the second part of the temple and look at deeper meanings of this astonishing place.

Devotional Questions

1. What is the most important religious or spiritual place where you go to be with God? The spiritual nature of the Christian faith does not require the believer to be grounded to a specific place for worship. Yet we establish a private sacred space when we go to worship God in nature or a quiet room in our house. Is there a place that stands out for you?

2. Think about what the temple was like in Jerusalem. Is there any place (office building, sports venue, shopping mall) that you go that is similar to it today?

3. How do you think the temple's immense size played on the minds of those who came to worship God? Think of our most beautiful churches. Why are they built with such great extravagance? What does this type of construction say about the people's view of God? Their view of themselves?

4. Where do you imagine Satan's temptation of Christ occurred on the temple grounds? Why did Satan take Christ there, of all places?

5. What is your reaction to what this chapter says about "eliminating the crow"? How can we eliminate the distractions that interrupt our worship of God?

6. For Christians, where is our Holy of Holies? How is it like or unlike that of the temple?

7. If Paul was imagining the temple at Jerusalem when he wrote
   of our bodies as temples of the Holy Spirit (1 Cor. 6:18–20),
   what comparisons can we make? What impact should this have
   on our self-images? How magnificent a creation are we?

CHAPTER 13

HEROD'S TEMPLE II
When a House of God is No Longer God's

As he approached Jerusalem and saw the city, he wept over it and said, "If you, even you, had only known on this day what would bring you peace— but now it is hidden from your eyes. The days will come upon you when your enemies will build an embankment against you and encircle you and hem you in on every side. They will dash you to the ground, you and the children within your walls. They will not leave one stone on another, because you did not recognize the time of God's coming to you."

LUKE 19:41–44

Jesus' Temple Experience

The gospels indicate Jesus truly loved Jerusalem and especially the temple of the Jews. Though he knew he had come to fulfill the temple's temporary role, he mourned its inevitable destruction as he wept over Jerusalem. Every word of the Lord's prophets and poets emote almost inexpressible joy for this sacred place.

I also believe Jesus was aware that the temple stood at the end of an architectural progression. He knew because he instituted it. This sequence was founded on principles imbued within the natural world just as God prompted specific individuals to stand stones and build outdoor altars. The sequence moved upward in architectural and ritual complexity to a tabernacle of wood posts and woven woolens, and ended with an assembly of stonework resembling the tabernacle footprint, a massive composite of standing stones. The temple edifice echoed the crude forms of its architectural genesis.

Finally Jesus ended this redemptive architectural progression by becoming the Lamb who was slain on our behalf. Through his sacrifice, Jesus symbolically embodied every spiritual and ritual aspect the temple possessed. In doing so, he infused its architectural principles within his person. In addition to being the unblemished sacrifice, Jesus became the succession of sacred inner spaces, nullifying the need for the exclusive restrictions of curtains, doors, or a priesthood operating on our behalf.

As the author of book of Hebrews famously put it, "Unlike the other high priests, he does not need to offer sacrifices day after day, first for his own sins, and then for the sins of the people. He sacrificed for their sins once for all when he offered himself" (Heb. 7:27). We never read of Jesus, as a man, demanding entry to the Holy of Holies or participating as high priest, though he was certainly qualified to do these things. But there was no need; he embodied all of those things. And through his death Jesus made the temple redundant.

Through Jesus' death and resurrection he became the first living temple (as he was the last Adam, 1 Cor. 15:45). Likewise, those who accept him as Savior become living temples in his very image. Architecturally then, we might say Jesus was a perfect version of the Vitruvian Man (see chapter 2) who infinitely encompassed spiritual truth in all its proportion and symmetry, the very tools we use to create, design, and build in his likeness.

Just as Jesus worked as a craftsman in human form, it must have been equally astonishing for him to physically climb the stairs to the summit of the Temple Mount. The sense of perspective must have hit him as he walked though its magnificent courts. Jesus must have been aware that he created this principle as well as those of dimension, aspect, proportion, shape, and measurement when he inhabited the primordial, boundless universe where everything requiring the need for these words did not yet exist.

The temple was the greatest structure, in size and affluence, he encountered during his life on earth. And as God and man, he must have loved to interact with and test his limited senses and divine perspective against its massive walls and great expanses. As a builder he must have appreciated the genius of its design and the height of artisan and engineering skills necessary to construct such a place.

To physically interact and worship in the structure he ordained to have built many centuries previous must been equally astounding as it was for him to cut and plane a piece of wood or set the courses of a stone wall. He did not have to appear in cloud form and take his place in the Holy of Holies. Christ could touch the stone, sense shade and sun under the colonnades and out in the Courts of the Gentiles and Women. He could see and smell the blood and smoke of the sacrifices. For that matter, can you imagine watching the Son of God bringing his sacrifice to the priests?

Jesus' earthly roots ran deep on the Temple Mount, as we might feel with a home with which we have marked the passages of time. Joseph and Mary consecrated him there to the Lord shortly after his circumcision (Luke 2:22–24). Simeon and Anna the prophetess blessed him and prophesized his auspicious future under the cover of its entrance and courts. Every year afterward Jesus travelled with his family from Nazareth to the temple to celebrate Passover. At age twelve he was in the temple courts sitting among the teachers and asking questions in what he called, "my Father's house" (Luke 2:41–49). He was tempted there by Satan at the advent of his ministry (Matt. 4:5–6), and in the famous episode of the cleansing of the temple, Jesus was compelled to take physical action against those who polluted its sanctity (Matt. 21:12–13; Mark 11:15–17; Luke 19:45–46; John 2:14–17). He spent many hours there teaching and walking about (Matt. 26:55; John 7:14; 10:23). I can't help thinking he was living the psalmist's words,

> Blessed are those you choose
> and bring near to live in your courts!
> We are filled with the good things of your house,
> of your holy temple.

> Ps. 65:4

The temple is categorized as one of the wonders of the ancient world, and Jesus' words proclaiming its doom must have been spoken with some melancholy. I can't pick up any joy in his voice. Despite the temple's grandeur and Jesus' abiding association there, the place possessed a dark, sinister side. It is time to look at a few of these troublesome symptoms and Jesus' work at exposing them. We should first look at the one who rebuilt the Temple Mount, King Herod the Great.

King Herod

When speaking of New Testament architecture we must discuss Herod the Great. It is important to speak a little about the one who is credited for rebuilding the Temple Mount in the style and splendor Jesus experienced.

Herod was born sometime around 73 BC (the exact year is uncertain) about one hundred and forty years before the Jews revolted against Rome and the temple was destroyed. His birthplace is unknown. Herod's father was from a wealthy and politically prominent Idumean family (from the Edomite nation) in southern Judaea. In 125 BC this area was annexed into the Jewish Hasmonean kingdom, and most of the Idumeans converted to Judaism and were assimilated into the Jewish population. Herod's mother, Cyprus, came from a distinguished Arabian family (likely of Nabatean lineage, whose capital was the great trade city of Petra). It is important to know Herod was not a Jew through lineage, but was grafted in through political expediency. We will come back to this important point below.

Due to high family connections, Herod was twenty-five years old when he became governor of the Galilee and thirty-three when he was appointed king of Judaea (40 BC) by the Roman Senate. Herod was a brilliant politician whose loyalties pin-balled off the ascending/descending Roman governorship of Mark Antony, the reign of Julius Caesar, and finally the reign of Octavian, who became Emperor Augustus Caesar. Herod's move to support Augustus secured his kingship (with the exception of one diplomatic mistake) for the remainder of his life and made him a loyal friend of Rome.

The relative empire-wide tranquility during Augustus' reign enabled Herod to express his brilliant gift of building and architectural design without interruption. Two of his greatest architectural achievements were the construction of the harbor at Caesarea (22 BC) and two years later, the temple in Jerusalem (20 BC). Earlier, Herod built a theater, a hippodrome, and a new palace for himself in Jerusalem. He later built a second palace in Jericho, where he experimented with water pools and building geometries that should put him on par with being an Archimedes of his time. Another notable project was his palace complex on a Dead Sea massif called Masada, a marvel that must be seen today to be believed.

The consensus among historians is that Herod was an architectural genius, a builder of builders, but unfortunately a homicidal maniac. Here we have another example of how a person possessing extreme aesthetics and artistic sensitivities can be brutally immoral.

According to Josephus, the construction of the temple building only took a year and a half. It was built solely by hundreds of skilled Levitical priests so as to not desecrate the holy space. During this time there was no interruption of sacrifice. The outer porticoes were finished in eight years. This seems like a very short time, especially when the Jews in John 2:19–21 claim it took 46 years to build the temple. It is likely the main structures were completed as Josephus states while the finishing touches in ornamentation and out-buildings went on for decades. The gold sheathing and sculpture-work were financed through years of taxation, generous offerings, and funds skimmed off the money changers and animal sellers.

The most poignant aspect to Herod was his inability to act as high priest in the temple. Josephus tells us,

> Into none of these courts did King Herod enter since he was not a priest and was therefore prevented from so doing. But with the construction of the porticoes and the outer courts he did busy himself, and these he

finished building in eight years. [99]

Because of his non-Jewish lineage, Herod could not take part in priestly rituals and was even prohibited from entering the Inner Enclosure beyond the narrow strip of the Court of Israel. I have to restate this for credulity. Herod could neither take part in administering the functions of the temple nor enter the Holy of Holies on the Day of Atonement. It is astonishing to think he could not even worship there. It would be as if you had designed and built a beautiful church but denominational requirements kept you from entering through its doors to worship.

Herod was an outsider to what was arguably the greatest achievement of his life. His Nabatean/Idumean lineage disqualified him from being a Jewish king under the Hasmonean kingly line. He could not be a priestly king as Solomon and the many others who followed. As a grafted-in Jewish citizen, he never could loose his alien status. He was more of a client-king of Rome than a Jewish king.

Israeli archaeologist Ehud Netzer asserts that the Royal Stoa, along the southern end of the Outer Court, was built in order to restore Herod's kingly status on the Temple Mount. I find this very compelling. Netzer believes it to be "the most secular building ever erected by Herod, and evidently the most monumental one of them all."[100] The size and splendor of the Stoa reflected his need to save royal face. It was a substitution, a place where Herod could officiate as a secular king since he could not in a religious context.

This bears out by simple observation. If we look at models of the Temple Mount from an aerial view, we see the two most dominant structures were the temple and the Royal Stoa (without considering the Antonia Fortress attached to the north wall's exterior face). These two great buildings sit across from each other; the edifices for worshipping God and honoring man exist in a permanent face-off, as if in spatial competition for overall control. Clearly this is a face-off between God's sovereignty and Man's self-determination. Into the fray steps Jesus of Nazareth, and let the sparks fly.

Closely related to this divine-human encounter is how the human need for remembrance is imbued within architecture. This is vital to understanding how the temple affected Herod, and particularly the behavior of the high priests, temple leaders, and Pharisees. We will elaborate on this critical factor to a great extent in the following section.

Jesus and the Architecture of Remembrance

Jesus knew the temple was temporal when he said, "As for what you see here, the time will come when not one stone will be left on another; every one of them will be thrown down" (Luke 21:5–6).

This must have seemed unbelievable to those who heard Jesus' proclamation. As we have seen, the temple's magnificence was almost beyond sensory comprehension. Josephus reveals King Herod's motivation to carry out this great work:

> And now Herod, in the eighteenth year of his reign . . . undertook a very great work, that is, to build of himself the temple of God, and make it larger in compass, and to raise it to a most magnificent altitude, as esteeming it to be the most glorious of all his actions, as it really was, to bring it to perfection, and that this would be sufficient for an everlasting memorial to him. . . .[101]

Josephus cuts to the core in defining the human drive to construct colossal structures, places that push the limits of engineering and creative design. Like the temple, massive buildings can become vision statements and living memorials. They obviously do not live as flesh, though they certainly interact with each other in spatial and aesthetic languages interpreted through our senses. In this way we come to know and appreciate particular places.

Buildings are geometric extensions of someone's vision, conceived by an architect's mind and fabricated by the hands of talented crafts-people. And if built properly they have much longer life spans than ours. This is critical for understanding how they work as a means of human remembrance.

It is commonly accepted in the architectural world that buildings convey messages. Great or small, functional utilitarian or aesthetically glamorous, buildings embody the intent, egos, and vision statements of those who directed their construction and commenced their dedications. We often don't have to search far for an interpretation of these things; their messages are often proudly revealed to us by their designers.

Recently Steve Jobs, the CEO of Apple Computers, gave a presentation to the Cupertino City Council for a new office building that would soon be submitted to the city for approval.[102] Along with statistical things, Jobs spoke heavily in environmental terms about the effect the building's soft circular shape would have on the landscape. It would look like a giant circular glass spaceship (the Mother Ship) suffused in tree-studded grasslands. The concept of infinitude contained in the ringed shape was a deliberate subconscious influence to think beyond restraint, to literally and architecturally work "outside the box." The design was rife with attitude and infectious self-image.

Like the new Apple complex, buildings reflect our preferences in design and have a potent effect on our sense of self. And if we know anything about the human character, anything affecting our self-esteem has the potential to be another fleshly, dual-edged sword wielded on behalf of blessing or curse. We will see how this played on the Pharisees, scribes, and temple administration operating under the temple's monumental shadow.

No matter how immense the building, the messages behind its design fade with the passing of human generations, much as the natural elements of rain, wind, and sun (the chemical processes in the atmosphere) work to dissolve a building's fabrics. To combat time's effects on eroding memory, commemoration plaques are often fixed to certain structures. They proclaim the human need to be remembered, honored, take credit. In whatever sense it may come, pride is at work here.

I know of a pastor who installed a plaque, commemorating himself, on a prominent wall of a church gym/multipurpose facility he fought for years to build. He had this done not less than a week before he moved across the U.S. to take over the pastorate of another church. His photo and inscription honoring his work express his desire to be remembered for this accomplishment long after he is gone.

Building for remembrance was not limited to King Herod. The concept was active in every ancient city as it is today. It is a human universal. I give you an example from the ancient city of Palmyra in Syria.

Remembrance:
An Example from Ancient Palmyra

Several years ago I walked through the ancient city of Palmyra (also known by the local ancient folks as Tadmor) in the central desert region of Syria. Out in a less kept area of the site, a fragment of what once had been a great support pillar caught my attention. It had stood upright for eighteen hundred years. Near its base, wind-borne sand had worked a soft area of its sandstone down to a perfectly formed pencil point. I imagine desert-beavers (which do not exist) coming at night to fell this stone tree for their lodge in the local oasis pool. Though the pillar was several feet in diameter, only an inch of stone kept it upright. Its fate was foretold by many nearby columns that had collapsed and spilled their drum cylinders across the ancient avenues where they once cast their long shadows. Now scattered pieces, they seem to be in stages of melding back into the desert sand from which they came, like the bodies of an ancient, lost stone-people processing through a "dust to dust" burial dirge.

Many monumental columns survive to their original height along Palmyra's main avenues. At a prominent elevation you can see, written in mostly ancient Greek and Palmyrene lettering (a variant of ancient Syriac and Aramaic languages), inscriptions written to honor the donors (called "notables") who financed civic projects. Just below the writing, empty shelves attached to the pillars once held the sculpted images of the honored persons.

Donor prestige was as important a facet of ancient civic life as it is today. Their generous gifts bought them local power, the best seats at the theater and at animal and gladiator contests, special service at the great bath complex, and after Rome fell, front seats in Christian churches when everyone else stood.

The need for remembrance extended into the realm of death. Wealthy Palmyrene families built tall, square-cornered burial towers (called tower tombs) with doors and windows, rising four and five stories in the air. A great many today stand in ruin, their sum composing a small city that, in their prime, would have compared only slightly less in scope to the metropolis itself. Several towers are fully restored so tourists can climb their stairways and see rooms lined with stone compartments that once interred the dead. The stairs end at rooftops surrounded by low parapet walls where, it is conjectured, the bodies were first carried for their funerary rites. The priests used the roof to elevate the person to the heavens for a presentation to their divinities before interring them below. In front of the tomb compartments, stone sculptures were cut to the likeness of the deceased in various reclining poses. Many of these have survived and can be seen in Palmyra's archaeological museum. Extreme detail was taken in presenting their individual ethnicities, clothing, jewelry, and hairstyles, which have provided a treasure trove of information for understanding the provenance of Palmyra's wealthy society (a melting pot of Greco-Roman, Syrian, and Mesopotamian peoples).

This ancient metropolis, this once great East-West crossroads, under constant assault by nature, will someday vanish into dust and follow the caravans of monarchs, traders, merchants, families, and soldiers that millennia earlier had traversed its streets and out its gates into the mists of time. Yet amidst the eroding remnants of empire, pillar inscriptions and funerary statues cry out for the need to be remembered and take credit for what is now dust.

Despite his PR campaign advertising this as an act of religious devotion, King Herod rebuilt the temple to be an everlasting memorial for himself. Despite its incredible dimensions and

The great colonnade along Palmyra's Cardo Maximus with decorative
shelves on which statues honoring city notables once rested.
Photo by C. March

A restored tower tomb at Palmyra.
Photo by C. March

extreme material affluence, today there is virtually nothing left of it. The surrounding walls and columned walkways exist in part; some are incorporated within later Crusader and Islamic structures. There are only enough altered vestiges of its past glory for archaeologists to incessantly argue over.

This lesson provides the ultimate commentary on Solomon's poetic verses in Ecclesiastes concerning the irony of life and building in vain—or building for vanity's sake. We will use his insights to contrast God's and man's intent for the temple, a contrast which will ultimately shed light on the destructive behavior of the Jewish leadership.

Contrasting God's Intent and Human Purpose

Isaiah shows us how the Lord enlivened its courts. We will let the Lord speak on his own behalf:

> *"To them I will give within my temple and its walls*
> *a memorial and a name*
> *better than sons and daughters;*
> *I will give them an everlasting name*
> *that will endure forever.*
> *And foreigners who bind themselves to the LORD*
> *to minister to him,*
> *to love the name of the LORD,*
> *and to be his servants,*
> *all who keep the Sabbath without desecrating it*
> *and who hold fast to my covenant—*
> *these I will bring to my holy mountain*
> *and give them joy in my house of prayer.*
> *Their burnt offerings and sacrifices*
> *will be accepted on my altar;*
> *for my house will be called*
> *a house of prayer for all nations."*

ISA. 56:5–7

It is significant the Great Architect infused his living name "within my temple and its walls." God is referring to its specific architectural elements; he is not speaking in vague symbolic terms. The temple was dedicated as a memorial to the Lord's name (a name better than any other name). Temple life came out of the reciprocal covenant relationship between the Lord and his people. Blessing and joy would come out of faithful worship, obedience, and love for the Lord. Herod stood in direct contrast to the Lord's intent for the temple. The Lord determined it to be a place of remembrance for himself, not for an earthly king.

To repeat, on the surface Herod presented the project to the Jews as a gift to their nation and their God, "to correct that imperfection" of the temple not at that time built according to the original model (not up to Solomon's proportions and splendor).[103] But what we can gather from Herod's ruthless actions (infanticide in Bethlehem, assassinations of his sons and family members, etc.) tells us that we should not accept his righteous intent at face value.

Okay, This Is the Really Important Part!

Josephus presents Herod's true motivation in rebuilding the temple as an inward act, "as an everlasting memorial to him." Herod clearly misunderstood the Lord's temple mandate. And this became a major philosophical shift behind the temple's purpose. Remove the Lord's name from Isaiah 56:5–7 and insert Herod's name, and you see the magnitude of the offense. For the first time, the temple was built to glorify a man. Everything in this chapter hinges on this point. Like a cancer, this humanist ideal for self-glorification also infected the Jewish religious elite with the same virus.

What I'm Not Saying

I must again be clear; I'm not condemning the many

thousands of Jews who came to the temple to worship God with righteous hearts. The same goes for the many priests who ministered there similarly. I'm talking about those in leadership at whom Jesus vented his indignation, the guys who wanted to discredit and kill him.

I'm also not saying that putting names on commemoration plaques is wrong. Nor is donating great sums to finance building projects. It is not a sin to be very proud of building something beautiful and costly, and feeling wonderful about the way it expresses deep creativity. Work of this sort pushes its creator and those who stop to observe its lines to higher aesthetic and spiritual thinking. Beautiful buildings enhance society in general. And this is a good thing. All of this boils down to intention, ego, and attitude.

I pick up where I left off. To build in Herod's example reflects a delusion that, though we live for a breath of time, we can extend our self-images beyond the time brackets of our lives and defeat the horrible anonymity of the grave. Clearly this is a humanist proclamation (frustration) against death, exposing the inherent desire to live beyond the limits of one's life. The mandate behind the Tower of Babel's construction could have easily come through Herod's lips: "Come, let us build ourselves a city, with a tower that reaches to the heavens, so that we may make a name for ourselves; otherwise we will be scattered" (Gen 11:4).

Like most ancient kings, Herod built to his egocentric fame, which flies in the face of earlier biblical temple constructions by King Solomon, Zerubbabel, and Ezra. In those cases, the Godhead was intimately involved and humility defined the builder's characters. I don't see this in Herod.

I think of Solomon, when he said in Ecclesiastes,

> *I undertook great projects: I built houses for myself and planted vineyards.*
> *I made gardens and parks and planted all kinds of fruit trees in them. . . .*
> *I denied myself nothing my eyes desired;*
> *I refused my heart no pleasure.*
> *My heart took delight in all my labor,*
> *and this was the reward for all my toil.*

Yet when I surveyed all that my hands had done
and what I had toiled to achieve,
everything was meaningless, a chasing after the wind;
nothing was gained under the sun.

ECCLES. 2:4–5, 10–11

Solomon, in great clarity, concluded that though building great projects was exhilaratingly rewarding, they did not fill the hole in the soul that only God can satisfy. Perspective was the problem. In light of the interminable onslaught of days, nothing matters, nothing lasts. And to think one can build everlasting memorials to oneself is the epitome of futility; it is the pointlessness of prioritizing temporal things—and crushing those who get in the way.

Next we will see how this lack of perspective among the Pharisees and temple leadership came to light in their confrontations with Jesus of Nazareth.

When a House Is No Longer a House

While Jesus was teaching in the temple courts, he asked, "Why do the teachers of the law say that the Messiah is the son of David? David himself, speaking by the Holy Spirit, declared:

"'The Lord said to my Lord:
"Sit at my right hand
until I put your enemies
under your feet."'
David himself calls him 'Lord.' How then can he be his son?"
The large crowd listened to him with delight.
As he taught, Jesus said, "Watch out for the teachers of the law. They like to walk around in flowing robes and be greeted with respect in the marketplaces, and have the most important seats in the synagogues and the places of honor at banquets. They devour widows' houses and for a show make lengthy prayers. These men will be punished most severely."

MARK 12:35–40

In that hour Jesus said to the crowd, "Am I leading a rebellion, that you have come out with swords and clubs to capture me? Every day I sat in the temple courts teaching, and you did not arrest me."

MATT. 26:55

Jesus entered Jerusalem and went into the temple courts. He looked around at everything, but since it was already late, he went out to Bethany with the Twelve.

MARK 11:11

On reaching Jerusalem, Jesus entered the temple courts and began driving out those who were buying and selling there. He overturned the tables of the money changers and the benches of those selling doves, and would not allow anyone to carry merchandise through the temple courts. And as he taught them, he said, "Is it not written: 'My house will be called a house of prayer for all nations'? But you have made it 'a den of robbers.'"
The chief priests and the teachers of the law heard this and began looking for a way to kill him, for they feared him, because the whole crowd was amazed at his teaching.

MARK 11:15–18

Every day he was teaching at the temple. But the chief priests, the teachers of the law and the leaders among the people were trying to kill him. Yet they could not find any way to do it, because all the people hung on his words.

LUKE 19:47–48

As Jesus looked up, he saw the rich putting their gifts into the temple treasury. He also saw a poor widow put in two very small copper coins. "Truly I tell you," he said, "this poor widow has put in more than all the others. All these people gave their gifts out of their wealth; but she out of her poverty put in all she had to live on."
Some of his disciples were remarking about how the temple was adorned with beautiful stones and with gifts dedicated to God. But Jesus said, "As for what you see here, the time will come when not one stone will be left on another; every one of them will be thrown down."

LUKE 21:1–6

Not until halfway through the festival did Jesus go up to the temple courts and begin to teach. The Jews there were amazed and asked, "How did this man get such learning without having been taught?" . . .

Then Jesus, still teaching in the temple courts, cried out, "Yes, you know me, and you know where I am from. I am not here on my own authority, but he who sent me is true. You do not know him, but I know him because I am from him and he sent me."

At this they tried to seize him, but no one laid a hand on him, because his hour had not yet come. . . .

The Pharisees heard the crowd whispering such things about him. Then the chief priests and the Pharisees sent temple guards to arrest him. . . .

Finally the temple guards went back to the chief priests and the Pharisees, who asked them, "Why didn't you bring him in?"

"No one ever spoke the way this man does," the guards replied.

JOHN 7:14–15, 28–30, 32, 45–46

We see in the passages quoted above that the temple leaders were paranoid of religious competitors and potential usurpers. They were clearly jealous of Jesus' popularity and superior scriptural knowledge. They were angered greatly at his occasional, annoying tendency of his hinting at divinity. Jesus could wield the Word of God like a Roman soldier's short sword, his *gladius* that sliced open arteries and veins that spilled anger born of humiliation, guilt, and conviction over the court's paving stones. Only the Son of God could do these things, but he did not present himself in the expected Messiah format of conquering king. It seems the leaders thought it best to kill this threat that can not be understood.

The Hebrew name for the Temple Mount was literally Mountain of the House.[104] The term was common in Jesus' time and was, with certainty, known by him. This adds another perspective to Jesus' reaction to the evil happening within the temple courts. The temple leaders had polluted the Mount, though not with pagan idolatry as Israel's evil kings had done. Rather, they were misled to believe they were protecting a sacred religious system based on meticulous procedure housed in a monumental architectural edifice. When we read of them plotting to kill the Son in the very home of the Father, we must ask ourselves, "At what point is a house no longer a house?"

This brings up their whole killing attitude. The people loved to come and be amazed at Jesus' teaching, and despite Jesus' claims, it is startling that this put temple leadership in a killing tizzy. It would be like having a popular, dynamic church lay ministry and then discovering a jealous board member lurking in your bedroom closet with a sharp metal pointy thing when you reach in for your pajamas at bedtime. It's pretty unthinkable.

Then there is the business of having a financial district on temple grounds. The problem of building a glorious temple—or church, for that matter—is the "glorious" amount of funding it takes to complete it. So enter the rich folk and the poor widow at the tithe chests in the Court of the Women. The trumpet-like funnels that amplified the money (or lack thereof) dropping into the chests was an amazing innovation. No question, there was an emphasis on giving and special (loud) recognition for those who did. A poor widow faithfully giving all she could was audibly sorted to the lower strata in this materially charged religious environment.

It takes a lot of money to build a temple. It must have taken many fortunes to pay for the gold plating, the golden grape arbor with clusters the size of a man, towering colonnaded courts, massive stonework polished to a glass finish, and great cedar beams. Money collection must have been a major focus on par with worship.

I'm reminded of the Crystal Cathedral church in Orange County, California that is presently being sold through bankruptcy. Years ago Cathy and I went there to attend church. All over their magnificent grounds, in the walkways and sides of buildings, are bricks and paving stones inscribed with donor names. The church property even has a cemetery. This is Palmyra all over again. The message was clear: give to this specific building program and you will receive permanent recognition. Yet there is certain risk in inscribing one's name on a building. What if the vision falters, the key leadership fractures, and the institution collapse to ruin? Those names are physically associated with failure. Do the donors who sacrificially gave now want their brick(s) removed and returned?

The Temple's Secular/Pagan Shape

Most temple discussions relate to its distinctly Jewish elements, all the specific features the Lord required Solomon to build and adapted over the centuries. These things were re-incorporated in Herod's design, but there were a number of alterations, mostly within the things we've discussed: the outer colonnades, the Royal Stoa, and the Temple Mount's general layout. Some of these elements were a direct consequence of Herod's psyche and his egocentric vision. To accomplish this, Herod borrowed architectural components from pagan religions and Hellenism (Greek secular culture) and infused them into the core of the Jewish worship environment.

First, the temple and its environs, in their newly reconstructed form, followed the basic template for pagan temple design. Though the temple itself was a magnificent representation of the original built by Solomon, the Temple Mount in its entirety had become very similar in design and size to the great pagan temples being constructed in the Roman East up until then and for the next two centuries.

Temples comparable in size and opulence to Herod's Temple Mount were: the temples of Jupiter and Bacchus at Baalbek (Lebanon), the Sarapeum at Alexandria, the temple of Bel at Palmyra; the temple of Artemis at Gerasa, and the temple of Jupiter-Hadad in Damascus. These temples typically had great columns standing in front of their main doors, and like the Jewish temple, their massive structures rose many feet into the air.

All of these temples were surrounded by great walls (called *temenos*) where one entered through massive gates into open plazas many acres in size completely surrounded by richly decorated colonnades. Along the covered colonnades business transactions and sacrificial animals were sold, much like what Jesus' reacted strongly to when he overthrew the money changers' tables.

Thus, the Temple Mount was a composite of Jewish and secular architecture. It reflected both authentic temple design and that of King Herod (seated in his Royal Stoa), a false Jew living within a pagan Roman context. The temple represented God's model handed down to Kings David and Solomon, yet the outer courts and colonnades were products of an Eastern pagan monarch. It's just as easy to call this place "Herod's temple" rather than "Yahweh's temple."

In fact, if you removed the temple and the *soreg* rail, the Temple Mount would be in the configuration of a Greco-Roman marketplace, called an *agora*. From what we see in Jesus' encounters there, the *agora* business influence had infiltrated its courts.

Clearly, from the verses quoted above, the chief priests' and Pharisees' behavior was an enigma. They seem morally conflicted. They conducted worship and administered the Levitical laws with exactitude, but the reality of their lives was quite different.

Here the egotism Herod infused in the Temple Mount reconstruction was fleshed out in the behavior of those who operated and maintained it. Herod's edifice was built for his vainglory, and this message was transmitted to and embraced by the Pharisees, scribes, and temple administration recorded in the gospels. The royal affluence of the place had worked into their minds. I am led to think they had accepted Herod's vision of remembrance as their own.

Their seeking to discredit and kill Jesus, their public conduct as well as within the religious arena—both of these are proof of this influence. They became like minor eastern monarchs, religious prima donnas dressed in costly robes seeking attention and honor in the marketplace. And as Herod often moved out of ruthless self-preservation to maintain his rule, the Pharisees and temple leaders too reacted brutally toward anyone who countered the status quo, much less threatened the temple's existence. Enter Jesus of Nazareth.

How We Might Miss Jesus Teaching in Our Courts

I wonder at this misconnection, this misconception of the Savior. We condemn the Jews of this time, but perhaps we too are guilty of not always recognizing him walking in the courts of our lives, preaching penetrating, difficult, eternal truth words we would rather not hear, prompting us to do righteous things we would rather not do. We would rather trip Jesus up with "that's not my spiritual gift" or "I'll pray about it" or call the temple guards to capture our Bibles and hide them under a sheaf of papers on the desk.

As Christians living in this state we possess dual natures in continuous conflict. We sincerely participate in our temples and enthusiastically do what is required spiritually, yet just across the court is Herod's Royal Stoa, where we go for a bit of secular fun. The Courts of the Women and Gentiles then becomes the DMZ between our flesh and the Spirit, a no-man's land of hidden traps and killing zones. We announce we are praying for specific things to advance a more Christlike lifestyle, but we keep one foot in Herod's place, and we are nothing more than self-righteous jerks. We are saved by faith, but if we allow the flesh a bit of free rein we become living dichotomies, internally polarized.

A Painful Example

Recently I've become closely aware of Christians whose spiritual and moral natures are in radical contradiction. I'm not talking about the sin-stuff that we earnestly struggle against or the attitude things my dear wife confronts me with on a daily basis. I'm referring to what I can only describe as someone with dual identities. It's in the way their Bible stuff is compartmentalized away from their lifestyle stuff. It's spiritual schizophrenia.

I am thinking of a Christian man I've known for twenty-five years who, I've discovered, lives in two moral worlds. The flipside to his identity is very dark. A bizarre instance of this behavior happened when we were traveling together researching a book on medieval English parish churches. While driving down English country lanes and sitting at meals, he spontaneously reminisced over an adulterous romance that I thought he had repented of years previous. He fondly related his sin and then, in the same breath, began discussing several of the five points of the Calvinist doctrine. It was like, "then we had great sex on the train all the way from Paris to Marseille—by the way, I tried talking to the guys at our men's Bible study breakfast about Calvin's unconditional election and limited atonement but, they just don't get it." And there's my all-time favorite line of his: "I may have a problem with (*expletive*), but God can't fault me for my theology!"

I'm trying to put into words the shock I felt when he said these things (obviously his loyal wife was not present). Here was a man who first explained to me a number of theological perspectives I still hold dear. I sat under his wonderful teaching in many Sunday school classes. Having a dear "brother" reveal his inner dark side is like seeing a beautiful pancake in its golden loveliness baking on the grill and then, after flipping it over, you scream the primordial scream when the sight and stench of the burnt side is exposed. Or to shift to nonfood analogies (which is difficult for me), it's like the young girl in those teen slasher movies who is lying in bed asleep, then her eyes flick open in terror when her subconscious mind puts 2 + 2 together and she realizes her new boyfriend, who has an acute fondness for sharp pointy things, is the one who's butchered half her high school. Or when Bruce Willis's character, John McClain, in the movie *Die Hard* (1988), dumped that terrorist's body out the window of the Nakatomi Building onto the windshield of Sergeant Al Powell's patrol car, and McClain's voice inside your head hollers, "Welcome to the party, pal!" You get my point.

It's so disappointing, because my friend could be wonderful to be around. His biblical insights are very deep, and we have conversed for hours over a wide range of positive interests. I confront him on his sin and I get an excuse or the finger of hypocrisy pointed back in my direction. Then there's the ultimatum, followed by hard feelings and a lost relationship. At the end of the day I must admit that, what I thought was a mature believer is one of those problematic soils and weed-choked plants in the parable of the sower (Matt. 13:3–23).

I found that at the core of his sin was his egocentric appetite for prestige, an arrogance that pushed him to temporarily abandon his faith. I believe he fabricated a theology that allowed him to temporarily depart to do his thing, because he knew Jesus and his beloved Scriptures would always be there when he came back. Or that somehow, God owed him. As he said, "God can't fault me for my theology." I can't think of a more delusional, Pharisaic mentality.

Conclusion: Time for Change

> *There is a time for everything,*
> *and a season for every activity under the heavens:*
> *a time to be born and a time to die,*
> *a time to plant and a time to uproot,*
> *a time to kill and a time to heal,*
> *a time to tear down and a time to build,*
> *a time to weep and a time to laugh,*
> *a time to mourn and a time to dance,*
> *a time to scatter stones and a time to gather them,*
> *a time to embrace and a time to refrain from embracing,*
> *a time to search and a time to give up,*
> *a time to keep and a time to throw away.*
>   ECCLES. 3:1–6

Nothing lasts. Nothing is meant to last. Cathy and I have just moved out of the apartment we've lived in for the last five and a half years. I had to dispose of some things that had simply worn out. The friction of time wears on stuff. At times like this I go to Solomon and the book of Ecclesiastes for some consolation.

After this long chapter I am left to consider the temple in a similar light. As a physical thing, it simply was not meant to last. Again, nothing physical does, no matter its size or how indispensible it seems.

It is a mistake to think the behavior of the chief priests and Pharisees forced God's hand to eliminate the temple, ultimately by the hand of the Romans. I am thinking of what "the fullness of time" means. At the time Christ was on earth, the ark was not present, and the chief priests and Pharisees were impersonating their kingly benefactor. They had gone native. The temple leaders didn't recognize the Savior when they heard him teach in wisdom, not even when they were standing a mere handbreadth away from the very Son of God's personal space. It was no longer God's House of the Mountain; it had become something else: a blind exactitude of Jewish sacrificial instruction surrounded by Greco-Roman architecture. It had become Herod's Temple. It wouldn't have mattered if Jesus had come like another David, holding a sling and a sword, promising to evict the Romans and bring about a Jewish Spring. They would have rejected that Messiah too if it meant reducing their Herodesque self-images. They were too far gone. It was time to tear down and scatter stones.

The temple was the high water mark in biblical architecture. From this point on the Scriptures relate to buildings in their base physical forms (home churches) and in very metaphorical and visionary terms: believers as temples and the fantastic City of God. To these we now turn.

Devotional Questions

1. How important was the temple in the life of Jesus? What was his history there?

2. Do you think he was sad when he thought of the temple's eventual destruction? Or was he content in knowing that it had served its purpose?

3. What was King Herod's underlying reason for remodeling the Temple Mount? What reason did he give the Jews? Were the reasons different or the same?

4. I write about the importance of remembrance and architecture. Why do some people desire to inscribe their names on certain buildings? Can you think of any you know where a commemoration (honorific) plaque is attached in someone's honor? Do you see evidence of this on Christian buildings? Is the reason the same for Christian and secular buildings? What is happening when this is done in a church setting?

5. We have seen how buildings are expressions of those who built and use them. Humility and grandeur in architecture are often expressions of the self-images of those who designed and operate within their spaces. They are expressions of who they are. The temple's magnificence mirrored King Herod's ego. According to Jesus, how were the Pharisees, temple leaders, and the overall Jewish leadership imitating the social behavior of an Eastern king? How were they similar to Herod in their treatment of Jesus?

6. What was the common name for the Temple Mount? How is this significant?

7. How was the temple likened to a house?

8. What destroyed that home?

9. How can we miss Jesus teaching in our courts?

10. What parts of his teaching do our wills choose to reject or ignore?

CHAPTER 14

STONE IMAGERY
Jesus, Peter, and Paul

THE APOSTLES PETER AND PAUL spoke openly of building imagery. I have mentioned those uses at the end of chapter 11, "A Carpenter's View of Jesus," and will return to them again in chapter 15, "The House Church at Dura Europos." In this chapter we will follow the thread of the biblical construction narrative through the epistles up to John's description of New Jerusalem in Revelation. For if Christianity were to have an architectural theology supporting the spiritual edifice of New Testament Christianity, it could very well be based on the following teachings of Peter and Paul.

We should not be mislead by thinking of this as entirely new, as originating from New Testament thought. Rather, Peter and Paul draw upon the Old Testament passages that speak of picking up stones, building foundations, and erecting walls—essentially everything we have been discussing to this point.

Centuries before Peter and Paul, the Lord spoke through Isaiah and compared his covenant faithfulness to Abraham with a stone quarry. God encouraged his people by telling them they were cut from the same stone; they were made of the same stuff as Abraham. In essence, the promises he made to Abraham he also made to each of his descendants:

> "Listen to me, you who pursue righteousness
> and who seek the LORD:
> Look to the rock from which you were cut
> and to the quarry from which you were hewn;
> look to Abraham, your father,

and to Sarah, who gave you birth.
When I called him he was only one man,
and I blessed him and made him many."

ISA. 51:1–2

The patriarchs who erected altars, heaps, and standing stones would have understood this imagery. They would have seen that though they were early forerunners operating in crude methods, nothing theologically had fractured and gone astray.

Peter and Paul were drawing on similar imagery when they wrote their "stone" references concerning Christ and the church. The concept of stacking stones for the purpose of glorifying Yahweh, now identified as Christ the Redeemer, runs in a continuous, uninterrupted movement from the sacrificial tithing of Cain and Abel, through the post-flood altar of Noah, through the tabernacle, Solomon's temple, the Old Testament prophets, Herod's temple, and up to the time of Peter and Paul. Later in this chapter we will advance this discussion to see Christ compared to cornerstones and capstones, which are critical to a building's viability. The apostles, prophets, and believers are personified as stones and take their assigned place within a metaphorical temple structure to form a unified whole. But let's begin our study of Peter and Paul with some much-debated words of Jesus.

"You are Peter, and On This Rock . . ."

Jesus told Peter and the disciples that the church was to be the next worship structure ordained by God. It followed in order after God's instructions to David and Solomon for the temple in Jerusalem. God mandated the construction of Noah's ark, altars and standing stones, the tabernacle, the temple, and now the church.

"But what about you?" he asked. "Who do you say I am?"
Simon Peter answered, "You are the Messiah, the Son of the living God."

Jesus replied, "Blessed are you, Simon son of Jonah, for this was not revealed to you by flesh and blood, but by my Father in heaven. And I tell you that you are Peter, and on this rock I will build my church, and the gates of Hades will not overcome it. I will give you the keys of the kingdom of heaven; whatever you bind on earth will be bound in heaven, and whatever you loose on earth will be loosed in heaven."

MATT. 16:15–19

Unfortunately, Matthew 16:15–19 has been the battleground over which Roman Catholics and Protestants have fought over for centuries—sometimes with sharp pointy things that draw much blood. Therefore I am compelled to take some time here to discuss the prickly issue of Peter and the reference to "this rock."[105]

Over the centuries, Christian theologians from all camps have filled many pages of commentaries with their different takes on this passage. The Catholic Church's view is to push the apostle Peter to prominence and from him assert a continual line of papal authority over the church. The Protestant evangelical position pushes Peter's confession to the forefront and claims that the rock on which the church will be built is Christ, yet Peter, through his beautiful confession of faith, is a driving force in its initial leadership. This passage presents an entirely new direction from the rock terminology established in the Scriptures up to this point. Rock metaphors have only referred to God, never to a man. This is a critical transition in the entire scriptural narrative.

It is popularly accepted that Jesus was referring to the meaning of Peter's name in the Greek as "stone," to that rock upon which Jesus would build his church. The grammatical ending of Peter in the Greek text has led many to assert that Peter was the "little rock" in respect to Christ as "the Rock."[106] This is a Protestant way of saying to the Catholic Church that neither Peter nor the succeeding popes of the church were ever intended to carry the divine equivalency of Christ on earth. Behind the Greek shuffleboard competition happening here, most Greek scholars will not stake their lives on whether this grammatical nuance was intended to hide a golden theological nugget.

Personally, I have always believed that there was a connection between Peter's name and the metaphorical foundation stone supporting the coming church. Yet I do not elevate Peter to an ultimate hierarchical position over the early church. Peter never alludes to himself that way, and the disciples never had the intention of doing so. This church leadership question with Peter is curious. Though Peter was likely the source behind the gospel of Mark and wrote the epistles of 1 and 2 Peter, we do not hear about him again after midway through the book of Acts. Early traditional writings have Peter active in the Roman East up until his dying the martyr's death after the great fire of Rome at the end of the year AD 64. However these post-Acts years of his biography are shrouded in uncertainty. I am led to believe that based on what we know of Peter's later life, Jesus had to be referring to something other than setting Peter as the metaphorical leader-stone upon which all others were to depend. Distilling this chapter down to its base properties, I make the stand that Jesus is the builder and the Rock upon which the church stands. All that the apostles do, they do through him. Christ made the affirmation about Peter because Peter had just given the example of faith necessary for him to become a pastoral leader with the strength and vision to perform his difficult ministry. In a moment, I will quote Peter (1 Peter 2:4–8), who will help clarify this rock terminology from his perspective.

The name *Peter*[107] may not have been a reference to his character at this stage in his life. Much has been made of the few very public mistakes that revealed his spiritual immaturity. Jesus was compelled to publically admonish him with some very severe words: "Get behind me Satan! You are a stumbling block to me; you do not have in mind the concerns of God, but merely human concerns" (Matt. 16:23; compare Mark 8:33). When Jesus was arrested and interrogated, Peter denied any affiliation with him three times and was called out by a young girl. Ouch.[108] This does not seem like foundation-stone behavior. Yet I identify with Peter more than the other disciples, out of conviction for the same errors in judgment. It gives me hope that I have so much space in which to mature.

Yet in Matthew 16:15–19, I think Jesus was speaking in a more visionary sense regarding Peter's temporal ministry until his martyrdom by Roman authorities. Many interpret Christ's reinstatement of Peter on the shores of the Sea of Galilee as a forgiving of the past and an affirmation of his pastoral ministry. In response to each of Peter's successive confessions of his love for Christ, Christ told Peter to feed and care for Christ's sheep.[109] For every denial there was redemption.

Jesus used the allegory of the shepherd and his sheep a number of times during his ministry years,[110] and it is clear to me that Peter was to assume the shepherd role (as were the other apostles) as Jesus' life had demonstrated. The image of the shepherd and his sheep was painted in fresco over the third-century baptismal font in the Dura Europos house-church (see chapter 15) and is still popular today.

Yet years later when Peter wrote in terms of "the Shepherd," Peter was referring to Christ:

> For "you were like sheep going astray," but now you have returned to the Shepherd and Overseer of your souls.
>
> 1 Pet. 2:25

We must keep at the forefront that the church was originally formed around a group of Jewish believers. Being well versed in the Scriptures, the disciples could not have missed the name changes of Abram to Abraham and Jacob to Israel. In their cases, as here with Peter, the change of name was a symbol of a promise about a community's perpetuity through the promises of God. As the disciples were to discover, the elevation of honor among them would not be that of earthly entitlement. All of them would, in various ways, follow Christ's example of selfless sacrifice, uncomfortable earthly existence, and heavenly glory.

The Rock and the High Winds of Persecution

Peter's rock symbolism is related to Jesus' reference to foundations in his Sermon on the Mount (see Introduction) and the battering of high winds and rising waters. It follows that in the first act of instituting his church (symbolized as a building), Jesus established the rock on which its foundations would rest. The storms would surely beat against it. The gates of Hades in Matthew 16:18[III] are important in this context, for the gates of ancient cities defined their power. Thus, if the church was founded on solid rock, the power of the underworld could never topple its walls. With the exception of John, the disciples listening to Jesus' blessing of Peter would all die, in very uncomfortable ways, for preaching the gospel. Peter's martyrdom would happen close to the apostle Paul's, under Emperor Nero.

We read and discern these passages in our time, which lets us take a tax deduction for a tithe. But back then, and sporadically for the next 280 years, there was a chance you could be turned in by friends and neighbors, publically interrogated by government officials, mauled to death by wild animals, covered in pitch and burned in Nero's gardens, mutilated and beheaded, stoned outside city walls, have hooks inserted in your flesh and be dragged though the streets, or die slowly in innumerable other ways for public entertainment. And to think, many Christians in this environment wore their white baptismal robes in public as a witness of their conversion. Talk about "in your face" belief!

These external forces were matched by the internal theological attacks that threatened to eliminate the Rockhood of Christ through endless philosophical wrangling. In order to exist under this type of pressure, a society's structure must be like a monumental edifice with an unshakeable symbolism of faith and hope.

In the following section we'll see how Peter and Paul incorporated Old Testament references into their concepts of Christ and the church. The language is of stones, buildings, and builders. I have stated this without much fanfare before, but the continuance of construction terminology since the first pages of

Scripture till now is astonishing. I cannot help but claim that the earliest and strongest metaphors in use during biblical time came from architects, architecture, and methodology from the building trades. If they were writing with their audiences in mind, the prevalence of this language makes me wonder how many in the early church were working in these fields.

Peter's Stone Imagery

As you come to him, the living Stone—rejected by humans but chosen by God and precious to him—you also, like living stones, are being built into a spiritual house to be a holy priesthood, offering spiritual sacrifices acceptable to God through Jesus Christ. For in Scripture it says:

"See, I lay a stone in Zion,
a chosen and precious cornerstone,
and the one who trusts in him
will never be put to shame."

Now to you who believe, this stone is precious.
But to those who do not believe,

"The stone the builders rejected
has become the cornerstone,"
and,
"A stone that causes people to stumble
and a rock that makes them fall."

They stumble because they disobey the message—which is also what they were destined for.

1 PETER 2:4–8

It is wonderful to see the deep progressive spiritual maturity in Peter. I cannot help but think he took the blessing of his new identity and any attention it may have gained, and quickly passed it on to Christ. Paul (quoted below) uses very similar terminology to express a unified church. Their Old Testament references are listed below.

Whatever self-image he may have had of himself as the rock of the church, Peter clearly identified Christ as the Rock as described in the Old Testament. He called him "the living Stone," "a chosen and precious cornerstone," "the stone the builders rejected," and "a stone that causes people to stumble and a rock that makes them fall." The believers he called "living stones" that form the walls of a "spiritual house." I appreciate the fact that Peter included everyone under Christ in stone metaphor; clearly, he did not glorify himself as the Rock. He expressed tremendous humility in these verses. Peter formulated a unified temple of stone imagery founded on the precepts of the Old Testament. We might call this bonding of the old and new a monolithic form.

"See, I lay a stone in Zion, a tested stone,
a precious cornerstone for a sure foundation;
the one who relies on it
will never be stricken with panic.
I will make justice the measuring line
and righteousness the plumb line."

Isa. 28:16–17

The stone the builders rejected
has become the cornerstone;
the LORD has done this,
and it is marvelous in our eyes.

Ps. 118:22–23

He will be a holy place;
for both Israel and Judah he will be
a stone that causes people to stumble
and a rock that makes them fall.
And for the people of Jerusalem he will be
a trap and a snare.

Isa. 8:14

Christ is the cornerstone upon which all of the structural load forces above bear down and ultimately reside. If the cornerstone fails, the entire foundation is put at risk. Thus, it is critical that Christ is planted here. The capstone is a wall stone specially crafted and placed to prevent doorway and window openings from collapsing. Thus, entry and the emission of light into this edifice are made possible by Christ. From the perspective of elevation, Christ is above and below. As cornerstone and capstone, he is ever present—a structural support continually operating within the edifice.

Rejecting Stones

The walls, which are entirely dependent on the chief cornerstone and capstones for their ability to stand, are metaphors for a spiritual priesthood. A wall is not a wall when it has collapsed to the ground; it is . . . a pavement. Peter also warns that this building is a stumbling block for those destined to stumble.

In the course of life we naturally accept and reject materials out of which we build our lives. Whether we realize it or not, we set the cornerstones of our lives based on what we accept as truth and build our structures on top of our perceived certainties. Some identities rest in orientation to pleasure, career, learning, science, and religion—things that should make us fulfilled, content, and happy. Yet the architectural blueprint Peter and Paul use is drawn on the metaphorical truth hidden within the principles of the cornerstone and capstone.

There are those who daily stumble over and reject the materials of Christ while loading up their trucks in the spiritual lumberyard. They approach the corner and capstone that rest neatly on their pallets, roll them over to inspect their surfaces and qualities, but set them aside and walk away to gather others more in the style of their way of life, more in line with their vision of themselves. We have seen this as a Babel mentality, a foundation-in-the-sand thing. I can demonstrate the effects of building the wrong way with an example from my construction past.

A Helpful Example from the Real World

In the first year of my apprenticeship (1984), I carried a ladder for an independent building engineer hired by a property management group to inspect a townhouse community that was suffering from a multitude of structural failures. We thoroughly studied a diverse test group of units by their overall construction methods and material qualities. Though the owners of these places had spent top dollars in a strong real estate market in an affluent area on the Monterey Peninsula, the houses were construction trash. A trailer park would have performed better. Original photos taken soon after their completion portrayed them as modern pristine buildings nestled in the midst of mature oaks.

The deception was impressive. The effects of wind and rain played havoc on these buildings because they consisted of mediocre materials and their exteriors covered over poor construction techniques. We found shallow foundations, improper wall connections to foundation sills, stucco coats that ran into the soil and allowed entry for destructive bugs of all types. Dry rot, mold, and mildew invaded the homes' inner walls. Sapwood, a cheaper but weaker and more unstable material, was often used for window, door, and roof fascia, which twisted and literally pulled nails out of their boards when exposed to heat and cold. The movement of materials and the buildings themselves made the tar and gravel roofs a moot point.

I had spent many days repairing these roofs under the employ of a very fine roofing company.[112] Amazingly, the roof structures were consistently under-supported, which caused some of them to sag in their middles, creating standing pools of water throughout the winter months. As we cut through the roofing membrane to repair leaks and reroof certain sections, my boss and master roofer, Roy Lambert, showed us that the roofing quality was minimal at best. Many residents had to replace their ceilings and ruined light fixtures; a few owners had their water-soaked sheetrock ceilings collapse in on them while they lay in their beds at night. The owners were not happy campers.

Truly, it would have been better had the homes not been built. The building contractor and the architect who had jointly developed the site had long closed their companies (rumor was they started up somewhere else in the United States under different identities). The county building inspector who signed off the final inspection that ensured everything was up to code had long since retired and moved away. The relatively few years it took for this place to evolve into a catastrophe were enough for the perpetrators to take the money and flee into obscurity. For the owners, there was only the county to sue for damages, and from the last I heard, they were struggling to summon the legal funds for a long battle. Most of them were in the process of either selling out for a pittance or hiring their own consultants and contractors to save what they could.

After a week of study, the summary opinion of the inspector I accompanied was that the entire complex had been "built wrong from the ground up." A sign with this epitaph could have stood at the community's entrance (as a tombstone), encapsulating the situation perfectly.

This book is a testimony to this truth. To live a full life is to build according to the precepts of Scripture, drawn to our scale by the Great Architect who set the code from which we should build our lives. He did this out of his love for us simply because he wants us to stand with him forever. God would rather that we not become a construction epitaph. The first step of failure, he says, is to reject him at the places we go to gather the stones to fabricate our lives. To reject God's truth is to build "wrong from the ground up."

Paul's Stone Imagery

Paul uses very similar building terminology in describing the continuity of the church, going back to the prophets in the Old Testament.

Consequently, you are no longer foreigners and strangers, but fellow

citizens with God's people and also members of his household, built on
the foundation of the apostles and prophets, with Christ Jesus himself as
the chief cornerstone. In him the whole building is joined together and
rises to become a holy temple in the Lord. And in him you too are being
built together to become a dwelling in which God lives by his Spirit.

EPH. 2:19–22

Again we have Christ as the chief cornerstone together with
the apostles and prophets, and fellow believers as stones laid in
courses. Similar to Peter's image, Paul's structure is a temple
built for worshipping the Lord. It is enlivened by the Holy
Spirit and becomes very much like the future New Jerusalem
as it is spiritually illuminated from within. The structure, by its
nature, tells us that we are part of an eternal plan. Its timeline
stretches from creation to eternity. We believers are an assembly,
a composite of kings, priests, apostles, and regular folks who, at
the end of the day, rest on a secure foundation. And because
of the saving grace of Christ, some carry certain honor, but we
are really no different from each other. We are stones firmly
set within the walls of the holy temple. If we are looking for the
antithesis of the Tower of Babel, there is no need to look further.

The Body as a Temple

I have become a fan of the television show "The Biggest
Loser." I am not sure how this happened; perhaps my interest
lies in the contestants' psychological battles over food more than
the competition itself or watching them puke on their treadmills.
Through the act of inserting mass quantities of food through
their mouths, these people have gained enough weight that their
sacks of skin can contain two, perhaps three, people. That is a lot
of weight to be carrying around. I try not to snack when I watch
the show, and I am convicted about the state of my body. My
metabolism has transitioned from the jackrabbit of my youth to
the mighty sloth in my adulthood. I would never have been able
to sit and think and write for hours as I do now. The downside is

that I do not burn calories as I once did, and photographs taken of me during the holidays are shocking. I have begun hiking the hills in Rancho San Antonio Park near where we live. This is helping to assuage the stress of being unemployed now for over a year. My body is a temple, and it is no mystery why Paul wrote about the human body in this fashion.

So much of how we treat ourselves is a reflection of our self-image, and this is critical to our spiritual life. Paul tactfully transitions into this topic by comparing ourselves to the highest order of built form of his time. As he related Christ and his believers to symbolic stones of a temple, he likewise used the temple metaphor for our fleshly bodies. This coincides with his admonition against sexual impurity in I Cor. 6:18–20:

> *Flee from sexual immorality. All other sins a person commits are outside the body, but whoever sins sexually, sins against their own body. Do you not know that your bodies are temples of the Holy Spirit, who is in you, whom you have received from God? You are not your own; you were bought at a price. Therefore honor God with your bodies.*

Dr. Phil should be happy here. Fragments of this section have been used throughout society in the promoting of a positive self-image. Granted, they are typically politically sanitized by taking out the Holy Spirit and God business, but no matter—the message is that we are a beautiful temple of the Lord. Despite the damage done by the advertising and entertainment industries and legalistic, critical family members, the fact that we are crafted by the Creator and eternally restored via the sacrifice of his Son should kill any words that attack us as being ugly, stupid, and not worthy. Perhaps the entire point of this book is not so much theological as it is in knowing that in God's sight we are accepted, loved, and considered physically and spiritually beautiful.

Paul confirms this when he writes that we are intimately involved in the eternal plan of the Creator who loves us infinitely:

For we are God's handiwork, created in Christ Jesus to do good works,
which God prepared in advance for us to do.

EPH. 2:10

We are his handiwork, his craftsmanship. What beautiful words. I must remind myself of this constantly when the world tells me that I should adopt another self-image or that I must implant rows of hair follicles on the receding California coastline that is happening on top of my head.

Summary

The New Testament's temple imagery ultimately breaks down to an intimate presentation of the individual as a beautiful creation. All of this biblically sanitized talk about rocks and temples pales in comparison with the fact that we are loved by the God who created every part of our bodies; we are temples made by his holy hand. Our temples are the metaphorical stones used to build the spiritual architecture of the church. I do not know how our self-esteem can be elevated any higher than this. We are redeemed by the Redemptor who restores.

Likewise, it takes an assembly of micro temples of believers to form a holy temple to the Lord. In this we become the tabernacle prototype as we are purposed to worship him with the illumination of the Spirit. We stand as memorial stones in testimony to this wonderful truth. Can you see the progression from the earlier chapters?

We house the Holy of Holies when Christ enters us, and conversely, we may tragically become like the sinful kings of Israel when we desecrate our bodily temples with destructive things. I wonder if any one of the kings of Israel ever thought that making the temple a place of pagan worship was a politically correct, multicultural thing to do. We discover, as temples, that purity is not a puritanical hate word; we must embrace the truth of Christ upon which purity is founded. It's time for a long walk in the hills.

Devotional Questions

1. How is Christ likened to the Rock? Where does this rock-language come from?

2. Why did Christ use rock terminology when he referred to the apostle Peter as the rock upon which the church would be built?

3. Where does Jesus speak of a house sitting on a rock foundation? What does the foundation represent?

4. What is the purpose for building on a rock rather than some other substance?

5. How important is it to have your life founded on rock? Relate this to Christ's and Peter's examples.

6. What storms did the early church have to weather that required a strong foundation?

7. What was Peter referring to when he said, "The stone the builders rejected is now the capstone" and "A stone that causes men to stumble and a rock that makes them fall" (1 Peter 2:4–8)? What Bible passages was he quoting? Explain this rock symbolism.

8. We have seen what happens to buildings when proper construction methods are not used. How does this relate to our rock imagery of setting foundations and rejecting and accepting stones when building our lives?

9. What does it mean to say we are God's workmanship?

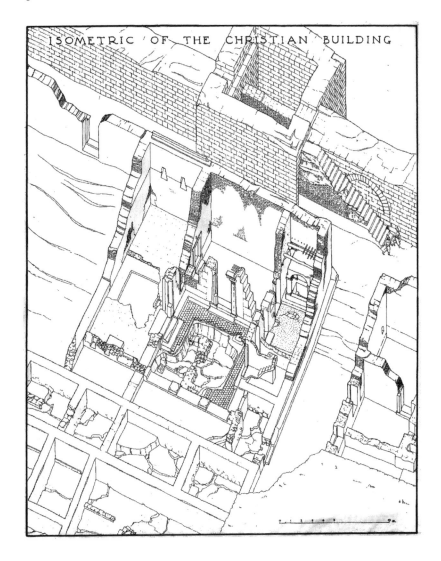

Christian Building, Isometric Projection of Extant Remains, by Henry Pearson, in *The Excavations at Dura-Europos*, Final Report VIII, Part II, The Christian Building, C.B. Welles, ed. Courtesy of the Yale University Art Gallery, Dura Europos, Archives.

Chapter 15

The House Church at Dura Europos

FOR THE FIRST SEVERAL CENTURIES of the church's life, communities of Christians often met in private homes. The following passages from the New Testament and early Christian sources mention the house in varied locations and contexts:

> *The churches in the province of Asia send you greetings. Aquila and Priscilla greet you warmly in the Lord, and so does the church that meets at their house.*
>
> 1 Cor. 16:19

> *Give my greetings to the brothers and sisters at Laodicea, and to Nympha and the church in her house.*
>
> Col. 4:15

> *To Philemon our dear friend and fellow worker— also to Apphia our sister and Archippus our fellow soldier—and to the church that meets in your home.*
>
> Philemon 1–2

> *Rusticus the Prefect said, "Where do you [Christians] assemble?" "Wherever is chosen and it is possible for each one," said Justin, "for do you think it possible for all of us to gather in the same place [of assembly]?" Rusticus the Prefect said, "Tell me, where do you assemble, that is, in what place?" Justin, said, "I have been staying over the baths of Myrtinus for the entire period I have resided in Rome for this the second time. And I know no other meeting place except the one there. If anyone*

wishes to come to me there, I am accustomed to share with him the words of truth."

Interrogation of Christian Justin Martyr in Rome, AD 164[113]

And while Paul was speaking in the midst of the church in the house of Onesiphorus, a certain virgin [named] Thecla, whose mother was Theocleia and who was betrothed to a man [named] Thamyris, sat down on a nearby window of the house and listened night and day to the words being spoken by Paul concerning chastity.

The Apocryphal Acts of Paul and Thecla,
written sometime before AD 190, somewhere in Asia Minor

Then turning his attention to Emeritus, the Proconsul said, "In your house the congregation had been gathered contrary to the order of the emperors?" Since Emeritus was filled with the Holy Spirit, he said, "In my house we conducted the Lord's Supper." The proconsul asked, "Why did you permit them to enter?" Emeritus answered, "Because they are my brothers, and I cannot prohibit them." "But you should have stopped them." "Certainly not," said Emeritus, "for it is not possible for us to exist without the Lord's Supper."[114]

The Idea of the House for a Church

Jesus never mentioned physical architecture in respect to his church. He did not sit down with Peter (the rock on whom he would build his church) and discuss floor plans and ritual movement within four walls. A builder with his pedigree might have made this a huge issue, and I have to say I am a little surprised with this after all that has been covered in this book. All we have from him (chapter 14) are symbolic images of stones and foundations. Jesus' institution of communion did not come with a dimensional model indicating where this ritual was to take place. We do not hear of a structural prototype that was put into the minds of any of the apostles as God did with Noah, Moses, and David. Instead, the Holy Spirit guided them in new ways. Yet, at the end of the day, we have a cup of wine, a loaf of bread, and a semblance of structured leadership.

Void an architectural mandate, the church was a fluid system. Worship could be conducted anywhere, and as the above quotations show, for the first several hundred years of the church, "anywhere" was an accurate locator for the home or room or hall of some type. The early church also met in graveyards, celebrating the martyrs who died for the faith. In time churches were built over them, as was St. Peter's in Rome. It should not be lost on us that some of what we know of Christian meeting places was admitted while under interrogation by Roman magistrates. The words of their testimony meant horrible torture and a death sentence. When I read the eyewitness accounts of the church martyrs, I think how much I take for granted the freedom to worship. I do not risk imprisonment and a horrible death for attending a church service. If I were risking being mauled by animals, burned at the stake, beheaded, or beaten to death by a howling mob for entering a church or reading my Bible, I would treasure worship and memorize the entire New Testament. I definitely would not complain about the air conditioning, the comfort of the seats, and a fussy child.

There was tremendous freedom in not having a building mandate from Christ. A Christian was technically free to worship at any place and any time of the day or night. Though congregations had leaders (elders, deacons, deaconesses), they were initially a priestless religion. Intercession was direct. Symbolically, their high priest operated at the right hand of the Father (see the book of Hebrews). The full range (not to be confused with "free range") of landscapes—natural, civic (downtown), urban (more dense housing), and industrial zones—became instantaneous places of worship.

Why the House?

Aside from the practical nature of the house structure, there are suggestions for the reasons why the home was chosen. Up until the fourth century, Christianity was seen by Romans as one of the many minority "mystery cults" in a vast religious marketplace. The scant historical evidence suggests that by the fourth century the faith had spread the full breadth of the Roman world, perhaps beyond—but in tiny pockets. The mass conversions that created large Christian population centers did not happen until after Emperor Constantine in the early fourth century. Thus, from a population standpoint, there was no need to build big. Also, with some exceptions among the Roman aristocracy, Christianity was made up primarily of the middle to lower classes of society. Financially and politically, they were not yet in a position to institutionalize.

The imminence of the rapture (the big eschatological event) was another likely reason they were not compelled to build permanent structures. After all, they had New Jerusalem waiting for them. If you read enough accounts of the Christian martyrs during the Roman period, you get a sense that, given a choice (and most were given a choice), entering the gates of heaven was a much better option than worshipping with the pagan status quo.

The church experienced its first persecutions and martyrdoms when its nonconformist message emanated from the home and began to affect the set patterns of civic life. Old school pagans who controlled the infrastructure of the cities were upset with this; nonparticipation in the festivals and sacrifices to their gods endangered their protective covering. Also the loss of revenue in the sales of idol paraphernalia and peripheral industries supported by the religious economy increased the tension, sometimes to the breaking point (Acts 19:23–41).

Make the gods angry, and then bad things happen. As we see in Justin's words above, the church could survive Roman persecution if broken into small anonymous worship groups (fragment and survive). Under interrogation Justin could only state that the location of his meeting room was over a bath complex, though there were likely many similar to it throughout Rome and in its subterranean catacombs.

Thus, the impending reality of the rapture, lack of wealth, occasional periods of persecution, and a faith-based religion without ornamentation and physical accoutrements are the reasons why we have virtually no physical evidence of the church for its first two hundred years (with exception of the textual remains of the New Testament and early Church Fathers). For this reason, the archaeological remains of the house church at Dura Europos that I will present below are of vital importance for Christianity.

The nomenclature I will, at times, use for the house church is the *domus ecclesia*[115] as the worship center for Christianity. The formal basilica-style church, recognizable by its rounded apse on its eastern end, was a later development, beginning in the fourth century AD. This was a sign that the church had become a governmental institution, approved by the emperor, who was likely a Christian (at least in generic terms). With the advent of a governmental system of bishops and priests came the theater of ritual and ecclesiastical law. After four hundred years, the *domus ecclesia* faded from existence.

The remainder of this chapter focuses primarily on the only house church to have been systematically excavated by archaeologists. It was found in an ancient city in Syria called Dura Europos that rests, long abandoned, on a plateau over the banks of the Euphrates River. Before I describe the Christian site, I will briefly mention its historical and physical contexts.

Dura Europos, Syria

In September of 2005 I visited Dura Europos in eastern Syria. It was way over one hundred degrees Fahrenheit, and the heat reflected off the rocky soil like an oven. Though this place took hours to get to, it was an amazing feeling to walk within the walls of this deserted ancient city and gaze over the Euphrates River below its plateau. I could see that the city, though relatively small, was inundated with religious cult sites. Rusted metal signs with faded lettering identified their locations; remnants of their mud-brick walls gave me the sense of the dimensions of their rooms and open courts.

In addition to Christianity and Judaism, pagan temples and

shrines represented deities from Mesopotamia, Syria, Palestine, and Greece, as well as those common with the Roman military. Archaeologists were able to determine that, as the city grew in size and wealth, the various religions expanded their worship centers. What makes this a gold mine for ancient religion theorists is that nearly all the cult sites were based on the footprint of the prototypical home.

The home in Dura was typical throughout Mesopotamia and Palestine. It consisted of a series of rooms surrounding an open court. Entries from the street were not overly elaborate, and internal walls were situated so there was no direct line of sight to the inner court from the street. A study on the majority of homes at Dura indicates the wealthier the house, the more it was insulated from the street by layers of walls and ancillary rooms. The poorest living spaces were closest to the streets, and the inner spaces of the wealthiest were the farthest from them. Divan benches, or what we might think of as perimeter couch seating in a living room, existed in rooms within pagan temples as well as residential houses. Here, the patriarch of the house resided and entertained his guests.

Three natural barriers protected the city at its walls. To the east lay the cliff over the Euphrates, and two deep wadis (small valleys cut by water erosion) cut gorges along the northern and southern perimeters. To the west, open desert ran flat to the city's fortifications. Impressive ramparts were erected to counteract this natural defensive weakness, perhaps giving the city its Aramaic name *Dura*, meaning "fortress." *Europos* is a Greek name honoring the Macedonian birthplace of the first Seleucid king, Seleucus Nicator, during whose reign Hellenistic Dura was founded.

Dura's greatest natural defense, the Euphrates River and the wadis running up into the city's west end, were the determining factors in the city's economic, political, and military importance over the course of its history. From earliest times, the Euphrates was one of the main trade arteries between the Eastern and Western worlds.

Very little is known about Dura Europos before the

Macedonian colony was founded in 300 BC by one of Alexander the Great's generals, Seleucus Nicator. The colony was probably a refoundation of an earlier settlement. A clay tablet discovered within the city dates from the reign of King Hammurabi of Hana (1900 BC) and refers to the site as *Damara*, possibly an earlier form of its present name.[116] Dura remained a Parthian outpost and Roman-Parthian buffer zone until AD 165, when the Roman armies of Lucius Verus and Avidius Crassius captured the city. It remained a Roman possession for less than a century; it was taken by a Persian people, similar to the Parthians, called the Sassanians during King Shapur I's second invasion of Syria in approximately AD 256. The Persians evacuated the population, briefly occupied the city, and then abandoned it. Late Roman historian Ammianus Marcellinus mentions that Dura was "a deserted town" when he and Emperor Julian's army passed by in AD 363.[117]

Dura's western city wall not only protected and separated, but also played a key role in the final desperate defense of the city. An unintended consequence of this defense was the preservation of the architecture and art that has brought a great measure of modern fame to the city. Anticipating Sassanian under-wall sapping, the Romans strengthened the western wall by dumping massive quantities of dirt against it, filling the interior street (named Wall Street by American archaeologists in the early 1930s) and the residential buildings paralleling it to the east. The Jewish synagogue and Christian house church, one block north and south of the main gate respectively, were among the buildings inundated. Further dumping required the demolition of roofs and walls protruding from the defensive buttressing. Despite this effort, the walls were breached, probably near the end of the year AD 256.[118] The fill protected the buried buildings from looting and decay and thus preserved them for posterity.

There is reasonable evidence that Dura was a prosperous place under Rome, especially in the good-quality domestic construction in the western neighborhoods that contained the Christian and Jewish centers. The expansion of the church and synagogue in the last decades of Dura's occupation may have taken advantage of entire blocks being "reorganized" by civic authorities.[119]

The synagogue and several pagan shrines and temples were very near to the Christian *domus*. The auxiliary gate on the west wall and the road that ran along it must have made foot and wheeled (and camel) traffic like a flowing river outside the *domus*'s walls. Excavators found remains of a bench attached to the house's outer wall on the Wall Street side of the church, and I speculate whether it was used as an evangelism tool by Christians in sharing the gospel.

The Christian Domus

The Christian site of Dura Europos stands immediately behind the city's western defenses. It was a corner property, along what excavators named Wall Street and Street 3, on Block 8 on the city plan. Tower 17 of the western wall was immediately to its west across Wall Street and only a block south of the city's main gate.

The character of the structure typifies the Durene private house with boxlike rooms surrounding an open center courtyard.[120] The main entrance was accessed by an inconspicuous doorway from Street 3 on the northeast corner of the building. This admitted one into a room similar to a vestibule whose interior door was completely offset and opposite that of the entrance to the inner courtyard. The main rooms open peripherally off an internal open court not visible from the street, though most of the rooms could be accessed by internal doorways without passing through the court. Accesses to the stairwell leading to the roof, the covered portico, and contact with the street through the vestibule were only attainable by passing through the courtyard. Exterior windows were limited to two at the southeast end of the extended assembly hall, which were thought to have been shuttered and possibly covered with glass or gypsum crystal.[121] No windows faced Street 3 or Wall Street. Two interior windows—one in Room 5 (between the assembly hall and the baptistery) and one in the assembly hall—allowed light to be cast from the courtyard. The footprint of the house measures 56.92 feet (17.35 meters) south wall, 57.25 feet (17.45 meters) north wall, 60.96 feet (18.58 meters) west wall, and 66.21 feet (20.18 meters) east wall.[122] Its footprint was 3,619.50 square feet. Geometrically, it was a trapezoid whose only right angle was interior to the residential block at its southeast corner.

In similarity with the synagogue and several polytheistic worship centers, the Christian *domus* was originally a residential structure built over a much smaller and earlier structure that was likely destroyed or in ruins when the residential block was systematically developed.[123] It required several minor modifications to transform it to a religious place.

The dating of the site rests primarily on a single inscription in wet plaster on the west wall of the assembly hall requesting that *Dorotheos* be remembered and giving the date of the year 544 of the Seleucid Era or AD 232–233.[124] It is the only text found on the site dated in the calendar year, and its importance is enhanced by it being etched in the first coat of plaster at a level above the floor that could only be reached from an elevated platform by one performing the work. Carl H. Kraeling, the leading archaeologist on the site in the 1930s and author of the excavation report, deduced that the inscribed plaster was consistent with the original construction of the pre-Christian house, thus dating it to AD 232–233. Though this evidence is tenuous, Kraeling puts the Christian conversion of the building in the mid 240s, between 232 and the city's fall in 256. No matter the efforts to place a date on the Christian *domus,* its lifespan was very short, possibly as little as ten to as much as twenty years, if the calculation based on archaeological evidences is accurate.

The conversion from residence to Christian building meant a shift in spatial perception, and this shift entailed only two minor remodeling efforts. First was the elimination of the south interior wall in the assembly hall that created a long rectangular room of 42.32 feet (12.9 meters) long by 16.9 feet (5.15 meters) wide, enabling room for sixty-five to seventy-five worshippers. Second, the bench seating in the assembly hall was eliminated and the floor level was raised with dirt infill to cover its remains.

A single raised platform or bema was built against and centered on the north wall (south wall of Room 3). It projected just over 3 feet (.97 meters) from the wall and was almost 8 inches (.20 meters) above the floor and was nearly 5 feet (1.47 meters) long. The purpose of the platform is debated, but it is highly likely that religious services were conducted from there. Early Syrian Christian documents mention teachers and missionaries teaching from a chair, and there was room here for one to be used.[125] There is no sign of a chancel screen that typifies later churches after Constantine the Great (AD 313) or a strong sense of hierarchy in elevation; the platform was modest and without ornamentation. Thus, it may have been a place for the teacher's chair taken from the symbolic image of the seated philosopher, the seat of Moses in ancient synagogues, and the episcopal seat of James described in the church at Jerusalem.[126]

The plainness of the assembly hall interior, void of a single touch of color or symbolic imagery, must be held in contrast to a particular room where every square inch of wall and ceiling surfaces was embellished. This room was set aside for the initiatory rites of Christianity, and it held different spatial connotations than what was found in the assembly hall. Unified within the modular *domus*, they stand as separate spaces with different functions and symbolic and visionary meanings.

Plan V, House Plan After Transformation into Christian Building,
Resotration, by Henrty Pearson, in *The Excavations at Dura-Europos*,
Fian Report VIII, Part II, The Christian Building, C.B. Welles, ed.
Courtesy of the Yale University Art Gallery, Dura Europos Archives.

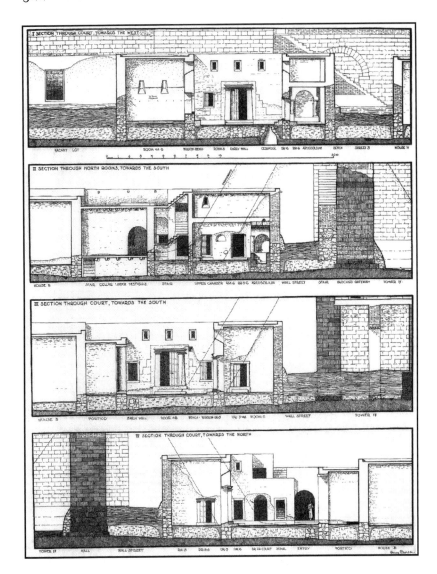

Plan VII, Christian Building, Sectional, Elevations, Restoration, by
Henry Pearson, in *The Excavations at Dura-Europos,* Final Report VIII,
Part II, The Christian Building, C.B. Welles, ed. Courtesy of the Yale
University Gallery, Dura Europos Archives.

The Baptistery

In the northwest corner of the Christian church, and standing adjacent to the assembly hall, was a room designated as the baptistery. It is the only room within this structure that can firmly identify the house as a Christian site. From a cursory perspective, this little Christian community prioritized its initiatory rites. During the house's remodeling, it received a more thorough transformation than any other room and was the most highly decorated. Originally, it could not have been more than an unlit storeroom whose walls were not plastered, and it is poignant that the room with the lowest functional esteem was elevated to the house's highest purpose.

The room was split horizontally into upper and lower stories that correspondingly lowered the ground floor ceiling height. The first floor was reached by an interior staircase behind the north wall of the baptistery. Several flights likely led to an entry landing to the "upper room," and at least one more flight led to the rooftop. The room had collapsed along with the ceiling when defensive preparations were being conducted in 256.

Kraeling made the case that that adjoining rectangular Room 5 worked in conjunction with the baptistery as a chamber for the first introductory procedure of the baptismal ritual.[127] Syrian sources describing the baptismal ritual led Kraeling to assert that Room 5 served (in part) as an *exorcisterium* that entailed the unction of oil being applied to the entire body, and the convert's confession of Christ and turning away from sin.[128] The past was "exorcised," and the anointing of oil was an extension of the Old and New Testament blessing for new life and identity. What was performed physically in Room 5 was carried out symbolically in the waters of the baptismal font.

However, with the economy of space and the periodic nature of the rite, it is doubtful that Room 5 had a single purpose. Kraeling reasoned Room 5 could have seated the women worshippers the way a similar separate space was used in the synagogue.[129] Seating in later basilicas separated women on opposite sides of the center aisle or to the rear of the nave. Ventilation added by the installation of a window would have suited a significant group seated for either worship or community meal purposes, though all of this remains speculative. However, the very ornate moldings around the doorway leading into the baptistery (rather than the nondescript nature of the courtyard entry) clearly make this space one of initiating a procession into a more intimate, sacred space.

The west end of the baptistery was excavated below floor level to reveal the font resting on bedrock. The font basin and canopy was a single brick structure without evidence of a drainage system. The canopy was in the form of a barrel vault, supported by two pilasters against the wall and two free-standing columns made of rubble and plaster. The front and side wall faces were arched, with the front arched face being raised higher than the sides. The walls were plastered, and a low bench was built on the east end of the room. In the far corner, an exterior door gave egress to the courtyard via a low doorstep.

A rectangular niche was installed in the wall between the two (interior and exterior) doors. Surviving fragments indicate that a small table or ledge projected below the niche, positioned slightly offset toward the door leading to Room 5. Holes dug in the floor close by, likely by vandals in search of buried money at the time the house was abandoned in 256, are thought to be the reason for the table's destruction, making it uncertain as to what role it or the niche played in the room. Kraeling thought the surface's purpose coincided with the meaning of the painted scene below the niche and above the table. The scene portrayed David's victory over Goliath. Syrian literary and liturgical sources interpreted this story symbolically as the believer's ability to defeat evil and overcome Satan, a defeat in which the rite of unction normally played a part.[130] Kraeling contends that the table and niche likely held the oil that was dispensed before entering or after exiting the water (we are uncertain about the exact practice from this time). Anointing one after baptism eventually became the liturgical procedure of the Eastern Orthodox Church. It also may have held a lamp for lighting, as the door to the courtyard was barred and the room did not have windows.

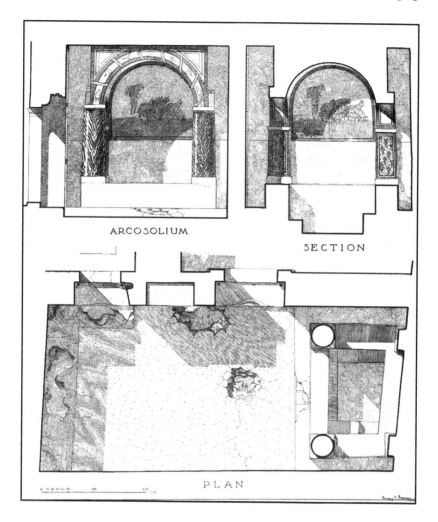

ARCOSOLIUM

SECTION

PLAN

Plan VIII, Christian Building, Baptistery, Plan, and Sectional Elevation, by Henry Pearson, in *The Excavations at Dura-Europos*, Final Report VIII, Part II, The Christian Building, C.B. Welles, ed. Courtesy of the Yale University Art Gallery, Dura Europos Archives.

After the structural modifications, the entire room was decorated with paintings of which fewer than half (eight) remained intact upon modern excavation.[131] On the font, the decorations consisted of geometric designs and plant-leaf motifs. The columns were faux painted to appear as marble stonework. Painted plaster ceiling fragments found during excavation and the remaining portion of the baptismal canopy indicate they were painted with white stars on a dark blue field. The guttering flames of oil lamps must have enhanced the sensation that the baptism was occurring at the dark of night and illumined by celestial light. The decoration and stylization of the canopy and ceiling is similar to the niche found in the *Dura Mithraeum* (a hall-like structure for the worship of the god Mithras) and the Torah Shrine of the later synagogue. This has led some to speculate that some artistic themes spread across religious boundaries within the city.

The biblical paintings must be understood in light of the scriptural material available to this community residing in Mesopotamia. It is not certain that this early third-century *domus* possessed a complete collection of Paul's letters and four separate gospels, or whether their scriptural canon was that of the western Mediterranean church. A critical piece of information assisting this discussion was a discovery of a fragment of the *Diatessaron*, a single gospel narrative or "harmony" formed out of the books Matthew, Mark, Luke, and John. The *Diatessaron* is attributed to Tatian, a second-century Church Father and apologist of Assyrian ancestry who was a pupil of Justin Martyr in Rome. From its compilation in the mid-second century, it became the standard gospel text in Syrian churches until the fifth century, when it was replaced by the four separate gospels. The fragment was found in the defensive fill in Wall Street, north of the city gate. The script (fourteen lines) is of Greek text, and it is assumed that during siege preparations this corner piece was torn from its scroll. It is unknown whether the scroll existed beyond the life and walls of Dura. The fact that it was not found within the *domus* is not surprising, considering the chaotic time of its provenance. The Greek text is comparable to the formal names in the graffiti inscribed on the walls of the building during its Christian period, and together they tell us that the membership of local Christians, or a significant segment of them, had Greek (or adopted Greek) names and were drawn from the Hellenized element of the city's population.[132]

From the time of the baptismal room's excavation to the present, the interpretation and meaning of its artwork (like the artwork in the synagogue) has been the focus of much discussion without an overall consensus. All the pictorial representations are of biblical narrative scenes and were organized in zones with a framework of lines. The font was built on the west wall; its opening was framed above by the canopy, at the sides by the pilasters, and at the bottom by the upper ledge of the basin. Painted inside this frame, the image of the Good Shepherd and His Sheep dominated the focus of the font. In the lower left corner of the Good Shepherd image, a sketch was made of Adam and Eve depicting the Fall in Genesis 3:1–7. The font was highlighted by red banding between black lines. The painted message hovering over the waters of baptism is about the saving nature of the Good Shepherd who gathers his flock and separates them from the original sin of Adam. Again we see the role of water, as in previous chapters, as active participant in deliverance, salvation, and passing over the void. The Christians' eternal hope is manifest in a comprehensible, relational Savior.

The painted images on the north, south, and east walls of the baptistery were organized in two ascending registers. The artist(s) had nearly ten feet of vertical wall space in which to work. The specific narratives and their locations are the following:

Upper Register, North Wall: The Healing of the Paralytic
Upper Register, North Wall: Jesus Walking on the Water
Upper Register, South Wall: Garden Scene or Paradise of the Blessed
Lower Register, South Wall: The Woman at the Well
Lower Register, South Wall: David and Goliath
Lower Register, East and North Walls: The Resurrection Sequence

Other images from the east and north walls have been

identified as a procession of either the Wise or Foolish Virgins or the Women at the Tomb (or the wise virgins carrying lamps to the bridegroom's tent).[133] They portray characters in motion from right to left, toward the font at the end of the room where the Woman at the Well is located.

It is not possible to establish a firm iconographic message in the baptistery room. Clearly, they are New Testament scenes pertaining to concepts of living water and the restoration of creation to new life in Christ through the celebration of death and resurrection through the waters of baptism. Overall, the elements of the room are as much a subject of water, oil, and Christ in the image of a shepherd as it was of people in procession. Perhaps it can be said that the path to Christ is one of men and women moving toward the loving arms of the Shepherd and becoming his lambs, which he carries through this life and into the next.

Also, this Christian community was focused on the oil of ritual unction and the water of baptism, rather than on the Eucharist (Communion).[134] There is not a single image of bread or a cup within the pictorial narrative. For Christianity, this emphasis was radically reversed less than a century later.

Other Texts Mentioning the Early Church

At Dura we see a small Christian community living on the very edge of the eastern Roman trade frontier. It is interesting that the only truly identifiable *domus ecclesia* has not been found in the thriving communities of the early church in Italy, Turkey, or Palestine. This lone example rests not far from the Syrian border with Iraq. There is a good reason for this. In its infancy, the *domus ecclesia* was not considered so much in a structural sense but in communal terms.

> To the church of God in Corinth, to those sanctified in Christ Jesus and called to be his holy people, together with all those everywhere who call on the name of our Lord Jesus Christ—their Lord and ours.
>
> 1 COR. 1:2

Paul, an apostle of Christ Jesus by the will of God,
To God's holy people in Ephesus, the faithful in Christ Jesus.

EPH. 1:1

To the church of the Thessalonians in God the Father and the Lord Jesus
Christ: Grace and peace to you. We always thank God for all of you and
continually mention you in our prayers.

1 THESS. 1:1–2

If we take Paul's introductions in several of his letters as examples, honor was not placed on buildings but on the faith and everyday lives of the believers who gathered together in homes.

Yet in the late third century we have one first-source quotation from a man named Porphyry of Tyre, writing during the years AD 268–270, who tells us Christians were building big even before Constantine:

But the Christians, imitating the construction of temples, erect great
buildings in which they meet to pray, though there is nothing to prevent
them from doing this in their own homes since, of course, their Lord hears
them everywhere.[135]

Porphyry was a pagan scholar, philosopher, and a severe critic of Christianity who wrote publicly, intending to defame the faith. His writings were burned by the church in the fifth century when he was condemned in 448. He noticed, painfully, that Christians were building monumental structures in order to pray, though I am sure other aspects of worship were happening there. It took a pagan to expose the essence of Christian behavior. A militant anti-Christian tells us that a defining characteristic of the early church was that it was on its knees in prayer. You do not need a giant elaborate building for that.

However, Porphyry's hatred became realized when Emperor Diocletian outlawed Christianity, and successive emperors, Galerius and Maximinus Daia, persecuted the church heavily until 312. During this period most of the churches Porphyry wrote of were destroyed, with land and property taken by the government. All this was reversed in the fourth century when the construction of formal basilica-style churches began. This construction rose to a crescendo in the sixth century, when churches in the thousands were built in Palestine, Jordan, Syria, and throughout the Mediterranean world. The magnitude of this era of construction is comparable to that of the earlier classical period in the second century AD; the Romanesque/Gothic periods in Germany, France, and in England throughout the twelfth through fifteenth centuries; during the Victorian period in the nineteenth century; and the post-war boom in the United States and western Europe in the mid-twentieth century.

However, the house presents a problem for historical Christianity. If not for the baptismal room at Dura, there would be nothing else to indicate the building had a Christian identity. A similar situation presents itself in Lullingstone, Kent, Great Britain, where a Roman manor house was discovered with a fresco in the shape of a (post-Constantine) *chi-rho* Christian symbol. Its fragments were found in the collapsed rubble of a ground-floor room thought to have been used as a meeting hall for Christian services. Signs of remodeling indicate an expanding Christian community in existence during the fourth century. A half-subterranean chamber below, where the fresco had fallen, bore signs of pagan imagery and a painted wall niche typical for a shrine. Archaeological dating has pagan rites and Christian worship happening literally one above the other during the fourth century. The house appears to have fallen out of use by the early fifth century, about the time the Romans evacuated Britain to protect Rome from the barbarian invasions. The pieces of the *chi-rho* mosaic were reassembled and can now be seen in the British Museum. Church historians were excited to recognize this as possibly the earliest Christian site known in Britain. However, care must be taken, for as at Dura, if the mosaic had not been found, there would be nothing to indicate the place was used for Christian worship . . . if that was the case at all.

I am a huge fan of ancient churches. I am in the midst of writing a tour book on England's parish churches for the

American tourist. They are masterpieces, little gems built when William the Conqueror invaded England, Richard the Lionheart went on Crusade, William Wallace was irritating King Edward I, and the plague swept over Europe. With a little study you can see the architectural transitions between the Saxon, Norman, and Gothic periods. Don't get me started. While I traveled through Jordan and Syria, I was enthralled by the remains of churches from the fourth through seventh centuries. In all these places I imagined the innumerable generations of believers who passed through the spaces where I stood, praying similar prayers as I prayed during uncertain times. I will likely study them for the remainder of my days.

Yet the New Testament church was primarily concerned with a heavenly dwelling. The following passages indicate the Christian vision of earthly and heavenly permanence.

> *My Father's house has many rooms; if that were not so, would I have told you that I am going there to prepare a place for you?*
>
> JOHN 14:2

> *For we know that if the earthly tent we live in is destroyed, we have a building from God, an eternal house in heaven, not built by human hands. Meanwhile we groan, longing to be clothed instead with our heavenly dwelling.*
>
> 2 COR. 5:1–2

> *And God raised us up with Christ and seated us with him in the heavenly realms in Christ Jesus.*
>
> EPH. 2:6

> *But our citizenship is in heaven. And we eagerly await a Savior from there, the Lord Jesus Christ, who, by the power that enables him to bring everything under his control, will transform our lowly bodies so that they will be like his glorious body.*
>
> PHIL. 3:20–21

In respect to the historical timeline, the *domus ecclesia* had a relatively short shelf life during the early Christian period (though it has been in various stages of revival in the United States since the late-twentieth century). With the exception of those located in very wealthy estates, by their nature home churches were not built to last many generations. They were rebuilt many times or destroyed completely as invaders repeatedly swept through like sea tides over a shore. And perhaps this best exemplifies the end game foreseen by the early church. They saw their existence on earth as for a breath of time.

After Constantine we see a change in this paradigm. The church morphed into a government. It correspondingly reoriented its architectural energy toward establishing a kingdom on earth until Christ returned and elevated it to its full glory. The remnants of its great fourth- through seventh-century monuments, the fragments of its ecclesiastical structures, remain in part to be categorized and admired along with pagan monuments.

However, the promises in the above verses do not envision a refined earthly home. The purpose was not to sink deep roots into the world's social systems but to draw people out of it. Symbolically, except for the lone example at Dura, the ancient *domos ecclesias* have vanished along with the believers who filled their rooms. They believed their destiny lay in the heavenly realm. And it is in heaven that we see a city, or a building that is a city. It is toward that we now turn.

Devotional Questions

1. What was the first type of church building?

2. Why do you think Jesus spoke of his church but not the church building? Isn't this odd coming from a builder?

3. Since God gave his servants specific instructions in how to build seemingly everything but a church building, what does this mean for the church? What opportunities does this give for churches to explore architectural exploration and creativity?

4. What is the most effective church building you've experienced during worship? What made it so effective?

5. Where is Dura Europos? Why is this ancient place important to us?

6. What type of church was there at Dura? What room was the most decorated and why? What priority did they place on the ritual that happened there?

7. From what we see of this little church, is there anything about it that appeals to you? Look at its floor plan and list and describe each room. What is Christian sacred space in its refined state?

8. Who destroyed Dura Europos? What kept the house church and other buildings from being destroyed completely?

9. Why are house churches so rare in archaeology?

10. How does the Dura house church relate to the churches we attend today?

CHAPTER 16

UNDER CONSTRUCTION
The City of Heaven

THERE IS A CITY with which we have no physical handholds to fully grasp its magnitude.[136] This city spoken of throughout Scripture and religious contexts is referred to properly and figuratively as the Holy City (Rev. 21:2), New (heavenly) Jerusalem (Heb. 12:22; Rev. 3:12; 21:2), celestial city, Mount Zion (Isa. 30:19; Heb. 12:22; Rev. 14:1), City of God (Heb. 12:22; St. Augustine, *The City of God*), and tabernacle (Heb. 8:5; 9:11; Rev. 15:5). The Greek word used in the earliest texts for "new" is *kainos,* meaning something renewed or refreshed. This is different from the Greek word *neos,* meaning something entirely new. Here we can connect our previous discussions of the term "redeemed" and Christ's work as *Redemptor* with this sense of "new" for the heavenly city. This may hint that what we have coming down from heaven is something with which we can make associations. The city is not totally alien to our perceptions; our minds will understand and be oriented to its geometric shapes, lines, and spaces. It is something we can only imagine.

With the information we have, there is really nothing to which we can compare this place, or if we do, we will likely be very surprised when we actually see it. The apostle John could only associate its characteristics with precious stones and metals and a psychological assessment that it will be void of pain and suffering. Please, sign me up now.

The City of Heaven's gates, foundations, tree of life, and river flowing through it are somehow integrated into its architecture, which is an immense cube. It appears astonishingly beautiful, beyond comprehension yet enigmatic in its specifics. Perhaps this is as it should be. I have enough on my plate understanding the basic functions of my laptop computer. What I will attempt here is to present what John wrote and make associations with our previous chapters.

Debate over whether its description in Revelation 21 is literal or figurative, occurring in the future or happening now, has become a literary fulcrum separating faiths, denominations, and splinter cults. The variances are so many that I will not begin to discuss them, as this will not be fruitful, and honestly, I just would rather not. Very generally, one side sees this city as a figurative representation of a heavenly reality and not an actual city with walls and so on. To those of this persuasion it is more of a spiritual restoration, a divine renewal of life that could very well be happening presently on earth, or has the potential to do so here as much as it could happen in heaven. As for me, and as I stated in the introduction, I believe the place to be real with specifics yet to be determined. The reality of it is beyond what feeble theorists have envisioned. I think we can safely take John's description and magnify it to the point where we will need new minds to comprehend it fully.

The side to which I have aligned myself takes the New Jerusalem event to be a logical progression that leads to the end of the biblical timeline. This new period or dispensation occurs after the end-times events: the final judgment of sin and the creation of a second heaven and earth where this "new" Jerusalem is the location where believers will live for eternity.

Presently, mainstream theology has Christians existing in a dual citizenship—as members of the church on earth and simultaneously as citizens in heaven. Their hope for a final reconciliation is secure. New Testament verses from Ephesians, Philippians, and 2 Peter speak to this.

> But our citizenship is in heaven. And we eagerly await a Savior from there, the Lord Jesus Christ, who, by the power that enables him to bring everything under his control, will transform our lowly bodies so that they will be like his glorious body.
>
> PHIL. 3:20–21

And God raised us up with Christ and seated us with him in the heavenly realms in Christ Jesus, in order that in the coming ages he might show the incomparable riches of his grace, expressed in his kindness to us in Christ Jesus.

EPH. 2:6–7

But in keeping with his promise we are looking forward to a new heaven and a new earth, where righteousness dwells.

2 PETER 3:13

Jesus' words directly imply a heavenly home. Shortly before Jesus' death on the cross, he spoke of a heavenly place to which he was going to prepare for his disciples:

"Do not let your hearts be troubled. You believe in God; believe also in me. My Father's house has many rooms; if that were not so, would I have told you that I am going there to prepare a place for you? And if I go and prepare a place for you, I will come back and take you to be with me that you also may be where I am.

JOHN 14:1–3

One of the great philosophical questions humanity has explored over the millennia has been: "Is this all there is in life?" A beer commercial (it seems the great philosophers of our modern era are writing beer commercials) I recall from the late 1980s proclaimed, "You only go around once in life, so you've got to grab all the gusto you can." And I think this may reflect the impulse we have either to embrace the promise of life after death or to not go there and focus on eating, drinking and being merry, for tomorrow we die.

The book of Ecclesiastes preaches the futility of pursuing the things of the world for the sake of those things. At the end of the day . . . is the end of the day. As with the temple in chapter 13, stuff wears out and so do we. An older cousin of mine recently mentioned to me that someone he knew would needle his simplistic lifestyle by occasionally informing him that her house and property were now worth five million dollars. Now that she has passed on, what is its value to her now? Is she in a place where dollars are converted into eternal perks? The house (and the stuff within it) still rests on its land, so I assume she did not take it with her. The irony is we will be buried under what we once strived to attain, under the things that had propped up our self-esteem. From a materialistic standpoint, burial is the ultimate statement that a material culture has kicked our butts.

But, do we lose in the end? What we see in the vision of the City of God is that this present life is a mere blip on our eternal timelines. Our sense of time is chopped up into years, months, days, hours, and minutes; yet in the context of heaven, the segmenting of time is irrelevant. Eternity does not come in bits and pieces but endlessly flows. John's point in writing about the city of New Jerusalem is to let us know that because of forgiveness in the sanctifying blood of the Lamb, the grave does not beat us. The striving for things of this earth is a temporary condition for an eternity coming—or I should say descending, from the heavens.

Jesus wanted his disciples to know at their darkest hour that there is a home after this life is over. Since I first worked in the trades, I have always loved the verses from John 14. What is amazing is Jesus spoke of a house with actual rooms in the heavenly realm. It is just like God to not make our adjustment to heaven difficult or weird. I know Hollywood is not at work here. It seems as though we will be able to slip in and carry on after we pass on. Rooms and a house—you've got to love it. And the best part is we will not need a GPS and a map to find it. Jesus will introduce us to our new home!

Beyond the Holy City there is nothing more in the works (that we know of anyway)—nothing more to design, no instruction to transmit to a chosen people.

The long stretches of Scripture I will quote cannot be summed up or paraphrased somehow. The descriptions are too amazing. I can visualize the apostle John being in the Spirit yet struggling with his first-century vocabulary to relate to other first-century folks the things he saw.

Then I saw "a new heaven and a new earth," for the first heaven and the first earth had passed away, and there was no longer any sea. I saw the Holy City, the new Jerusalem, coming down out of heaven from God, prepared as a bride beautifully dressed for her husband. And I heard a loud voice from the throne saying, "Look! God's dwelling place is now among the people, and he will dwell with them. They will be his people, and God himself will be with them and be their God. 'He will wipe every tear from their eyes. There will be no more death' or mourning or crying or pain, for the old order of things has passed away."

He who was seated on the throne said, "I am making everything new!"

REV. 21:1–5

In the introduction I mentioned that one of the attributes of God is that he is a God who builds. I heard an architect interviewed on the Charlie Rose television program who stated essentially what the Roman architect Vitruvius wrote a generation before Jesus in his treatise *On Architecture*. He stressed that the architect should know how to build as much as he or she knows how to design and draw. Architects must understand the demands they are putting on the builders as much as they understand the materials' limits and capacities. They must be versed in the arts and sciences, possessing a broad body of knowledge, which is critical in the mental process of bringing forth a solid form from the imagination. From the ancient to the medieval periods, the master builder was responsible for design and overall fabrication. He possessed a dual gifting of vision and ability. I see God as the ultimate, perfect fulfillment of the Master Builder. "I am making everything new!" are the joyful words of a builder in his rhythm on a wonderful job on the eighth fairway on the Pebble Beach Golf Course with no strange, tormented supervisors to torment him.

The fallen city of Lachish, destroyed by the Assyrians and Babylonians, is an anti-metaphor for the City of Heaven. There will be no more death, crying, or pain. No armies with sharp pointy things surrounding the walls of our lives, building siege ramps to get close enough to relentlessly pry away the stone barriers that protect our most intimate selves. There will be no more nightmares of tearing appliances out of our kitchens and throwing them out our windows on the heads of the killers on scaling ladders propped against the walls protecting our very souls. We will never be led away to captivity by the psychosis of our subconscious minds or hear the tortured screams of victims we cannot save, who hang impaled on sharpened poles or are flayed alive outside the range of our medicating slings and arrows. What a relief to not have to be wary, to not have to screen our phone calls, no one looking for a way in to scan our electronic information, no identity theft.

We turn to the Lord's final building project—at least what we know of. The apostle John describes this new city:

> And he carried me away in the Spirit to a mountain great and high, and showed me the Holy City, Jerusalem, coming down out of heaven from God. It shone with the glory of God, and its brilliance was like that of a very precious jewel, like a jasper, clear as crystal. It had a great, high wall with twelve gates, and with twelve angels at the gates. On the gates were written the names of the twelve tribes of Israel. There were three gates on the east, three on the north, three on the south and three on the west. The wall of the city had twelve foundations, and on them were the names of the twelve apostles of the Lamb.
>
> The angel who talked with me had a measuring rod of gold to measure the city, its gates and its walls. The city was laid out like a square, as long as it was wide. He measured the city with the rod and found it to be 12,000 stadia in length, and as wide and high as it is long. The angel measured the wall using human measurement, and it was 144 cubits thick. The wall was made of jasper, and the city of pure gold, as pure as glass. The foundations of the city walls were decorated with every kind of precious stone. . . . The twelve gates were twelve pearls, each gate made of a single pearl. The great street of the city was of gold, as pure as transparent glass. I did not see a temple in the city, because the Lord God Almighty and the Lamb are its temple. The city does not need the sun or the moon to shine on it, for the glory of God gives it light, and the Lamb is its lamp. . . . On no day will its gates ever be shut, for there will be no night there. . . . Nothing impure will ever enter it, nor will anyone who does what is shameful or deceitful, but only those whose names are written in the

Lamb's book of life. . . .
Then the angel showed me the river of the water of life, as clear as crystal,
flowing from the throne of God and of the Lamb down the middle of
the great street of the city. On each side of the river stood the tree of life,
bearing twelve crops of fruit, yielding its fruit every month. And the leaves
of the tree are for the healing of the nations. No longer will there be any
curse.

REV. 21:10–19, 21–23, 25, 27; 22:1–3

After reading and thinking about this description of the New Jerusalem, I can only say that the Lord loves hand tools. I think he took care to have it precisely measured by a carpenter's rule and have the numbers relayed to us. This is to let the builders, masons, and woodworkers among us know that when we actually see this place, we will be able to make associations with what we have built on earth. The angle cuts will be well joined, corners set square, its lines running true and symmetrical to the eye. Vitruvius would find geometric symmetry in its features.

Structural measurements in the Scriptures remind me of the figures the Lord gave Noah to build the ark, Joshua the tabernacle, and David and Solomon the temple in Jerusalem. God is concerned about dimension, and with him construction is not random. His numerics are rhythmic in sets of twelve imbued within a perfect square and three-dimensional cube. The square of 12 (representing Israel's tribes, the apostles, and layers of foundations or foundation stones) is 144, which is the thickness of the city's wall in cubits. The Golden Mean of dimension that was used in the fabrication of the ark of the covenant is used in the overall design and specific assembly of the City of Heaven. The numbers here are symbolic and carry deep meaning.

If the Holy City is a 1,400-mile cubed cube suspended in space over a cleansed earth, the cube would have about half the volume of the moon, and its footprint would cover more than the twenty-five states of the European Union, 79 percent of the area of the Middle East, and about two-thirds the size of Australia. If resting on the earth, the ceiling of the cube would extend into the exosphere. Someone took time out of their lives to estimate that the volume of the city divided by the approximate number of monotheists since Abraham would give one individual about a cubic mile of personal space. For some people I know, this is not enough. But at least, there will be no rubbing shoulders there, like sitting in coach seating on a nonstop flight from San Francisco to London. If you get there and only see Aunt Sue, then enjoy the space!

The uniformity of the city's geometry presents a nonhierarchical space. No one will be working to attain the corner office or the penthouse floor. There is no tipping for a room upgrade. Only the Lamb of God is adored everywhere, all the time, and what a relief to have selfish selfhood dispensed with. No idiots demanding constant attention. Worship is spontaneous and seemingly building-free. And I suppose this would be the ultimate aim of architecture: to create something so vastly magnificent that its function perfectly melds with its aesthetics, thereby transcending its form.

We can see the city as a fulfillment in a progression of the tabernacle and temple types. The perfect sacrifice of Christ has made the veil separating the inner tabernacle and Holy of Holies obsolete. There is no need to stack stones for an altar, no fire to light the kindling, no sacrificial animal standing off to the side, no mercy seat (atonement cover on the ark), and no light stand, for light is everywhere. I don't read of curtains or veils anywhere.

The place is reminiscent of the garden of Eden: a flowing river and a tree standing at its center. This may also speak to the human phenomenon of constructing paradise gardens, particularly in the ancient Near East, Babylon, and later in Moorish Spain and England. We see a consistency in linear movements of water, planting areas geometrically subdivided by trees, and spans of water enclosed within walls with gates. For the intrepid gardener, perhaps there is an inherent motivation to construct a personal heavenly garden allowing one a temporary relief from a world gone mad. Like the builder, the gardener will find natural associations with this natural setting. I now know where my wife, Cathy, will be spending much of her endless time.

From the wonders of the natural world, we see the Lord's

infinity in conceptual, material, and decorative design imbued within the elements of the city. His color palette is beyond description, and I think John struggles with it here. The best he can do is to compare it to precious elements: gold, silver, pearl, jasper. As far as night and day is concerned, it looks as though the whole planetary system is either not there anymore or completely redone, but in either case, we will not have to hunt for a light switch. The place is continuously self-lit. John attributes it to the glory of the Lamb of God.

If you are looking for the Architect and Builder of the ultimate green environment, you can start here. The river and tree of life speak of eternal continuance, sustenance, and a complete reset of the garden of Eden error. With all the craziness in the world (can you say nuclear?), musing on New Jerusalem brings a lot of peace. I think I will pause here for a while and be refreshed before starting the last chapter.

Devotional Questions

1. What is your vision of the City of Heaven? What do you imagine it being like? Do you believe it's a real place?

2. How does the apostle John describe it? Are there any rocks there? How is it lit? How is it founded? What role does water play?

3. How many colors does John mention? What impression of it does this give you?

4. Does John mention its measurements? Are the symmetrical? What other object we have discussed is also symmetrical?

5. What building forms and images from the Bible exist in the City of Heaven?

6. How is the City of Heaven like Eden? What kind of life awaits us there?

CHAPTER 17

SAWDUST
Last Words from the Job Site

THE LAST WORDS of this book are aimed to sort through the threads—the warp and weft[137] stretched across the biblical loom—to identify a coherent pattern from the last sixteen chapters. As the shuttle works under and over the scriptural narratives pertaining to sacred space, the pattern it weaves is a tapestry of the "home." I would have thought a temple or a massive basilica church would be dominant. Over the centuries, Christianity has focused great wealth on embellishing our churches. Yet what we see emerging from the pattern of threads is the humble home. The image is not forced from the text; it emerges subtly from what seems an integration of random thread colors. It is simply, irrepressibly, there.

Now that I am in my fifties, I find myself extremely reminiscent of the past; home pulls at my heartstrings. God established the home as a familial-societal core and devised the geometry from which it was to be built. Jesus of Nazareth completed the proverbial circle by building homes with his physical hands before his followers began to gather within them to worship him. He also made a huge effort, as shown particularly in the gospel of Luke, to meet and dine with people in the sanctum of their dining rooms and reception halls.

One of my favorite books from childhood is *The Wind in the Willows* by Kenneth Grahame. I reread it the other week, and a few sections struck me as appropriate in helping to summarize some last words.

The weary Mole also was glad to turn in without delay, and soon had his head on his pillow, in great joy and contentment. But ere he closed his eyes he let them wander round his old room, mellow in the glow of the firelight that played or rested on familiar and friendly things which had long been unconsciously a part of him, and now smilingly received him back, without rancor . . . but clearly too, how much it all meant to him, and the special value of some such anchorage in one's existence. He did not at all want to abandon the new life and its splendid spaces, to turn his back on sun and air and all they offered him and creep home and stay there; the upper world was all too strong, it called to him still, even down there, and he knew he must return to the larger stage. But it was good to think he had this to come back to, this place which was all his own, these things which were so glad to see him again and could always be counted upon for the same simple welcome.[138]

Little Mole understood that no matter how strongly the enticements of the world pull on one's heart, it is the enclosure of the home that founds one's life. To be anchored is to be placed, and this strength enables one to operate in the world. I am reminded of the tent stake in the hands of Jael and those that held up the fabric walls of the tabernacle. We know we must go back out to pursue our work and chase our dreams (have our time in the sun), but we have the home in which to gather and strengthen our resolve, to be ourselves. The closet where we are told to go to pray is there. As Mole relates, the home interacts with how the firelight illumines the things that make up who we are, the assemblage of our identities.

My mother is now in her eighties; her husband went to be with the Lord in 1996, and she is still in the home that she shared with my dad for nearly twenty years. She is managing it very well. The dogwoods my dad planted are now massive with thick trunks, and in the springtime they flower with unbelievable pageantry. A dogwood tree that did not bloom in his lifetime is doing so now—a delayed horticultural blessing for my mother, a flowering, communicating extension of my dad's love. My dad's old work boots, worn and dusty with time, rest under the sitting bench by the front door where he last pulled them from his feet. I gave them to him in 1977 after I came back from Israel, the summer I worked on Tel Lachish. Homes are more than a functional necessity; they become the accumulation of memories and physical memorabilia. They, in a way, become breathing entities. Designing and building a home is a natal event.

The image of the home is ever present in Scripture. In previous chapters I referred to the home in terms of tents of habitation: the Tent of Meeting; the tabernacle and temple (literally, the Mountain of the House); Jesus, the *tekton* home builder; and the house church of Dura Europos. The last image in the book of Revelation is of an immense house, or equally, a city of rooms.

I made a simple search for *house* in the Bible Lexicon and was surprised at the number of entries throughout the Old and New Testaments (971 times in 865 verses in the New International Version). *House* most commonly refers to a literal home, a family household (its affairs) and dwelling; a family of descendents (Aaron, Levi, Abraham, David) in a tribal sense as well as a nation or kingdom (Israel, Egypt); *sheol*, the house of the underworld; and in figurative/metaphorical terms for the body and receptacle.

Ecclesiastes uses *house* in poetic imagery to describe the vessel of the human mind and how its "keepers" tremble in old age:

> *Remember your Creator*
> *in the days of your youth*
> *before the days of trouble come*
> *and the years approach when you will say,*
> *"I find no pleasure in them"* . . .
> *when the keepers of the house tremble,*
> *and the strong men stoop.*

Eccles. 12:1–3

Proverbs uses *house* in parallel terms between one's life and the wisdom in which it was constructed:

> *By wisdom a house is built,*
> *and through understanding it is established;*
> *through knowledge its rooms are filled*

with rare and beautiful treasures.

PROV. 24:3–4

And Solomon likely penned this wisdom statement as he lived in the daily reality of several thousand wives and concubines:

Better to live on a corner of the roof
than share a house with a quarrelsome wife."

PROV. 21:9

It would also make little Mole happy to know that Jesus spoke of the house as the shelter of animals, a shelter he lacked. Jesus never sought to build himself a mansion in Nazareth, Capernaum, or Jerusalem, to settle down, sit on the porch—as the pioneer Daniel Boone did at the end of his days—and watch life go by: "Foxes have dens and birds have nests, but the Son of Man has no place to lay his head" (Matt. 8:20).

I thought that since Jesus used the metaphor of animal architecture to express his lack of earthly home, I would finish by presenting several verses along similar lines.

A Return to the Beginning: Making Connections

The prophet Isaiah tells us that animal habitation is part of judgment on the nations who oppose Israel and seek its destruction:

The desert owl and screech owl will possess it;
the great owl and the raven will nest there.
God will stretch out over Edom
the measuring line of chaos
and the plumb line of desolation.
Her nobles will have nothing there to be called a kingdom,
all her princes will vanish away.
Thorns will overrun her citadels,
nettles and brambles her strongholds.

She will become a haunt for jackals,
a home for owls.
Desert creatures will meet with hyenas,
and wild goats will bleat to each other;
there the night creatures will also lie down
and find for themselves places of rest.
The owl will nest there and lay eggs,
she will hatch them, and care for her young
under the shadow of her wings;
there also the falcons will gather,
each with its mate.

ISA. 34:11–15, EMPHASIS ADDED

The inclination for animals to adopt abandoned human architecture by divine mandate is fascinating. However, I find this passage sobering. Again, I pause in my line of thought to reflect on construction metaphor, "the measuring line of chaos and the plumb line of desolation." Ouch. The same tools God uses to create (Job 38:5) he likewise applies, in equal effectiveness, toward destruction. I imagine the ancient Assyrians and Babylonians storming Lachish.

From a naturalist's perspective, I like the idea of animals inhabiting a place made desolate by a God-versus-human societal encounter. God likes to keep the ball rolling and inserts the rhythm of the natural world when humanity morally falters and abdicates its place on a landscape. Yet we see an affirmation of the transference between animal and human architectures. We adopt our architectural principles from nature's examples, and when we abandon our spaces, the animals move in and assume residence. We understand how they might feel at home within them.

Some months ago I looked out of the window next to my desk, and I saw a small bird perched on a branch with root webbing in its beak. It quickly flitted off to work on its nest. Another bird had made her nest in one of the planters on our deck and sat for several weeks on her eggs. The chick hatched and developed its wings and feathers. Several weeks later I opened the curtains and saw our chick sitting on the leaves of an iris. The next day it left with its mother. Presently, we believe the mother and her young fledgling visit our deck and feed on the fallen seed from our birdfeeder. Their nest is abandoned—it was only a temporary but critical necessity to the pattern of life. Nature continues, with an invariable cadence.

I cannot help but relate the Dura Europos church baptismal room and its connecting rooms to our little bird's nest. Deep within the chambers of thick brick walls and central court, a person entered new life, emerging from the baptismal font wet from its waters. They were anointed with oil in the rite of unction. Slowly, through instruction and council, the wing structures of their faith were developed and they became self-sufficient outside the spiritual nest. The pull to go out into the commercial world was irresistible and necessary, yet the Christian *domus* would remain as a place of spiritual refuge.

Jesus of Nazareth spent most of his adult life before his ministry years building places very similar to the Dura house church. The majority of residential homes in Palestine and the Middle East were stone and/or mud brick buildings surrounded by a wall, their inner courts sometimes containing a well. The buildings consisted of a residence for the family, housing and open pens for animals, and storage for grain. These were places of walled refuge and self-sustainability, an enclosed composite of nature and human habitation, perhaps an ark fixed on the landscape.

We search for the first church prototype and we find the Savior building it long before generations of his little lambs worshipped him in similar structures. Jesus' last words indicate he is building still. I visualize him at this very moment running string lines for a section of wall on the New Jerusalem or perhaps on another structure in the vastness of heaven we are not yet aware of. I cannot imagine him ever dropping his tool bags.

APPENDIX

HOW I CAME TO WRITE THIS BOOK

THE TOPIC OF GOD as architect and builder has come to me because of how my adult life has proceeded within the fields of carpentry and academia. It is inspired by my autobiography and a search for identity in the Scriptures that I have known since childhood. I did not intentionally (with forethought and purpose) chart this dual course between the two widely disparate worlds of carpentry and academia. Believe me, having a prearranged schedule for what I wanted to do with my life would have saved me from a lot of stress. I have been more than a little envious of those I have known who have organized their lives by knowing what they wanted to become, and then set about doing it. My daughter, Jennifer, knew she wanted to be a teacher when she was ten years old while in fourth grade. I was wistfully envious.

Unfortunately, at the end of my undergraduate college years I did not know what I wanted to do with my life, and after I tried and failed at a number of things, the strong gravitational force of unemployment, marriage, two babies, and a mid-1980s building boom pulled me into the high-end residential construction industry. I became an apprentice carpenter on the central coast of California. My parents, who funded most of my college education, had higher professional hopes and were not pleased that I had become a blue-collar worker. Now that I have the wisdom of years behind me, I must not blame them for this. However, their feelings introduced me to a strange deprecating class bias toward those in the building trades that I had not previously known.

In particular, I found the commonly spoken phrase "thinking with one's hands instead of one's brain" an unbelievably ignorant statement. In this business, if the brain is disconnected from the hands, get ready for blood and missing fingers. I found the progression of fabricating an object in the mind, then forming it with the hands and body, an extremely complicated task requiring great concentration, hand-eye coordination, and thinking in series of processes. Over the years I found that as the body's kinetic memory stores each construction event, the tasks gradually become more intuitive. Yet different contexts required adjustments in technique, creative problem solving, and awareness in how change may affect the overall structure. Thus, a single construction task is not performed in isolation but is fluid with the whole. The end must be known and every cut, nail, attachment, and bond is performed in order to accomplish this end. Carpentry might be considered visionary as a dual physical and mental discipline. If, for some reason, none of this makes sense or does not apply to how you build, make sure you have some sort of demolition tool nearby. And if you need one, you can borrow one from me.

The issue of class takes me back to my early school days when the teacher asked what your daddy did for a living. I grew up in Menlo Park, close to Stanford University, and it was fun to hear from a third-grade friend that his dad was one of those building Stanford's Linear Accelerator, or about the father of a buddy in fourth grade who was a gynecologist. It was extremely interesting, albeit somewhat life-changing, when this buddy occasionally explained the responsibilities of this job in the language of a nine-year-old. All I knew was that his family was the first to get a color television and got to swim and play tennis at a place called a country club. He grew up to be a neurologist. My dad was a flight engineer for Pan American Airlines (a really prestigious job back in the 1960s and early '70s). Happily, I got to explain the places he went, to the astonishment to those in my classes.

I was and still am sensitive to working-class bias. Personally, I wish I could happily float over and be unaffected by this issue. After all, "the Lord heals all wounds," doesn't he? (All those carrying a measure of bitterness may now raise your hands.) Yet, this working-class business was dumped on my doorstep with some regularity, and since I'm the one at the keyboard, I think now is a good time to expose it.

I can't help but think that those who deprecate others' professions are insecure in theirs. I enjoyed what I did—the sportslike challenges, the teamwork and physicality, and the fulfillment of seeing physical progress at the end of the day were very rewarding. The wonderful, strange, and unique personalities I have worked with over the years could inspire a Tolstoy-sized epic. Knowing those people was, in itself, worth having the career. To relegate them to a lesser status is to discredit their personhood and says something about those who do so.

The issue of professional prestige was sometimes present on Sunday mornings at church. Occasionally, introduction time in men's groups became something of an anthropological study involving a newly assembled group of great apes and chimps determining their hierarchical place by loud grunts and chest thumping. I often mused on what it would be like to have Jane Goodall act as group leader.[139]

During one of these Sunday school hours, we were sitting in a communal circle reciting our professions one by one before beginning our biblical study on Christian manhood. "I'm a doctor." "I'm a captain in the US Navy researching the infrared tracking systems in ship-to-air missiles during inclement weather." "I own an investment company." Suddenly, I felt this unusual feeling of freedom rush over me, as if I were running like Julie Andrews[140] over an alpine meadow grasping some sort of banner over my head proclaiming, "Free the Carpenters!" (None of this is actually possible; I have tendonitis so that I can't run, and grass allergies so that I can't breathe—but let's not destroy the fantasy.) I decided to be whatever I wanted to be, so when it came to my turn, a state of euphoria swept over me as I said, "Hi, I'm Charlie March and I am a poet and dreamer of dreams and visions!"

The Miracle Part

In 2000, after the answers of many prayers, Cathy and I

moved from where our children, Jennifer and Ben, grew up on the central coast of California to attend Fuller Theological Seminary to pursue a master's degree in biblical studies. It began the fulfillment of a dream I had nurtured since I started teaching the Bible at our church in Carmel Valley in the early 1990s. A job was seemingly waiting for me at Fuller's maintenance department, as an employee named Richard DeMeyere, with similar construction experience, had just given notice.

Cathy and I were not sure how we would pay for my expenses and tuition. We had moved in faith, knowing that the Lord would find a way. I remember the two of us loading the storage room we had rented in Pasadena on a hot September day (thanks for helping, Mason!) with the things of our former life (putting them to rest for who knew how long) without knowing how we were to support ourselves, much less pay for school. I had listened to sermons and taught lessons for years on trusting God when there were no handholds to grasp and no immediate solutions to immediate issues, knowing God would bless those who moved in faith. And we were literally . . . moving.

During my employment interview we were informed that Fuller had full "tuition remission" (free tuition) for night classes for fulltime employees (now no longer available). The way was set: I would work four ten-hour days while taking night classes and have a three-day weekend to read and write. Cathy and I simultaneously turned toward each other as we walked from the interview and smiled and commented that we were flowing in the deep water of God's river. Abundance was added when Cathy found work at Fuller's School of Psychology as their clinical coordinator. After three years of forty-hour work weeks and year-round night classes, I (we) graduated with a master's in biblical studies.

While at Fuller Seminary I made contact with Professor Richard Alston who was, at that time, head of Classics at the University of London, Royal Holloway. I had sent out a brief synopsis of my professional and academic life and further interest in a degree in archaeology to universities throughout England. I felt that it would aid my academic employment prospects if I could attain another degree in a field connected to my interest in early Christianity. Going to school in the UK would give me a better international perspective on life elsewhere and firsthand reality of what a foreign student faced. The Classics Department secretary Margaret Scrivner (a wonderful woman whom I would share tea with over the next three years and who would counsel me through the PhD process) read my e-mail and forwarded it to Professor Alston. He responded by saying he had a project in mind and in particular was interested in my perspective as a builder paired with my Christian studies background. As he explained the parameters of the project, I immediately became drawn to its possibilities, as its goals were to discuss the architectural transition between the pagan and Christian periods during the end of the Roman Empire. I was to observe this change within two cities in the Middle East: the first within a city in the Decapolis region of modern Jordan called Gerasa (modern Jerash), and a city called Dura Europos in eastern Syria that had been a Roman trade hub and the modern archaeological site of the earliest excavated Christian church. This was a flat-out miracle. Of all things, it was my construction background that gave me access to the highest pursuit in academia. God loves good irony.

After nearly four years of research and trips traveling the length and breadth of Jordan and Syria, I completed my PhD in classics/archaeology. My PhD thesis is published by Archaeopress in the British Archaeological Reports (Oxford), and I have read papers at conferences at the Institute of Classical Studies, London, and the ARAM Society at Oxford University. I opened a publishing company, March Winds Publishers, Inc. to put my writings in print. The current of God's river relentlessly sweeps us forward, yet we must, in faith, paddle diligently to remain midstream.

BIBLIOGRAPHY

BIBLICAL TEXTS

Holy Bible, New International Version. Colorado Springs, CO: Biblica, 1973, 1978, 1984, 2011.

Holy Bible, New King James Version. Nashville, TN: Thomas Nelson, 1982.

Tanakh, Philadelphia: Jewish Publication Society, 1999.

PRIMARY SOURCES

Ammianus Marcellinus, *History,* trans. John C. Rolfe. Cambridge, MA: Loeb Classical Library, Vol. I, (1935), Vol. II, (1940), Vol. III, (1939).

Diodorus Siculus, *Historical Library.*

The Octavius of Marcus Minucius Felix, trans. G.W. Clarke. New York: Newman Press, 1974.

Heraclitus, *Fragments: The Collected Wisdom of Heraclitus,* trans. Brooks Haxton. New York: Penguin, 2001.

Herodotus, *The Histories.*

Philo of Alexandria, *On the Creation of the Cosmos According to Moses,* trans. David T. Runia. Leiden, The Nethlands: Brill, 2001.

The Works of Philo, trans. D. D. Yonge. Peabody, MA: Hendrickson, 1993.

Plato, *Timaeus,* trans. R. G. Bury. Cambridge, MA: Loeb Classical Library, 1929.

Porphyry's Against the Christians: The Literary Remains, trans. R. Joseph Hoffmann. New York: Promethius, 1994.

Proclus's Commentary on Plato's Parmenides, 947, trans. Glenn R. Morrow and John M. Dillon. Princeton: Princeton University Press, 1987.

Sextus Empiricus, *Against the Physicists, Against the Ethicists,* trans. R. G. Bury. Cambridge, MA: Loeb Classical Library, 1936.

Strabo, *Geographies.*

Tertullian, *De Spectaculis,* trans. Jeffrey Henderson. Cambridge, MA: Loeb Classical Library, 1931.

Vitruvius, *On Architecture: Books I–V and Books VI–X,* trans. Frank Granger. Cambridge, MA: Loeb Classical Library, (1931), and (1934).

Secondary Sources

Alexander, Christopher, *The Nature of Order, An Essay on the Art of Building and The Nature of the Universe, The Phenomenon of Life*, Book 1. Berkeley. CA: The Center for Environmental Structure, 2002.

Allara, Anny, "Les Maisons De Doura-Europos: Questions De Typologie," *Syria*, LXII, 1986, 39–60.

Berleant, Arnold, *The Aesthetics of Environment.* Philadelphia: Temple University Press, 1992.

Bloomer, Kent C. and Charles W. Moore, *Body, Memory, and Architecture.* New Haven: Yale University Press, 1977.

Bradshaw, Paul F., *The Search for the Origins of Christian Worship: Sources and Methods for the Study of Early Liturgy*, 2nd edition. Oxford: Oxford University Press, 2002.

Carlson, Karen M. "Why is His Only Word "No!?" Questions About Kids Series, *CEED*. Minneapolis: University of Minnesota, 2001.

Chadwick, H., *The Early Church.* New York: Penguin, 1967.

Cloud, Dr. Henry and Townsend, Dr. John, *Boundaries.* Grand Rapids, MI: Zondervan, 1992.

******* *Safe People.* Grand Rapids, MI: Zondervan, 1995.

Connerton, Paul, *How Societies Remember.* Cambridge, England: Cambridge University Press, 1989.

Corbier, Mireille, "Child Exposure and Abandonment," *Childhood, Class, and Kin in the Roman World,* Suzanne Dixon, ed. London: Routledge, 2001.

Cauvin, Jacques, *The Birth of the Gods and the Origins of Agriculture*, trans. Trevor Watkins. Cambridge, England: Cambridge University Press, 2000.

Dripps, R. D., *The First House*, Cambridge, MA: The MIT Press, 1997.

Esler, Philip E., *The Early Christian World*, Vols. 1, 2. London: Routledge, 2000.

Giles, Doug, "Girls Just Wanna Have Guns," www.townhall.com, 12/04/2010.

******* *Raising Righteous and Rowdy Girls*, White Feather Press, 2011.

******* *If You're Going Through Hell, Keep Going!"* Bridge Logos Foundation, 2009.

******* *A Time to Clash, Papers from a Provocative Pastor*, Townhall Press, 2007.

Grahame, Kenneth, *The Wind in the Willows.* New York: Sterling, 2005.

Guidoni, Enrico, *Primitive Architecture.* New York: Harry N. Abrams Publishing, Inc., 1978.

Heidegger, Martin, "Building Dwelling Thinking," *Basic Writings,* David Farrell Krell, ed. London: Routledge, 1993.

Hodder, Ian, "Architecture and Meaning: The Example of Neolithic Houses and Tombs," *Architecture and Order: Approaches to Social Space,* Michael Parker Pearson and Colin Richards, eds., London: Routledge Press, 1994.

Holtcamp, Wendee, "Mimicking Mother Nature," *National Wildlife,* Grand Rapids: The National Wildlife Federation, (Dec-Jan 2010); (Vol. 48, No. 1); pp.46–51.

Hopkins, C. and P.V.C. Baur, *Christian Church at Dura-Europos: Preliminary Report of Fifth Season of Work, October 1931—March 1932.* New Haven: Yale University Press, 1934.

Hopkins, Clark, *The Discovery of Dura-Europos,* New Haven: Yale University Press, 1979.

Hurtado, Larry W., *At the Origins of Christian Worship: The Context and Character of Earliest Christian Devotion.* Grand Rapids, MI: Eerdmans Publishing, 1999.

Johnston, Sara Iles, "Magic", *Religions of the Ancient World, a Guide,* Sarah Iles Johnston, ed. Cambridge, MA: Belknap Press, 2004.

Kosslyn, Stephen M. and Koenig, Oliver, *Wet Mind: The New Cognitive Neuroscience.* New York: The Free Press, 1995.

Kraeling, Carl, H. *The Excavations at Dura-Europos, Final Report VIII, Part II, The Christian Building.* New Haven: Dura-Europos Publications, 1967.

Lloyd, Robert, "Cognitive Maps: Encoding and Decoding Information," *Annals of the Association of American Geographers,* vol. 79, No.1, Mar., 1989, 101–124.

Malina, Bruce J. and Richard L. Rohrbaugh, *The Social-Science Commentary on the Synoptic Gospels.* Minneapolis: Fortress, 1992.

Matheson, S. B. "The Tenth Season at Doura-Europos 1936–1937," *Syria 69,* 1992.

Meeks, Wayne. A., *The First Urban Christians: The Social World of the Apostle Paul.* New Haven: Yale University Press, 1983.

Meiss, Pierre von, *Elements of Architecture: From Form to Place.* London: E &

FN Spon, 1998.

Musurillo, Herbert, ed., *The Acts of the Christian Martyrs,* Vol. II. Oxford: Clarendon, 1972.

Netzer, Ehud, *The Architecture of Herod the Great Builder.* Grand Rapids, MI: Baker, 2006.

Patai, R., *Man and Temple in Ancient Jewish Myth and Ritual.* London, 1947.

Patrich, Joseph, "Reconstructing the Magnificent Temple Herod Built," *Bible Review,* Oct. 1988.

Pinker, Steven, *The Blank Slate: The Modern Denial of Human Nature.* New York: Viking, 2002.

Rappaport, Roy A., *Ritual and Religion in the Making of Humanity.* Cambridge, England: Cambridge University Press, 1999.

Reisberg, Daniel and Heuer, Friderike, "Visuospatial Images," *The Cambridge Handbook of Visuospatial Thinking,* Priti Shaw and Akira Miyake, eds. Cambridge, England: Cambridge University Press, 2005.

Ries, Julian, *The Origins of Religions.* Grand Rapids, MI: Eerdmans, 1994.

Ritmeyer, Leen, *The Quest, Revealing the Temple Mount in Jerusalem.* Jerusalem: Carta, 2006.

Rowland, Ingrid D., and Thomas Noble Howe, *Vitruvius, Ten Books On Architecture.* Cambridge, England: Cambridge University Press, 1999.

Rubenstein, Jeffrey L., "From Mythic Motifs to Sustained Myth: The Revision of Rabbinic Traditions in Medieval Midrashim," *The Harvard Theological Review,* Vol. 89, No. 2, Apr., 1996.

Runia, David T., *On the Creation of the Cosmos According to Moses.* Leiden, The Netherlands: Brill, 2001.

Sawicki, Marianne, *Crossing Galilee, Architectures of Contact in the Occupied Land of Jesus.* Harrisburg, VA: Trinity Press International, 2000.

Schama, Simon, *Landscape and Memory.* New York: Vintage Books, 1995.

Sharples, Robert W., and Anne Sheppard, eds., *Ancient Approaches to Plato's Timaeus.* BICS Supplement 78, London: Institute of Classical Studies, 2003.

Silverstein, Murray, "The First Roof: Interpreting a Spatial Pattern," *Dwelling, Seeing, and Designing, Toward a Phenomenological Ecology.* David Seamon, ed. New York: State University of New York Press, 1993.

Smith, Jonathan Z., *To Take Place.* Chicago: University of Chicago, 1987.

Spirn, Anne Whiston, *The Language of Landscape.* New Haven: Yale, 1998.

Stahl, Lesley, "Mind Reading," produced by Shari Finkelstein, CBS, June 30 2009.

Stein, Murray, "How Herod Moved Gigantic Blocks to Construct Temple Mount," *Biblical Archaeology Review,* May/June 1981.

Sutton, Robert I. *The No Asshole Rule: Building a Civilized Workplace and Surviving One that Isn't.* New York: Business Plus, 2007.

Swenson, Richard A., M.D. *Margin.* Colorado Springs: NavPress, 1992.

Tversky, Barbara, "Functional Significance of Visuospatial Representations," *The Cambridge Book of Visuospatial Thinking,* Priti Shaw and Akira Miyake, eds. Cambridge, England: Cambridge University Press, 2005.

Ussishkin, David, *The Conquest of Lachish by Sennacherib.* Tel Aviv: Tel Aviv University, 1982.

Van Pelt and Westfall, *Architectural Principles in the Age of Historicism.* New Haven: Yale, 1991, 23.

Wharton, Annabel Jane, *Refiguring the Post-Classical City: Dura Europos, Jerash, Jerusalem and Ravena.* Cambridge, England: Cambridge University Press, 1995.

White, L. Michael, *The Social Origins of Christian Architecture, Vol. I., Building God's House in the Roman World: Architectural Adaptation among Pagans, Jews and Christians.* Valley Forge, PA: Trinity, 1990.

Zeki, Semir, *Inner Vision: An Exploration of Art and the Brain.* Oxford: Oxford University Press, 1999.

Endnotes

Introduction

1   God's name *Yahweh* is rendered as "the Lord" in most Bible
    translations.

2   *JPS Hebrew–English Tanakh* (Philadelphia: Jewish Publication Society,
    1999).

Chapter 1

3   Wendee Holtcamp, "Mimicking Mother Nature," *National Wildlife*
    (The National Wildlife Federation), 48, no. 1 (Dec./Jan 2010):
    46–51.

4   Eli Wiesel, "To Remain Human in Face of Inhumanity,"
    condensed from an address, *The Jewish Digest*, XVII (September,
    1972), 44.

5   Vitruvius, *On Architecture* 2.1.2.

6   Vitruvius, 2.1.2.

7   Vitruvius, *On Architecture*, 2.1.6–7 frag.

8   Anne Whiston Spirn, *The Language of Landscape* (New Haven: Yale,
    1998), 16.

9   Martin Heidegger, "Building Dwelling Thinking," *Basic Writings*,
    ed. David Farrell Krell (London: Routledge, 1993), 349.
    "That is, *bauen, buan, bhu, beo* are our word *bin* in the versions: *ich
    bin*, I am, *du bist*, you are, the imperative form *bis*, be. What does *ich
    bin* mean? The old word *bauen*, to which *bin* belongs, answers: *ich
    bin, du bist* mean I dwell, you dwell. The way in which you are and
    I am, the manner in which we humans are on the earth, is *buan*,
    dwelling. To be a human being means to be on the earth as a
    mortal. It means to dwell."

10 Spirn, 15.

Chapter 2

11 Nancy Pelosi, Catholic Community Conference on Capitol Hill,
    Washington, DC, May 6, 2010.

12 Plato, *Timaeus*, 32 B. The text has λόγον interpreted as *ratio*

13 Plato, *Timaeus*, I 5.11–17.

14 Vitruvius, *On Architecture*, 1.1.12, 15–16.

15 Sextus Empiricus. *Against the Physicists*, 1.78–80, LCL.

16 Sara Iles Johnston, "Magic," *Religions of the Ancient World, a Guide*, ed. Sarah Iles Johnston (Cambridge, MA: Belknap Press, 2004), 148–149.

17 Philo Judaeus, *On the Creation of the Cosmos According to Moses*, trans. David T. Runia, (Leiden, The Netherlands: Koninklijke Brill, 2001), 50–51 (paragraphs 16–24).

18 Proclus has similar ideas to Philo's here. See *Proclus's Commentary on Plato's Parmenides*, trans. Glenn R. Morrow and John Dillon, III, 839–840, (Princeton: Princeton University Press, 1987), 211–212.

19 Morrow and Dillon, III, 164.

20 Morrow and Dillon, IV.843–34 (frags.), 214–215.

CHAPTER 3

21 The Hebrew name for Noah's ark and Moses' basket is *tebah* (Strong's #8392); Ark of the Covenant is *'aron* (#727).

22 To calculate the equal ratio of sides with the ark, we begin by adding 2.5 cubits (side) to 1.5 cubits (width) to equal 4.0 cubits. Then we divide the sum (4.0) with the longest side (2.5) and we have 1.6. If we divide its length (2.5) with its width (1.5), we have 1.666 or precisely the square root of 2; this is an irrational number that has no end. Though 1.6 is different from 1.666 . . . , we can say that though the dimensions are not precise (God was not using his micrometer here) enough to split straws, the ratio of the ark's sides were equal.

23 Again, the Hebrew name for the ark of the covenant is 'aron (#727) meaning chest or coffin.

CHAPTER 4

24 Sarah Netter, "Oops! Georgia Family Distraught After Contractor Destroys Wrong House," *ABC News*, June 12, 2009, http://abcnews.go.com/Business/story?id=7823594&page=1, accessed August 31, 2011.

25 Josephus, *Antiquities of the Jews*, 4.2–3.

CHAPTER 5

26 I would like to thank the docent at Pershore Abbey, Gloucestershire, UK, for this expression. She was referring to the evangelical praise hymn music sung at the Baptist Church she attends in Pershore. Obviously, she is not a fan and misses the classic old hymns.

CHAPTER 6

27 Pierre von Meiss, *Elements of Architecture, From form to place* (Lausanne: E & FN Spon, 1998); Simon Unwin, *Analysing Architecture,* 2nd ed. (London: Routledge, 2003); Simon Unwin, *An Architecture Notebook* (London: Routledge, 2000); Kim Dovey, *Framing Places, Mediating Power in Built Form* (London: Routledge, 1999); Christopher Alexander, *The Nature of Order, Book One, The Phenomenon of Life* (Berkeley, CA: The Center For Environmental Structure, 2002).

28 Irwin Allen, *The Time Tunnel,* episode 20, 1550 BC, 20th Century Fox, broadcast on ABC, Jan. 27, 1967, summarized in "The Time Tunnel," *Wikipedia,* http://en.wikipedia.org/wiki/The_Time_Tunnel#Episodes, accessed September 10, 2011.

29 Kathleen M. Kenyon, *Digging up Jericho* (London: Ernest Benn, 1957); "British School of Archaeology in Jerusalem, Excavations at Jericho, 1957–58," *PEQ,* 1958.

30 John Garstang, and J.B.E. Garstang, *The Story of Jericho* (London: Marshall, Morgan and Scott, rev. ed., 1948).

31 Bryant G. Wood, "Did the Israelites Conquer Jericho? A New Look at the Archaeological Evidence." *Biblical Archaeology Review,* Mar/Apr 1990, 44–59.

32 David Neev and K. O. Emery, *The Destruction of Sodom, Gomorrah, and Jericho, Geological, Climatological, and Archaeological Background* (Oxford: Oxford University Press, 1995).

33 Josephus, *Antiquities of the Jews,* 5.1.2.

34 Joyce Landorf Heatherley, *He Began with Eve,* (Georgetown: Balcony Publishing, 1989).

35 Corrie ten Boom, *The Hiding Place* (Grand Rapids, MI: Chosen, 2006).

36 Louis Kahn, *Essential Texts,* ed. Robert Twombly (New York: W.W. Norton, 2003), 231.

CHAPTER 7

37 Jacques Cauvin, *The Birth of the Gods and the Origins of Agriculture*, trans. Trevor Watkins (Cambridge, England: Cambridge, 2000), 98, 128.

38 Ian Hodder, "Architecture and Meaning: The Example of Neolithic Houses and Tombs," *Architecture and Order, Approaches to Social Space*, eds. Michael Parker Pearson and Colin Richards (London: Routledge Press, 1994), 80–81.

39 The Greek word here for *room* is ταμείον: secret, hidden room; an earlier Greek definition is "treasury."

CHAPTER 8

40 The word for *mind* (*nephesh*) is used alternatively in 1 Chron. 22:19; 29:9 as "soul" and "mind" respectively, in devotion with heart and soul to seeking the Lord, and giving with a willing mind. However, there is another inference going on here.

41 Lexicon reference numbers: *Sakal*: #7919; *Hayah*: #1961 and #346; *Nephesh*: #5315; pattern: #8403; Works: #4399; Hand: #3027.

42 Philo, *On the Creation of the Cosmos According to Moses*, trans. David T. Runia (Leiden: Brill, 2001), 4.16–19, p. 24.

43 Semir Zeki, "The Pathology of the Platonic Ideal and the Hegelian Concept," *Inner Vision* (Oxford: Oxford University Press, 1999), 93, pp. 95–96.

44 Steven Pinker, *The Blank Slate: The Modern Denial of Human Nature* (New York: Viking, 2002).

45 Stephen M. Kosslyn and Oliver Koenig, *Wet Mind: The New Cognitive Neuroscience* (New York: The Free Press, 1995), 54–55.

46 Plato's understanding of the eyes as receptors fusing visual information into a similar substance by the process of "inner fire" is remarkably similar to Kosslyn's and Zeki's descriptions.

47 Daniel Reisberg and Friderike Heuer, "Visuospatial Images," *The Cambridge Handbook of Visuospatial Thinking*, eds. Priti Shaw and Akira Miyake (Cambridge, England: Cambridge University Press, 2005), 43.

48 Kosslyn and Koenig, 89.

49 The ventral system is located deep in the midbrain. In addition

to processing cognition, it is where we process our sense of reward, motivation, and issues of addiction.

50 Kosslyn and Koenig, 366.

51 Lesley Stahl, "Mind Reading," produced by Shari Finkelstein, *60 Minutes*, CBS, 06/30/2009.

CHAPTER 9

52 Tertullian, *De Spectaculis*, trans. Jeffrey Henderson, LCL (Cambridge, England: Cambridge University Press, 1931). VII, VIII.

53 *The Octavius of Marcus Minucius Felix*, trans. G.W. Clarke (New York: Newman Press, 1974), 70.

54 *Octavius*, 122.

55 Herodotus, *The Histories*, I.179.

56 Strabo, *Geographies*, 16.1.5

57 Diodorus Siculus, *Historical Library*, II.10.

58 Mireille Corbier, "Child Exposure and Abandonment," *Childhood, Class, and Kin in the Roman World*, ed. Suzanne Dixon (London: Routledge, 2001), 63–64. The Greek is: εχ (απο) κοπριασ.

59 2 Kings 19:9; Isaiah 37:9.

60 David Ussishkin, *The Conquest of Lachish by Sennacherib* (Tel Aviv: Tel Aviv University, 1982). All background information on tel Lachish comes from this wonderful book published five years after I worked at the Lachish excavation.

CHAPTER 10

61 Simon Unwin, *An Architecture Notebook* (London: Routledge, 2000), 26.

62 Unwin, 25.

63 "Gotta Serve Somebody," *Slow Train Coming*, Copyright © 1979 by Special Rider Music.

64 Other capital cities were: Ecbatana, Persepolis, Pasargadae, and less often Babylon to the south.

65 Or *sommeliere* (fem.) a French word for "head wine waiter."

66 Seneca, *On Anger*, III, 40.

67 Karen M. Carlson, "Why is His Only Word 'No!?'" Questions

About Kids Series, *CEED* (Minneapolis: University of Minnesota, 2001); Dr. Henry Cloud and Dr. John Townsend, *Boundaries* (Grand Rapids, MI: Zondervan, 1992); Cloud, Dr. Henry Cloud and Dr. John Townsend, *Safe People* (Grand Rapids, MI: Zondervan, 1995); Richard A. Swenson, M. D., *Margin* (Colorado Springs, CO: NavPress, 1992); Robert I. Sutton, *The No Asshole Rule: Building a Civilized Workplace and Surviving One that Isn't* (New York: Business Plus, 2007).

68 Jim was eventually fired from the company and less than ten years later died of alcohol poisoning. Jim was a sweet, gentle guy to be around. Several of us witnessed to him, and he said he accepted Christ in his heart as a child. Blessings to you Jim; see you on the "other side."

69 Doug Giles, "Girls Just Wanna Have Guns," www.townhall. com, December 4, 2010, http://townhall.com/columnists/ douggiles/2010/12/04/girls_just_wanna_have_guns/page/full/, accessed September 14, 2011; *Raising Righteous and Rowdy Girls* (White Feather Press, 2011). *If You're Going Through Hell, Keep Going!"* (Bridge Logos Foundation, 2009); *A Time to Clash, Papers from a Provocative Pastor* (Townhall Press, 2007).

CHAPTER 11

70 The Greek word for carpenter is *tekton* (Greek: Matt.: τεκτονος; Mark: ο τεκτων; Latin: *tector*).

71 "Residential Building from the Time of Jesus Exposed in Nazareth," *Israeli Ministry of Foreign Affairs*, December 21, 2009, http://www.mfa.gov.il/MFA/History/Early+History+- +Archeology/Residential_building_time_Jesus_Nazareth_21- Dec-2009.htm, accessed September 14, 2011.

CHAPTER 12

72 R. Patai, *Man and Temple in Ancient Jewish Myth and Ritual* (London: 1947); Jonathan Z. Smith, *To Take Place* (Chicago: University of Chicago, 1987), 84; f.n. 47–48; 164–165. Jeffrey L. Rubenstein, "From Mythic Motifs to Sustained Myth: The Revision of Rabbinic Traditions in Medieval Midrashim," *The Harvard Theological Review*, Vol. 89, No. 2, (April, 1996), 131–159.

Tanhuma Qedoshim 10: "The Land of Israel sits in the middle of the world, and Jerusalem in the center of the Land of Israel, and the temple in the center of Jerusalem, and the Sanctuary in the center of the temple, and the Ark in the middle of the Sanctuary, and the foundation stone, from which the world was founded, in front of the ark."

"The foundation stone traditions do not express the idea of geographic center as such, but rather the motif of the temple as a fulcrum or "center" of order against chaos, and the idea of the beginning point of creation."

73 Jeffrey Rubenstein (1996), 14–15, f.n. 66. Sanhedrin 17.2, 29a. Also: Pirqei de-Rabbi Eli'ezer 10. "...he [the fish] showed Jonah the foundation stone fixed in the Deeps below the Sanctuary of God."

74 Rubenstein, 7, f.n. 24.

75 Images from http://store.ritmeyer.com are used by permission.

76 Leen Ritmeyer, *The Quest, Revealing the Temple Mount in Jerusalem* (Jerusalem: Carta, 2006); Ehud Netzer, *The Architecture of Herod the Great Builder* (Grand Rapids, MI: Baker, 2006); Joseph Patrich, "Reconstructing the Magnificent Temple Herod Built," *Bible Review*, Oct. 1988, 16–29. See also Murray Stein, "How Herod Moved Gigantic Blocks to Construct Temple Mount," *Biblical Archaeology Review*, May/June 1981, 42–46.

77 Josephus, *The Jewish War*, 1.401.

78 Josephus, *The Jewish War*, 5.186–187.

79 Josephus, *Antiquities*, 8.97.

80 Josephus, *Antiquities*, 15.390.

81 Josephus, *The Jewish War*, 5.190-192.

82 Josephus, *Antiquities*, 15.411-416.

83 Mishnah, *Eduyiot*, 8:6; found in Ehud Netzer (2008), 140. The *soreg* which bounded the inner enclosure and the Court of Women was exquisitely crafted. This court within the Outer Court is commonly believed to be 500 X 500 cubits (759 ft. each side): approx. 739,600, sq ft.; Court of Women: 135 cubits square: 53,917 sq ft., less the four segregated, referred to as offices in the Mishnah with dims. of 40 cubits (4,733) sq. ft: 4,733 sq. ft. X 4 = 18,933 sq ft. 53,917 – 18,933 = 34,984 open sq ft in the shape of a cross.

84 Josephus, *The Jewish War*, 5.193–194; *Antiquities*, 15.417.

85 *Middot* 2.5.

86 Josephus, *The Jewish War*, 5.201–206.

87 Josephus, *Antiquities*, 15.421.

88 Josephus, *The Jewish War*, 5.207–226.

89 *Pterugion*, meaning small wing (winglet); figuratively "top corner."

90 A kerfuffle is a commotion. I love this word.

91 Josephus, *The Jewish War*, 5.208.

92 Josephus, *The Jewish War*, 5.210.

93 Josephus, *Antiquities*, 15.394–395.

94 Josephus, *The Jewish War*, 5.211–214.

95 Mishnaic tractate *Shekalim* 8.5.

96 Josephus, *The Jewish War*, 5.219.

97 Yoma, 5.2 (Order of festivals of the Talmud and Mishnah).

98 John 2:21

CHAPTER 13

99 Josephus, *Antiquities*, 15.420.

100 Ehud Netzer, *The Architecture of Herod the Great Builder*, 167–171.

101 Josephus, *Antiquities*, 11.380.

102 "Steve Jobs Presents to the Cupertino City Council," June 7, 2011, Youtube.com, www.youtube.com/watch?v=gtuz5OmOh_M; www.youtube.com/watch?v=qT-4qQ96Qo, accessed September 15, 2011.

103 Josephus, *Antiquities*, 11.387.

104 Ritmeyer, *The Quest: Revealing the Temple Mount in Jerusalem*, 144. It is seen in the Jewish tract called the *Middot*, compiled just after AD 70.

CHAPTER 14

105 Several good commentaries: Donald A. Hagner, *Matthew 14–18*, Word Biblical Commentary (Dallas: Word, 1995); W. D. Davies & Dale C. Allison, Jr., *Matthew Volume II*, The International Commentary, (Edinburgh: T&T Clark, 1991). The feminine ending in the Greek of Peter's name has gained strength to nuance the text to read him as being "little" and Christ as THE ROCK. Many scholars see this as very creative (urban pastoral

myth) and cannot be fully substantiated by the Greek Lexicon.

106 The feminine ending in the Greek of Peter's name has gained strength to nuance the text to read him as being "little" and Christ as THE Rock. Many scholars see this as very creative (urban pastoral myth) and cannot be fully substantiated by the Greek Lexicon.

107 Πέτρος; *Petros*.

108 Matt. 26:69–75; Mark 14:66–72; Luke 22:54–62; John 18:15–27.

109 John 21:15–17.

110 Matt. 9:36; 26:31; John 10:14, 16.

111 See Isa. 38:10.

112 Lambert Roofing, Monterey, California (1983–1985).

CHAPTER 15

113 Herbert Musurillo, ed., *The Acts of the Christian Martyrs*, Vol. II (Oxford: Clarendon, 1972), 44–45.

114 The Martyrdom of Saturninus and company, AD 304.

115 *domus* = house; *ecclesia* (εκκλησία) = assembly, community.

116 S.B. Matheson, "The Tenth Season at Doura-Europos 1936–1937", *Syria 69* 1992, 133.

117 Ammianus Marcellinus, 23.5, 7–8.

118 Clark Hopkins, *The Discovery of Dura-Europos* (New Haven: Yale University Press, 1979), 247. Hopkins dates the fall of the city using coin hoards and coins found on three soldiers trapped under the western wall, near Tower 19.

119 In the last years of Dura's occupation, there is some evidence that housing came under pressure. Houses expanded into the streets, but rather than the poor being pushed to form a ghetto, the well-constructed buildings contained many independent dwellings, often with open peristyle courts, within rectangular street grids.

120 The primary source for the Christian *domus* is: Carl Kraeling, 'The Christian Building', *TED, Final Report VIII, Part II, The Christian Building* (New Haven: Dura Europos Publications, 1967). Also, Clark Hopkins, *Christian Church at Dura-Europos*, TEAD, VI (New Haven: Yale University Press, 1934).

121 Carl Kraeling, *The Christian Building*, 16–17.

122 Kraeling, 9.

123 Kraeling, 32–34.

124 Kraeling, 10, inscr. 10; Ἔτους δυφ' Μν(ησθῇ) Δωρόθεος.

125 Kraeling, 143.

126 Eusebius, *Hist. eccl.*, VII, 19.

127 Carl H. Kraeling, *The Christian Building*, p.153.

128 Kraeling, 153. Kraeling used the baptismal accounts within the Syrian, *The Apocryphal Acts of Judas Thomas* as his primary source.

129 Kraeling, 155.

130 Kraeling, 150–151, 190.

131 Kraeling, 163.

132 Kraeling, 113–114

133 Annabel Jane Wharton, *Refiguring the Post-Classical City: Dura Europos, Jerash, Jerusalem and Ravena*, (Cambridge: Cambridge University Press, 1995), 60, 177, n. 134.

134 Kraeling, 146.

135 Porphyry, *Against the Christians*, fragment 76.

Chapter 16

136 Okay, I tried, but I don't have anything to footnote in this chapter. I free-wrote whatever came into my mind from the years of thinking about the City of Heaven and applying lessons from my studies and the previous pages of this book. Sources for this topic run from stale commentary to some really exotic, lunatic fringe stuff. It seems every faith, domination, cult, and freak show has a take on this place. So I thought I would give it a go.

Chapter 17

137 The vertical and horizontal threads stretched on a loom, respectively.

138 Kenneth Grahame, *The Wind in the Willows* (New York: Sterling, 2005), 74.

Appendix

139 (http://www.janegoodall.org/chimp_central/default.asp); see also her book: *The Shadow of Man* or someone from: The Great Apes Survival Project (GRASP)

140 See *The Sound of Music* on DVD; the first few minutes are all you need here.

Made in the USA
Charleston, SC
17 December 2011